T0261350

Technology Strategy Patterns
Architecture as Strategy

Eben Hewitt

Beijing · Boston · Farnham · Sebastopol · Tokyo

Technology Strategy Patterns

by Eben Hewitt

Published by O'Reilly Media, Inc., 1005 Gravenstein Highway North, Sebastopol, CA 95472.

O'Reilly books may be purchased for educational, business, or sales promotional use. Online editions are also available for most titles (*http://oreilly.com/safari*). For more information, contact our corporate/institutional sales department: 800-998-9938 or *corporate@oreilly.com*.

Acquisitions Editors: Brian Foster, Mary Treseler
Development Editor: Alicia Young
Production Editor: Nan Barber
Copyeditor: Rachel Monaghan

Proofreader: Sharon Wilkey
Indexer: Ellen Troutman-Zaig
Interior Designer: David Futato
Cover Designer: Karen Montgomery
Illustrator: Rebecca Demarest

October 2018:   First Edition

Revision History for the First Edition
2018-10-02:   First Release

See *http://oreilly.com/catalog/errata.csp?isbn=9781492040873* for release details.

978-1-492-04087-3

[LSI]

Table of Contents

Part III. Communicating the Strategy

Preface

Welcome

Thank you for picking up *Technology Strategy Patterns*.

This book came out of a paper I gave at the O'Reilly Software Architecture Conference in New York City in the spring of 2018, called "The Architect as Strategist." I'm grateful for the many conversations it sparked. At the conference, a number of the architects in attendance asked if it could become a book. And so it is.

Intended Audience

This book is for anyone in information technology who wants to do more strategic, relevant, important work for their organizations. Therefore, there is no code in the book, and nothing too technical. People who will get the most out of it include:

- Architects
- Principal developers or tech leads who wish to become architects
- Technology managers in engineering, testing, and analysis, whether on the product development side or the IT back office
- Product managers
- Project and portfolio managers
- Business consultants
- Technology executives

- Strategy analysts and managers
- Anyone interested in strategy, architecture, and leadership

Whether you are a senior developer, enterprise architect, or CTO, or have never read a line of code in your life, I know you'll find something useful, and feel welcome and at home here.

Purpose of the Book

The book has two aims. The first is to help architects, product managers, and executives at technology companies or in technology organizations who are charged with producing technology strategies. This stuff works across industries. My hope is that with these practical tools and guidance, your strategies will be deeper, stronger, and clearer, and you'll get approval, support, and funding to make your ideas a reality. The primary assumption of the book is that you're in technology management of some kind, or want to be, and want to think more holistically and incisively about your technical roadmaps. The second aim is to help you in your career. I suppose an alternate, but less becoming, title for this book could be *How to Become the CTO*.

If you're familiar with patterns-oriented books, such as the Gang of Four classic *Design Patterns* (Addison-Wesley), this book takes inspiration from them without adhering too tightly to the template they typically employ. One of my favorite books, and one that changed how I think about software and the evolution of ideas, was *A Pattern Language* by Christopher Alexander (Oxford University Press). I have devised and refined this *bricolage* of ideas over several years from this and many sources. This book is, in a sense, just a written record of how I've approached this aspect of my work, as much an intellectual memoir as anything else.

While I've written books before on Cassandra, the Java programming language, software development, architecture, SOA, and web development, *Technology Strategy Patterns* is my first real book in nearly a decade. That's on purpose. I've been developing these ideas for the better part of that decade in my work conceiving and executing strategy as CTO, CIO, and Chief Architect at global tech companies. It represents a synthetic fabric of three areas:

- The first is a set of frameworks borrowed from the world of business strategy consulting as it is conceived in McKinsey,

Bain, BCG, and Harvard Business School. We technologists are often told that if we want to be heard, be understood, and get funding, we must "speak in the language of the business"—without quite being told what that is or how to do it. This book serves as the translation—the Rosetta Stone, if you will—for the language of business executives to teach you what they know to strengthen your work and help it succeed.

- Second, I borrow from the world of philosophy, having studied and fallen in love with it in graduate school, and finding its rigors and explosive power very helpful in my 20-year career in tech.

- Finally, there are many perhaps idiomatic tools and frameworks that I developed myself while running large teams of engineers, helping grow businesses, instituting organizational and cultural changes, and designing and implementing globally scalable, mission-critical, distributed software systems running thousands of transactions per second. Together, they form an array of lenses that you can variously employ over time in different contexts as needed. They'll help you define, create, elaborate, and refine your architecture goals and plans, and communicate them in rhetorically powerful ways to an audience of executives who must approve them as well as the teams who must implement them.

I recommend that you read the book front to back. As the Mad Hatter says, "Begin at the beginning, and when you get to the end, stop." The ideas build on each other, refer to each other, and are carefully organized in a logical architecture of their own to reveal to you the beautiful world of strategy one peek at a time. After you're done, keep the book handy to refer back to later as needed. You won't make a new strategy every day, but I think you'll see how many of the techniques can be woven into your daily work.

The tools in this book are proven. They work. I've used these techniques for years, in many contexts with many different leaders in many different organizations. Employing these techniques has repeatedly helped me win technology strategy funding for $1M, $10M, $30M, $50M, $75M, and more. If you employ these tools, your ideas will be sharper, your plans more accurate, relevant, empathetic, and fruitful. Executives will approve and fund your work, and your teams, your company, your customers, and your partners will benefit.

I truly hope that you find this book useful and inspiring for years to come, and that it serves you. It was written with affection and care. May it strengthen and deepen your work, and help you, your company, and your customers succeed.

Conventions Used in This Book

The following typographical conventions are used in this book:

Italic

Indicates new terms, URLs, email addresses, filenames, and file extensions.

`Constant width`

Used for program listings, as well as within paragraphs to refer to program elements such as variable or function names, databases, data types, environment variables, statements, and keywords.

`Constant width bold`

Shows commands or other text that should be typed literally by the user.

`Constant width italic`

Shows text that should be replaced with user-supplied values or by values determined by context.

This element signifies a tip or suggestion.

This element signifies a general note.

This element indicates a warning or caution.

Using Code Examples

Supplemental material (code examples, exercises, etc.) is available for download at *https://www.aletheastudio.com*.

This book is here to help you get your job done. In general, if example code is offered with this book, you may use it in your programs and documentation. You do not need to contact us for permission unless you're reproducing a significant portion of the code. For example, writing a program that uses several chunks of code from this book does not require permission. Selling or distributing a CD-ROM of examples from O'Reilly books does require permission. Answering a question by citing this book and quoting example code does not require permission. Incorporating a significant amount of example code from this book into your product's documentation does require permission.

We appreciate, but do not require, attribution. An attribution usually includes the title, author, publisher, and ISBN. For example: "*Technology Strategy Patterns* by Eben Hewitt (O'Reilly). Copyright 2019 Eben Hewitt, 978-1-492-04087-3."

If you feel your use of code examples falls outside fair use or the permission given above, feel free to contact us at *permissions@oreilly.com*.

O'Reilly Safari

 *Safari* (formerly Safari Books Online) is a membership-based training and reference platform for enterprise, government, educators, and individuals.

Members have access to thousands of books, training videos, Learning Paths, interactive tutorials, and curated playlists from over 250 publishers, including O'Reilly Media, Harvard Business Review, Prentice Hall Professional, Addison-Wesley Professional, Microsoft

Press, Sams, Que, Peachpit Press, Adobe, Focal Press, Cisco Press, John Wiley & Sons, Syngress, Morgan Kaufmann, IBM Redbooks, Packt, Adobe Press, FT Press, Apress, Manning, New Riders, McGraw-Hill, Jones & Bartlett, and Course Technology, among others.

For more information, please visit *http://oreilly.com/safari*.

How to Contact Us

Please address comments and questions concerning this book to the publisher:

O'Reilly Media, Inc.
1005 Gravenstein Highway North
Sebastopol, CA 95472
800-998-9938 (in the United States or Canada)
707-829-0515 (international or local)
707-829-0104 (fax)

We have a web page for this book, where we list errata, examples, and any additional information. You can access this page at *http://www.oreilly.com/catalog/0636920175155*.

To comment or ask technical questions about this book, send email to *bookquestions@oreilly.com*.

For more information about our books, courses, conferences, and news, see our website at *http://www.oreilly.com*.

Find us on Facebook: *http://facebook.com/oreilly*

Follow us on Twitter: *http://twitter.com/oreillymedia*

Watch us on YouTube: *http://www.youtube.com/oreillymedia*

Acknowledgments

I would like to thank my friends and colleagues at Sabre who shared important insights and supported this work.

First, to our wonderful enterprise architecture team of Andrea Baylor, Holt Hopkins, Tom Murray, Jerry Rossi, and Andy Zecha. You're such a joy to work with every day. I'm grateful to get to hang out with such knowledgeable, sharp, funny, dedicated, passionate, good people.

President Clinton Anderson, previously of Bain & Company, and Sabre Hospitality VP of Strategy Balaji Krishnamurthy, previously of McKinsey, both inspire me, are such fun to work with, and teach me every day. I'm so grateful to work with you and know you. Thank you for sharing your thoughts and methods, and in so doing, helping inspire this book. You both get stickers.

A special thank you to Justin Ricketts for his support on this project and for being so terrific to work with. I am grateful to my colleagues across Sabre, especially Tom Winrow.

Thank you to Brian Mericle, enterprise architect, and my longtime friend and colleague, for his valuable edits to this book.

Thank you to my old friends and mentors Todd Davis, Deryl Heitman, Steve Miller, and Ted Taylor for the many opportunities you afforded me to grow and learn.

Thank you to Mike Loukides, my longtime friend and editor at O'Reilly, who always pushes me to see farther. I'm grateful for your help in developing this book and these ideas. Thank you for our sprawling, fabulous conversations. Thank you too to Brian Foster for welcoming this book at the Software Architecture Conference and your guidance of this work. Thank you to my development editor, Alicia Young, whose diligence and care improved this work. Thank you to all my friends at the wonderful O'Reilly Media, including Mary Treseler, Nan Barber, Rachel Monaghan, and Sharon Wilkey for your terrific work that improved this book. I am grateful for what you do in the world to help spread the knowledge of innovators. What a beautiful company you created, Tim; may it ever flourish.

I am most indebted to my wife, Professor of Philosophy Alison Brown, for her wisdom, better ideas, revisions, suggestions, summations, expansions, explanations, expiations, encouragement, tenacity, and love. You are the *sine qua non*, as ever.

Introduction

This Is Water

My favorite joke is told by philosopher and author David Foster Wallace in his address to the graduating class of Kenyon College (*http://bit.ly/2wapscd*) in 2005. It goes like this: One morning two young fish are swimming in the ocean. They come across an older fish who waves happily and calls out to them, "Morning, friends! How's the water?" They nod in acknowledgment and swim on. Once they're out of sight, one turns to the other and asks, "What the hell is water?"

With this joke, Wallace reminds us that the most obvious, important realities are often the ones hardest to see, that we can lock ourselves in mental models so complete that we don't even know we're imprisoned by them.

As technologists, we can be perhaps particularly susceptible to this. Our work is engaging and requires a watchmaker's attention to detail. Yet, as technologists, we are businesspeople. A hammer doesn't exist to be a hammer. It's a tool to construct something else. Technology is one tool with which businesses are constructed, rise, and fall. We operate in wide spheres of ever-farther-reaching impact on the world around us. In a sense, this book is about constructing a new mental model within this water of business.

Discovering Strategy

The roles that are ultimately valued at an organization tend to be the people who do what the boss did. If the boss used to be a salesperson or deal-maker, that's who she'll recognize, side with, empathize with, reward, understand, and listen to most. If you want your voice to be heard, you must make a concerted effort to empathize with people, and employ the tools, techniques, and language that they respond to.

At one point in my career I was running the enterprise architecture department of a large corporation. My manager, the CTO, asked me to help him estimate a large project. He wanted me to go off and determine the "incrementals." I didn't know what he meant. But in my stupidity, I didn't want to *look* stupid, so I didn't ask him, thereby enthroning myself as truly stupid. So I went off and tried to figure it out myself and came back to him three or four times with something different than he needed. I was a pretty good technologist, but I didn't sufficiently understand the language of business. And therein lies the problem. It's hard for people to know what they mean themselves, much less express it to others in a way that achieves their aims. After all, that's the secret to happiness in life: figuring out what you want, and learning how to ask for it.

As I have progressed in my career from developer to architect to CTO and CIO and Chief Architect, I have been asked to create a technology strategy many times. Concluding that no one asks the not-as-clever people to craft strategies for stuff that doesn't matter, I was always delighted at the prospect. It felt like an honor, sounded really cool, and seemed important and big, like I had been asked to help make decisions about how to guide the organization. So I was over the moon for a moment. And then suddenly scared. Because I realized for all the times I'd heard people say the word as if they knew what they were saying, I had never seen anything that I thought looked like a strategy. My concern grew as I realized many of my (accomplished and perfectly reasonable) bosses hadn't either. They didn't know exactly what they were asking me to do, or what the result should look like. Perhaps the strategists were the only people left in the world with a higher room in the Ivory Tower than architects and academics. Eventually we all bumbled our way through it and got to something good enough. But in some cases this process took a year and wasn't always optimal.

Yet I was intrigued, in part because it wasn't lost on me that the clever people, and the people running the organization (only occasionally the same thing), were keenly interested in strategy.

While trying to discover what a good strategy should look like, I grew more concerned at being able to construct this seemingly critical but elusive and mystical document. Companies do not tend to publish their strategies externally since they contain revealing secrets about their plans and fears. So it is hard to find any recent, good, complete, relevant examples. I therefore took it upon myself to go to the source: strategy consultants. They are devoted to publishing their work and excitedly talking about it nonstop to anyone.

But once you've devised a strategy, it languishes on the shelf if you can't make people excited to hear it, understand it, care about it, approve it, and execute it. Any technology strategy is, in a sense, a request to spend millions of dollars of someone else's money. If you think of your work as a technology strategist in this way, you'll do it differently. By which I mean better.

I have known many smart people, wonderful technologists, who do not get their ideas heard by upper management. They state what the problems are and where the problems are going to be, write that up, and put it on the wiki—and nothing changes. Once it's too late and the platform is burning, those same architects get called in to rescue the situation. While people love to say, "I told you so," no one likes to hear it. These well-intentioned souls may have had the best recommendations, but it never mattered. These folks can become alienated, feeling misunderstood and unappreciated. And the business loses out on their great ideas. This is precisely what I don't want to see happen to you, and the reason I wrote this book.

Driving Strategy with Patterns

This book employs, albeit loosely, a suggestion of patterns that is likely familiar to you from the realm of software design patterns such as Decorator, Factory, Visitor, and Pub/Sub. They're used as shorthand for known, proven solutions, to provide an easy way for us to communicate to each other. I chose patterns to represent the ideas in this book because of that familiarity, and because that structure makes it easy for you to look up these ideas for years to come. To aid in this, they're divided into logical concept architectures.

Analysis
> First we explore foundational and general tools for critical thinking that will underpin the other patterns in the book.

Creation

These are the patterns that help you directly create your tech strategy. If you implement all of these patterns, you'll have a comprehensive, compelling annual tech strategy. But you don't need to always implement all of them. You can also pick and choose individual patterns to take a strategic approach to more local, specific project work.

Communication

These patterns help you to organize the components of your strategy in a way that your colleagues and executives can understand, get excited about, and support.

I'm sorry to repeat an old saw, but it's true: increasingly, it is impossible to distinguish between business and technology. But that distinction is still more powerful than it deserves to be, given typical organizational structures and the resistance to change, and an uncertainty about how to do so. I hope that in part this book will help you, your colleagues, and your organization to embrace this cross-pollination. I hypothesize that in the future, people who can learn quickly as synthetic interdisciplinarians will be highly effective, and highly prized, because maintaining that distinction is increasingly a barrier to progress, creativity, and innovation.

This book, I hope, gives technologists, strategists, product managers, executives, technology managers, and the architects who frequently mediate these worlds all a shared language. In this, may you be more fruitful.

PART I

Context: Architecture and Strategy

All models are wrong; some models are useful.
    —Statistician George Box

The Origins of Patterns

Christopher Alexander was a professor at the University of California, Berkeley. With a group of graduate students in the mid 1970s, he set out to catalog common practices he saw throughout architecture. He noted that many problems in architecture are inveterate, and that recording a set of optimal, or at least frequently employed, solutions to these problems would help elevate architecture as a field and expedite the work of architects. He called these common solutions "patterns," and his most excellent book, *A Pattern Language*, catalogs dozens of them.

Inspired by Alexander's work in the architecture of houses, buildings, and city planning, the Gang of Four applied the idea of patterns to software in their book *Design Patterns*. Since then, many books have employed patterns in a variety of technological domains, and the present work expands on this idea, taking repeated solutions found in the work of business strategists and illustrating how we can apply them to better our work as technologists.

The use of patterns as a structuring mechanism here is intended to make the book easy to use later as a reference after you've read it.

Applying the Patterns

There are five basic steps to follow in formulating your strategic technology analysis. Here is a simplified outline:

1. Establish context

   a. Analyze the trends happening in the world outside.

   b. Analyze the forces at work across your industry, your organization, and your department.

   c. Gain a view on your stakeholders.

2. Understand your competition, the market, and the technology landscape.

3. Identify strategic options in your products, services, and technology roadmap.

4. Evaluate those options.

5. Make a compelling recommendation with a coherent, cohesive, comprehensive strategy to gain approval and resources to execute your plans.

With this process in mind, let's turn our attention to how to view your technology work through the lens of architecture and strategy, so we have a shared understanding and vocabulary.

CHAPTER 1

Architect and Strategist

This chapter provides an overview of three different, somewhat traditional business strategy examples from different industries. We'll then look at the role of the architect and the role of the strategist in modern business, to see how strategically minded technologists can be a catalyst for real, meaningful change in their organizations.

Business Strategies

Business strategies reveal how companies allocate resources toward a certain aim. Let's take three examples: Michelin, a tire-company-turned-dining giant; Oracle, a dominant name in software; and Xerox and Canon, companies whose strategies set them on very different paths in the copy industry. Our brief look at these strategies will provide you with context for the concept of "strategy" and illustrate the business implications different strategies can have.

Marketing at Michelin

The Michelin Guide has been in circulation for nearly 120 years. It is known across the globe as the gold standard for fine dining restaurant ratings and reviews. The world's top chefs work year-round in pursuit of the coveted Michelin star, because being awarded one means that your restaurant is worth a detour, worth making a special trip just to eat there. And thousands of diners trust the guide as a well-known authority on the best restaurants. Such excitement is created in France each year upon its publication that the media frenzy it ignites has been compared to that for the Academy Awards.

But Michelin is a *tire* company. How in the world, and why, did a tire company come to hand out the highest honors in fine dining?

In 1900, there were only a few thousand cars in France. Cars were new, they were relatively expensive, and the culture had not yet shifted toward the idea that everyone needed to own a car. For tire manufacturer Michelin, that presented a problem. How could it sell more tires and thrive as a company when there were so few cars?

There are only two ways to create more demand for its product: sell more cars to outfit with tires, or find a way to make people who already have cars drive more so their tires would need to be replaced sooner. The company created the Michelin Guide and gave it away for free. In doing so, Michelin got its name out across France, then Europe, then the world as an excellent advertisement, and positioned itself as an approachable, authoritative company. It created inspiration for drivers and a reason for more people to have cars, and sold more replacement products as a result. The company also made money on the guide once it started charging for it.

This was an innovative, counterintuitive, winning business strategy that worked well for decades.

The guides, known affectionately as the "red books," grew the value of the brand overall and seem to be a real asset. Yet today, published on paper and sold in bookstores, the guides lose Michelin €19 million per year. These days, with the ubiquity of cars, and the joys of the open road firmly ensconced in the popular imagination, the guides don't act as powerfully in their original capacity. Yet they're still obviously important. They became disconnected from the idea of getting people to drive more, and started to have to run as their own business. Perhaps a new strategy better supported by, and better integrated with, technology could help make it profitable again.

Acquisition and Integration at Oracle

In 2007, Oracle Corporation determined a business strategy with a simple principle: either make its software number one or number two in every product category, or buy the market leader. In other words, if you can't beat them, buy them. Between 2008 and 2013, Oracle bought nearly 60 companies—a rate of almost one per month. Oracle spent $45 billion acquiring companies between 2004 and 2014.

When Thomas Kurian assumed leadership of the product teams for Oracle Fusion Middleware in 2008, his technology strategy was made clear to everyone at Oracle and to its customers: all products would use Oracle's middleware stack and must be modified to interoperate with it.

This technology strategy has turned out to be a mixed bag. On the one hand, it's a terrific example of how a technology architecture decision was made to directly support the business strategy of aggressive acquisitions, and that's a strong lesson to learn.

On the other hand, Oracle spent considerable time over many years on refactoring and redoing the internals of many products to comply with this architecture. That time was not spent on innovation or features for customers. In that time, Oracle entirely missed the critical revolutions in the cloud and machine learning, putting it years behind competitors in those crucial areas. More than 10 years later, the technology strategy and architecture within products remains unchanged.

Published Reference Architecture

A few years ago, Oracle published its set of technology strategies, reference architectures, and practitioner guides in a fairly comprehensive website (*http://bit.ly/2PLP1cr*). This is an excellent example of working to help educate your community on how to best take advantage of your strategy once you've published it.

Differentiation at Xerox and Canon

In 1968, Xerox introduced the 914 copying machine, which was capable of copying at what then was the astonishing rate of 120 copies per minute. With this product, it became the world's fastest company to grow to a billion dollars.

By the early 1970s, Xerox had a 95% market share in the global copier market. The large Xerox machines sold to large corporations with high-volume copy needs. The price: a whopping $80,000 to $129,000 each.

Xerox had a sophisticated and sizable sales force, all armed with deep product knowledge. Its mission was to build close, long-term customer relationships with all the Fortune 500.

Reliability was paramount: a stop in the copiers could mean a stop of the customer's business. Because of the centrality of the copiers in the business, Xerox built sturdy machines, but also touted its 24-hour customer service network. It required an extensive capital investment to create, train, and maintain such a capable network and build out the logistics. Such folks commanded hefty fees. Xerox enjoyed a large revenue stream from the service of its copiers, which required highly trained and skilled technicians. The company was at the top of its game, a seemingly impenetrable fortress with a sizable moat around it. In the same way that "to google" has become synonymous with "to search the web," people didn't copy documents, they Xeroxed them.

But within five years, the company's market share fell from 95% to 14%. By the end of the decade, profits from Xerox's $7B copying business had sunk by 40%. Today Xerox represents 17% of the market it once dominated. What happened?

Canon entered the market.

Canon had dedicated technology research in the 1960s to develop an alternative to Xerox's patented photostatic copying process. To create what it called the "New Process," Canon drew on two of its existing capabilities and techniques: micro-electronics, which it knew from its existing calculator business, and optics and imaging, which it drew from its camera business. This allowed it to make smaller copiers.

Canon designed its copiers for high reliability. They had only eight basic parts, making them orders of magnitude simpler than Xerox's products. In a shocking move, Canon made the primary assembly (toner, copier drum, charger, and cleaner) to be disposable. This was unthinkable, that you would design a key component of a critical piece of technology to be disposable. But Canon had its customers in mind: customers could easily remove and replace the assembly. This meant there was no need to build out, train, and manage the logistics for an extensive service department, keeping Canon lean and its costs down.

Furthermore, Canon designed its copiers around the manufacturing process—an inversion of conventional wisdom. The copiers could be made by robots on an assembly line, which dramatically reduced production costs. This meant Canon could redefine the market: instead of having to make a product that only the richest and largest companies would need or could afford, Canon designed its copiers this way to capture the individual and small business markets, selling them for $700 to $1,200. This opened up a new revenue stream, one that the market leader could not compete with. It quickly eroded Xerox's large corporate business, because companies realized they could have a hundred Canon copiers for the same cost, reducing their risk if anything went wrong, and they could budget for them much more easily.

This story illustrates how a technology strategy can work hand in hand with the business strategy, how they can drive as copilots. It represents a combination of technology and business strategy wonderfully aligned and interlinked. This is the essence of what a technology strategist does. With that in mind, let's look now at the role of the architect followed by the role of the strategist.

The Architect's Role

There are two jobs in the world that people want to do the most while knowing the least about: architect and strategist.

I should start by saying that this section does not offer a treatise on how to do architecture. I'm offering an overview of my perspective on the field, which I hope is a unique and interesting take on it, in order to provide context for the work at hand: devising a winning technology strategy for your business.

Technology systems are difficult to wrangle. Our systems grow in accidental complexity and complication over time. Sometimes we can succumb to thinking that other people really hold the cards, that they have the puppet strings we don't.

This is exacerbated by the fact that our field is young and growing and changing, and we're still finding the roles we need to have to be successful. To do so, we borrow metaphors from roles in other industries. The term "data scientist" was first used in the late 1990s. In 2008 or so, when "data scientist" emerged as a job title, it was widely ridiculed as a nonjob: the thought that people who just worked with data could be scientists, or employ the rigors of their time-honored methods, was literally laughable in many circles. By 2012, *Harvard Business Review* published an article by Jeff Hammerbacher (of Facebook and Cassandra fame) and DJ Patil called "Data Scientist: The Sexiest Job of the 21st Century." Today, it's one of the most desired jobs, with pundits declaiming the terrifying state that we do not have nearly enough of them to tackle our most central technology problems.

Likewise, the term "architect" didn't enter popular usage to describe a role in the software field until the late 1990s. It, too, was ridiculed as an overblown, fancy-pants misappropriation from a "real" field. Part of the vulnerability here is that it hasn't always been clear what the architect's deliverables are. We often say "blueprints," but that's another metaphor borrowed from the original field, and of course we don't make actual blueprints.

With such origins, and with the subsequent division of the architect role into enterprise architect, solution architect, data architect, and so forth, the lines have blurred further. The result is that decades later, the practice and the art of the architect in technology varies dramatically not only from one company to the next, but also from one department and one practitioner to the next.

So we will define the role of the architect in order to proceed from common ground. This is my tailored view of it; others will have different definitions. Before we do that, though, let's cover some historical context that informs how we think of the role.

Vitruvius and the Principles of Architecture

Architecture begins when someone has a nontrivial problem to be solved. The product management team states *what* must be done to solve the problem, and the architect describes *how* to realize that vision in a system.

The first architect of record is a fellow named Vitruvius, who worked as a civil engineer in Rome in the first century BC. While you may not know his name, during the Renaissance, Leonardo da Vinci popularized the "Vitruvian Man" with perfect proportions based on Vitruvius's ideas. Everyone who goes to architecture school learns his work.

Vitruvius is the author of *de Architectura*, known today as *Ten Books on Architecture* (*http://bit.ly/2ChIAv0*). It's a delightful, engaging read, and had a strong influence on Renaissance artists such as Michaelangelo as well as da Vinci. In it, Vitruvius expands on the three requirements that any architecture must demonstrate:

Firmitas
> It must be solid, firm.

Utilitas
> It must be useful, have utility.

Venustas
> It must be beautiful, like Venus, inspiring love. This is sometimes translated as "delightful."

It's a given that we must design a system, including a local software architecture, that actually runs, that it's "solid." It may need to run for many years, even decades, and be maintainable to adapt to changes over that time. Solid doesn't mean inflexible. Skyscrapers are built on purpose to sway slightly with the wind, specifically to be more durable. The Sears Tower in Chicago regularly sways between six inches and a foot; taller buildings in America sway as much as four to five feet. Your architectures, and your strategies, must be similarly flexible in order to endure. We'll look at this later when we discuss how to support evolutionary architectures through our strategies.

It must also be fit to purpose, which means understanding deeply what the real purpose of the system is, and how to manage user expectations. This is supported in real terms through standards and consistent application of conventions, both in the information architecture (i.e., the user experience and design), and within the software construction itself.

Beauty, for Vitruvius, isn't really in the eye of the beholder. It is about harmony of proportion. One suggestion we can deduce from this for our current purposes is that we must rightsize our architecture and strategy work for the task at hand.

Vitruvuis states—without irony—that an architect must concern himself with and become educated in several diverse fields of study, such that they find their way into the work. He outlines them in Chapter 1 of *de Architectura*:

- Skill in manual labor as well as in theory
- Proclivity and desire for continuous learning
- A dexterity with tools
- An understanding of optics—how the light gets in
- History, such that you can emphasize and not misinterpret signs of cultural significance
- A strong understanding of philosophy, in order to practice abstract thinking as well as honesty and courtesy
- Physics, to help make things sturdy
- Art, music, theater, drawing, painting, and poetry, to help make things beautiful and well suited to their human purposes
- Math
- Medicine
- Astronomy
- Politics

He concludes that absent a degree of education and even lay practice in any one of these areas, one cannot refer to oneself as an architect. These are excellent guides for us in technology today. For those of us concerned with the business of making software and setting the direction for other technologists, to hold ourselves to account in these ways would serve us very well.

In a recent conversation I had with Ben Pring, philosopher, noted futurist, and director of The Future of Work Center at Cognizant, he underscored the importance of beauty in software, pointing out that historically our most culturally significant buildings have been not merely adorned, but specifically built with beauty in mind as a central, driving narrative. I conclude from this that such foregrounding reinforces in the popular imagination the power of the institutions that build them. I base this conclusion on the preface in the *Ten Books*, in which Vitruvius writes openly and directly to Emperor Caesar, stating:

> But when I saw that you were giving your attention not only to the welfare of society in general and to the establishment of public order, but also to the providing of public buildings intended for utilitarian purposes, so that not only should the State have been enriched with provinces by your means, *but that the greatness of its*

power might likewise be attended with distinguished authority in its public buildings, I thought that I ought to take the first opportunity to lay before you my writings on this theme. (emphasis mine)

Realizing these broad dicta into an architecture means, I think, finding the concentrations of power, and determining how to best support and ultimately inspire the human factor in the forms we create. I hope once you're done with this book, you'll have some ideas for how to enable and reveal the three facets of firmitas, utilitas, and venustas in your own work.

Three Concerns of the Architect

Whereas developers are typically focused on delivering working code for a user story within the next two weeks for one system within their one team, architects are concerned with how technology can fulfill business goals given a long-term outlook across a variety of interrelated systems across many teams. It's analogous to a project view versus a portfolio view. They should have their visors raised much higher. The architect is hopefully not concerned with low-level details of the code itself inside one system, but is more focused on where data-center boundaries are crossed, where system component boundaries are crossed.

Here's my definition of an architect's work: it comprises the set of strategic and technical models that create a context for position (capabilities), velocity (directedness, ability to adjust), and potential (relations) to harmonize strategic business and technology goals. Notice that in this definition, the role of the architect and technology strategist is not to merely *serve* the business but to play together. I have been in shops where technology was squarely second fiddle, a subservient order-taking organization to support what was deemed the real business. That's no fun for creative people who have something to contribute. But more importantly, I submit that businesses, now more than ever, cannot sustain such a division, and to create greater competitive advantage must work toward integration with co-leadership.

Over my 20 years in this field, I've come to conclude that there are three primary concerns of the architect:

- Contain entropy.
- Specify the nonfunctional requirements.

- Determine trade-offs.

There are many different roles that architects legitimately play in different organizations. But the primary struggle I have seen comes when they are not focused on a deliverable, on what could be conceived as a "blueprint." Without that focus, they tend to weigh in at project meetings or make declarations informally that can't be remembered or followed. To stay pertinent to the project, and to help guide it in a way that others may not have the purview to do, drawing a line at these boundaries seems to work out pretty well. The definition remains, of course, rather open to interpretation, in grudging deference to the machinations of the real world.

Let's unpack each of those responsibilities.

Contain entropy

This viewpoint on the architect's work I learned in a fun conversation over dinner in New York with the very smart and funny Cameron Purdy, the founder of Coherence, who at the time ran Java at Oracle. "Entropy" refers to the second law of thermodynamics, which roughly states that systems over time will degrade into an increasingly chaotic state, such that the amount of energy in the system available for work is diminished.

The architect defines standards, conventions, and toolsets for teams to use. These are common practices, and generally idiosyncratic to any given organization. As application or solution architects, they help within a system, within an ecosystem, and across an organization to create a common set of practices for developers that help things both go quicker and be more understandable and maintainable. This is a form of containing entropy. As we mature, we realize that picking one tool or framework or language or platform is not a matter of personal taste, but rather a choice with broad ramifications for future flexibility, mergers and acquisitions, training, our ability to hire future supporting teams, and our future ability to directly support—or subvert—the business strategy.

Those with more business-oriented concerns and technologists cannot ignore each other's fields. Working as a pattern-maker and a synthesizer, the architect-as-strategist broadens and ennobles these concerns, creating technology strategies that both are rooted in the causes and concerns of the business and recognize its constraints and opportunities. In collaboration with product management, and with colleagues in strategy, business development, finance, and HR, the architect works to ensure that there is alignment between the systems, yes, but also between those systems and the organization, and between the organization and its stated aims.

In short, for far too long we architects have thought we were in the business of making software. But we're in the business of building a business.

The architect who is containing entropy is stating a vision around which to rally; showing a path in a roadmap; garnering support for that vision through communication of guidelines and standards; and creating clarity to ensure efficiency of execution and that you're doing the right things and doing things right.

I love this definition of containing entropy because it offers something to both the software-minded and the business-minded architect (which I hope are two categories this book will help collapse). One cannot be successful as an architect without thinking of not only *what* to do, but *how* to get it done within an organization, which requires knowing *why* it should matter to someone who isn't a technologist.

We often hear of architects with failed dreams of how the system should have been. They are consumed by writing documents and those documents are subsequently ignored, leading them to give up. Left with only the most informal conversational avenues to offer insufficient direction to teams, they become frustrated and even marginalized.

Knowing that you're in the business of building a business, and that technology is just an avenue by which you enable that, is a critical first step to being not only useful but powerful as an architect and strategist.

Specify nonfunctional requirements

Knowing what you're on the hook for, letting others know it, and making sure that it's a concrete deliverable will all go a long way to ensuring your vision is understood and realized.

Product management is responsible for specifying what the system must do for the end user. They might state functional requirements in user stories and epics.

The nonfunctional requirements are properties of the system that do not necessarily appear directly to the user. They are typically described as the "-ilities." The ones I focus on most are scalability, availability, maintainability, manageability, monitorability, extensibility, interoperability, portability, security, and performance.

The architect is responsible for specifying how the system will realize the functional and nonfunctional requirements in its construction. In order to do so, she must write a document that specifies how these will be realized.

This document, the *architecture definition*, serves as the technologist's answer to the blueprint. It should be structured in four broad categories to include business, application, data, and infrastructure perspectives, and expressed with clarity and decisiveness, using primarily testable statements as valid propositions (which we'll examine in the next chapter) and math.

Finding ways to make those expressions concrete and executable is too often overlooked. In addition to writing and publishing a formal architecture definition document to the teams, you can do this by adding nonfunctional requirements to user stories as acceptance criteria.

Determine trade-offs

You can never try to escape one danger without encountering another. Prudence consists in recognizing the different dangers and in accepting the least bad as good.
—Machiavelli, *The Art of War*

As we know, every action produces an equal and opposite reaction. Adding security reduces performance. Sharding and partitioning the database affords greater performance and distribution but creates complexity that is difficult to manage. Adding robust monitoring can generate huge volumes of log data to be stored, rotated, secured, and cleansed. Keeping the design "simple" often defers the interests of flexibility until later, where it becomes very expensive.

The role of the architect is to see where those challenges may lurk, seek to make them explicit, and make value judgments about how to balance the solutions and the new problems they occasion, under the guidance of the broader business strategy. As English poet John Milton wrote in *Paradise Lost*, you make "the darkness visible."

In short, you're never quite solving a problem. You're only trading it for one that you'd rather have. We solve our need for shelter by assuming a mortgage that we then must pay for. Paul Virilio, the French cultural theorist and philosopher, reminds us lucidly, "When you invent the ship, you also invent the shipwreck...Every technology carries its own negativity, which is invented at the same time as technical progress" (*Politics of the Very Worst*, Semiotexte). Your architecture and strategy work will do well to examine not only how you are addressing the problems you've been given, but also what new problems your solutions precipitate.

Any trade-off eventually reduces to a trade-off of time and money.

Absent a strategic mindset, many technologists left to their own devices create what amounts to little more than shopping lists of shiny objects. These can include the latest and most fashionable tech because it's popular or because it might bolster their résumé. We hear this frequently described as "a solution looking for a problem." Moreover, the less shallow or cynically minded among us are still rather prone to chasing exciting technology for its own sake, not unlike a dog chasing a squirrel. Intellectual curiosity is a wonderful thing, a best thing. But to ensure that your technology and architecture decisions are truly supportive of the business—that is, give it the best chance to create competitive advantage—they need to be not shopping lists of shiny objects, but squarely *strategic*.

So let's look at the role of the strategist.

The Strategist's Role

Strategy is about getting more power than the starting position would suggest. Strategy is the art of creating power.
—Lawrence Freedman, *Strategy: A History* (Oxford University Press)

The word *strategy* originates from the Greek *strategos*. The term first appeared in fifth-century Athens as a conflation of the words meaning the expansion of the military general, and came to be used to refer to the offices or science of the general—the general's work. But the word *strategy* entered general use only at the start of the 19th century in Antoine-Henri Jomini's writing on Napoleon's methods.

Jomini was of Swiss origin; he started out as a banker in Paris, later joined the French army under Napoleon, and eventually got promoted to general. Jomini began writing down Napoleon's methods in such a lucid manner that they came to be published as a book, entitled *Treatise on Major Military Operations*, in 1803. Jomini's strategies were employed in the US Civil War and eventually taught at West Point Academy. He is considered the founder of modern strategy by many military historians.

Jomini's definition of strategy helpfully divides the word. He writes, "Strategy decides where to act; logistics brings the troops to this point; tactics decides the manner of execution." In other words, means (resources) are allocated and subjected to a method in order to achieve a goal.

Yet definitions of strategy vary. One of the more abstract definitions comes from Sun Tzu, a Chinese general and philosopher, and author of *The Art of War* in 500 BC. His book was not translated to English until the 20th century, at which point it began serving as a foundational text for guiding military strategies. It entered the popular imagination once it got adapted and marketed for business purposes.

He writes, "Strategy is the art of making use of time and space." This is a tall order, and while aesthetically I appreciate the definition, we can break this down further in order to come to something practically executable.

The History of Strategy

If you're interested in the intellectual history of strategy, its origins, and its evolution from military thought to game theory to business, I highly recommend Lawrence Freedman's *Strategy: A History* (Oxford University Press). It's a fascinating read, and offers a much richer view than we need here.

For our purposes, strategy is about determining the problems and opportunities in front of you, defining them properly, and shaping a course of action that will give your business the greatest advantage. Balancing problem solving with creating and exploiting new opportunities through imagination and analysis is the cornerstone of a great strategy.

Echoing Jomini, we'll say that strategy is about determining the best balance between a set of goals, the method used to achieve them, and the resources available as means. With the current rate of change in business, we can't set it and forget it, expecting that a three- or five-year strategy will go unrevised. At the same time, constant revision amounts to a reactionary collection of tactics, which is no strategy at all.

Most business strategies will concern themselves with the following:

- The goals of the organization
- The operating model: processes and how your company conducts its business
- Culture: the mores and value system, the modes of communication
- Talent strategy: how you source and retain talent, how you train them
- Facilities strategy: where you do business, relevant local laws, and cost concerns

Strategies should be created at different levels: broad corporate-level strategies, business unit or division strategies, departmental strategies, and portfolio strategies. These will be more or less formal, and be revised more frequently according to the climate and what you find yourself in (see "Life Cycle Stage" on page 111). (Life cycles are discussed in Chapter 5.)

The Triumvirate: Strategy, Culture, and Execution

Culture eats strategy for breakfast.
 —Management professor Peter Drucker

Any business aims to do one or many of these things:

- Grow shareholder value
- Grow earnings per share
- Increase revenue
- Manage costs
- Diversify or create new revenue streams
- Cross-sell more products

- Increase market share
- Increase share of wallet
- Increase yield
- Improve customer retention
- Reduce product error/defect rates
- Improve safety
- Improve time to market/speed of operations
- Grow through acquisition

Of course, there are different emphases at different times. To achieve these aims, broadly speaking, the strategist asks these questions:

- Are resources devoted to the right areas, to the most important customers?
- Are we creating products and services that can thrive in a market in different time horizons?
- Where should we spend money? Where should we cut costs?
- Where do skills need to be added or strengthened?
- Where can productivity be improved?
- What culture, attitude, and skills are required?

Many companies have a Chief Strategy Officer or VP of Corporate Strategy. Strategy season frequently begins in the spring, giving this person and her team a couple of months to prepare a deck to present to the executive leadership team in the late summer. This will be discussed, revised, and eventually approved and used as input for budget season, which begins in the fall and continues until the budget for the following year is approved. We in technology tend to like to see our ideas realized moments after we have them. Being aware of this calendar and corporate planning process will help you plan for adding any big-ticket items to the slate in time for them to receive the necessary attention, support, and budget allocations.

That said, the evolution of agile software methods, the preponderance of "disruptive" startups, and a growing global economy have all aligned variously to dilute the formality and rigidity of the strategist's role in such a process, leading her to rely more on regular conversations with the executive team, and create reports with tighter scopes on an ongoing basis.

Depending on her level of power and position within the organization, the strategist finds herself concerned with some or all of the following:

- Identifying business development opportunities, such as partnerships, joint ventures, cooperative arrangements with competitors, and the like
- Finding, proposing, and validating mergers and acquisition opportunities
- Building strategic capabilities within certain areas of the organization, such as helping create a sustainable AI practice in the face of growing trends
- Performing research based on data to recommend long-term directions for the company (generally 1–3 years)

This last one is very common, and how many strategists are trained as consultants entering the field at the venerable strategy firms such as Bain, Boston Consulting Group (BCG), and McKinsey. They likely work with business analysts, marketing, sales, technology, and operations teams in a cross-functional working group to develop hypotheses for how the business climate might be enabling or impinging upon their competitive advantage, and how they should define a goal and direction and allocate resources to win in the marketplace.

According to one McKinsey report (*https://mck.co/2PtDZry*), 40% of strategists responding to their survey are most focused on "using fact-based analysis to spot industry shifts and to understand their own companies' sources of competitive advantage as a foundation for clear, differentiated strategies."

But spending months researching and creating data-driven decks is no longer enough. Because the world is moving so fast, the traditional strategist has taken the driver's seat in building capabilities. As the walls between business and technology continue to fold in on each other, the strategist may well find himself leading a team of data scientists to create an analytics platform to help themselves and customers gain precious insights into their business operations. My colleague Balaji Krishnamurthy, the VP of Strategy at Sabre Hospitality, who was previously in strategy roles at McKinsey and LinkedIn, offers this observation:

> To be a good strategist, you need to be ready to deal with ambiguity. You need to be ready to pivot. You must form a hypothesis quickly about what must be done, then synthesize lots of data. You must then see options and possibilities available, determine a goal, and present your findings clearly with a recommendation on how to allocate resources to achieve that goal.

Ultimately, companies are looking to grow and gain some distinctive competitive advantage. They can do this through technical innovation properly applied to real-world business problems. One assertion of this book is that the roles of Chief Architect and Chief Strategist are more blurred, and more aligned, than ever, and that their mutual understanding of each other's concerns and methods will be an increasingly important driver for winning organizations.

Learn from your executive and product leadership teams what areas of focus they have for their business strategy and product roadmaps, so you can be prepared to match your technology to them.

For example, if your business is in cost-cutting mode, as companies tend to be when revenue is soft or they're preparing for an IPO, then your technology strategy should match. You can do that by examining the people angle: Can you move workers or ramp down in expensive cities in order to hire programmers in lower-cost development centers? Can you examine your delivery and release processes to add automation and reduce manual labor there? Can you use free and open source libraries in place of expensive commercial software? These are examples from people, process, and technical perspectives of how you can map your technology strategy to the business strategy.

A *Strategy Deck* is analogous to an architecture definition document for the organization. Neither will achieve the desired aims if you assume it lives in a vacuum.

The culture of your organization comprises your stated principles, and to a far greater extent, the actual lived principles as reflected by the attitudes, communication styles, and behaviors of your teams. If your teams are territorial and competitive, an integrative platform strategy must identify and address that challenge.

Finally, your teams must be ready and capable of executing on your strategy. A Strategy Deck that states lofty, exciting aims will fail if it also doesn't include diligent, consistent execution and clear metrics to measure its success. This triumvirate is illustrated in Figure 1-1.

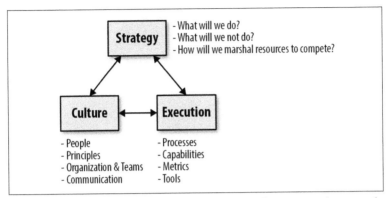

Figure 1-1. The triumvirate dominating forces of strategy, culture, and execution

Find ways to work with your leadership and across teams to ensure all of these forces are aligned. A good first step for doing so is to create two versions of the strategy: one that provides an honest and detailed examination of all three factors to share with the executive team, and another shorter version that communicates only the changes you're driving in a way that you can share publicly with teams. In long-range planning there are financial, business transaction, and personnel matters that obviously can't be disclosed.

Summary

In this chapter, we defined the roles of the architect and strategist. We highlighted key responsibilities and practices for these fields and set the context for the next part, in which we begin our exploration of the pattern language, starting with strategy creation patterns.

Creating the Strategy

Part II of this book is organized around the "creation" patterns—those that help you define components of your technology strategy.

A Logical Architecture of the Creation Patterns

Here I present 19 creation patterns to help you turn a vision into a holistic, strong technology strategy. They bridge the gap between an idea and an executable plan that has taken all key aspects into account.

The following is a kind of logical architecture of the 19 creation patterns. They are divided into five categories, starting with the broadest scope and narrowing from there, each of which corresponds to a chapter in this part:

- Analysis
- World
- Industry
- Company
- Department

Figure II-1 illustrates the logical architecture of how these patterns work together.

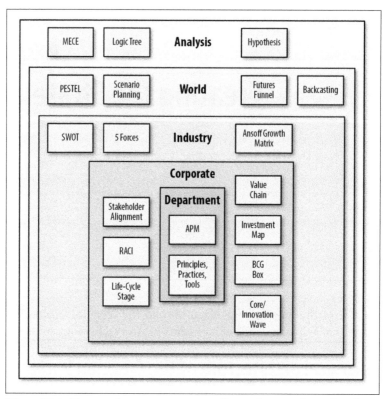

Figure II-1. The set of creation patterns all together in a logical architecture

This architecture is organized into concentric shapes representing increasingly narrow scopes of influence, impact, and relevance. This should help you to match the problem to the set of applicable patterns. The divisions are not strict; they're just a guide. Consider this a visual table of contents for all the patterns relating to creating your technology strategy. It's meant to act like a high-level, logical system architecture. Its purpose is to offer you an overview of the patterns all together and show where they operate in their different spheres. It gives you a quick reference point to select the tool that might help you for the job at hand.

Your boss might simply ask you to "make a technology strategy," because she felt she didn't have one, or didn't know what it was, and thought it would be a good idea to create one. This has happened to me several times in my career. In these cases, you need to ask clarifying questions about the concerns she expects you to address, and the scope of the recommendations she expects, so that you aim at the right level.

Consider the following situations.

You need to make a strategy to upgrade the online database. In this case, you've got a clear, localized, specialized problem. But it may have high impact if things go wrong. So you'll need a plan, and you'll need to contact some folks in different organizations if you miss the cutover window. So maybe this is a small project, and you only need to employ the MECE, Logic Tree, Stakeholder Matrix, and RACI patterns, along with elements of Principles, Practices, and Tools, to make your plan.

Or, you've been asked for a strategy to migrate from your home-grown legacy billing system to a new off-the-shelf product. This is a larger project that has impact and constraints outside your tech department and requires more analysis and understanding of your application portfolio and trends in the industry.

Maybe your boss asked if your software development method is right, or if you should switch to a new architectural model. These are larger problems, and you should expect to employ many or all of the patterns in the scopes of Department, Company, and Industry.

If you're the CTO, CIO, or Chief Architect, or you're on the enterprise architecture team and have been tasked with creating the technology strategy for your company, expect to employ all the patterns here. This work will take weeks and involve a lot of reading and writing and refining.

You don't design software by opening the classic *Design Patterns* book and dutifully making one component for every pattern. It's the same here. Use what pattern you need when you need it, and they'll be different for different strategy problem scopes.

But unless you're creating an overarching, multiyear strategy for your entire technology organization, you don't need to use all of them all of the time. That would be overkill, incredibly time-consuming, and silly. Of course, keep this book around as a reference and use the ones relevant for the scope and type of the job at hand.

Now let's look at the patterns.

CHAPTER 2

Analysis

To use language is to enter into the territory of categories, which are as necessary as they are dangerous.
—Rebecca Solnit, *The Mother of All Questions*

The only cost that matters is opportunity cost.
—Larry Page

This chapter covers foundational patterns for analysis that you can broadly apply. They are *MECE*, *Logic Tree*, and *Hypothesis*.

MECE stands for "Mutually Exclusive, Collectively Exhaustive." It represents a kind of metapattern. It offers a quick way to check that the building blocks of your strategy work are valid and complete. I call it a metapattern because it doesn't produce any direct output that you can drop right into your strategy like many of the others. It's a light form of analysis that's broadly applicable across all the other patterns we'll explore.

Logic Tree is used by strategy consultants as a simple tool for determining a set of relevant problems and possible causes. It helps organize your ideas, making quick work of examining any problem.

The *Hypothesis* pattern is a way of making a guess, based on some supporting suppositions and data, about what the root problem might be.

The patterns we're starting with are the most abstract. These are tools for analysis that will act as the underpinnings of any strategy work.

In the world of strategy consulting, analysis of this kind is performed on what they call cases. A *case* is a particular industry problem to be solved, like a detective "on the case." Job candidates for consultant positions at McKinsey or Bain or BCG must go through the case interview, in which they use a framework of tools and a certain approach to analyzing a problem to properly define and understand it, so they can make good recommendations or solutions. This is not dissimilar from when we are asked to envision a project or an architecture or define a technology solution within a business context. It's about how to make great choices from competing viable alternatives.

In business, *opportunity cost* refers to what happens when you pick one alternative from many: you may realize a gain from the one you pick, but forfeit any potential gains that could have been realized by the opportunities you didn't pick. If the returns on the choice you picked are more than the returns you could have had otherwise, you made the best decision from the available options.

There are obvious questions we get asked a lot. Do you choose to upgrade the current data center, or move to the cloud? Should you build or buy? Should you train your teams on artificial intelligence in-house, or execute an "acqui-hire" (buy a company not for its technology or customers but to get its knowledgeable employees)? What database vendor should you go with? Do you rush to be first to market and get customer feedback even if your product is a bit buggy, or make it solid and delay the launch?

Answering these questions well is hard, because these are complex problems with many moving parts, and because there is considerable risk involved when decisions are hard to reverse, when they're costly, or when you get only one shot at them. As architects, we're asked to make recommendations with imperfect knowledge, and need to do research, try some stuff out, and make a call. The more times we show good judgment, make the right call through a fog of business uncertainties, and minimize opportunity cost and maximize returns, the more our own stock price goes up in the organization.

As a technology strategist, you have many jobs:

- Survey the landscape across your industry, organization, customers, stakeholders, competitors, and employees.

- Examine trends in technology.

- Determine what current priorities, problems, and possible opportunities are presented to your company.

- Analyze and synthesize these problems and opportunities into a course of action: decide what to do, and what not to do.

- Make strong recommendations for how to allocate your company's resources, in what way, in what places, to what extent, and to what end.

That is the work of the technology strategist, whether you're an architect, director, VP, CTO, or CIO.

Because there is not unlimited money and time to invest in everything, strategy is about making the right recommendations to minimize organizational damage and positional disadvantage, and maximize advantage, profit, and benefit. The better you are at raw analysis, the more often you'll make choices with higher probabilities of winning.

MECE

MECE, pronounced "mee-see," is a tool created by the leading business strategy firm McKinsey. As stated previously, it stands for "Mutually Exclusive, Collectively Exhaustive," and dictates the relation of the content, but not the format, of your lists. Because of the vital importance of lists, this is one of the most useful tools you can have in your tool box.

The single most important thing you can do to improve your chances of making a winning technology is to become quite good at making lists.

Lists are the raw material of strategy and technology architecture. They are the building blocks, the lifeblood. They are the foundation of your strategy work. And they are everywhere. Therefore, if they are weak, your strategy will crumble. You can be a strong technologist, have a good idea, and care about it passionately. But if you aren't practically perfect at list-making, your strategy will flounder and your efforts will fail.

That's because everything you do as you create your technology strategy starts its life as a list, and then blossoms into something else. Your strategy is, at heart, a list of lists. Thinking of your work from this perspective is maybe the best trick to creating a sane, organized, productive context for your work. Let's talk about lists for a moment.

There are two parts to a practically perfect list: it must be conceived properly, and it must be *MECE*, which we will define in a moment.

In a properly conceived list, two things are crystal clear:

- Who the audience is
- Why they care

You can determine who your audience is by asking the following key questions:

- Upon reading this list, can the audience make a decision they could not make before having the information in the list?
- Upon reading the list, can the audience now go do something they could not have known to do before?

These are the two reasons to bother creating any kind of information in a strategy. In this context, there is little point, time, or patience for a document that merely helps a general audience "understand" something. Your lists must be lean. That means making them directive toward work that someone will go and do, or providing the data that allows a decision maker to decide the best course of action. The RACI is a list. It answers the question for the project team of who is assigned to what role so that everyone knows who is in charge of what, who is the decision maker for what, and who is doing the work, and if someone sees his name on the list with an "R" by an item, he can go do that work. The Stakeholder List is primarily for the project manager. It lets him decide whom to include in what meetings and whom to contact for certain questions. But if these, and all the many other lists you create as part of your technology strategy, are not MECE, your building blocks will be weak and your strategic efforts will crumble. Let's look at some examples to make this clear.

This formula is MECE:

Opportunity Cost = Return of Most Lucrative Option – Return of Chosen Option

This formula is MECE:

Profit = Revenue – Cost

Revenue – Cost = Profit is MECE. That's because together those three items make a complete thought, divided across lines that don't overlap, and nothing is left out. All of the parts of the money are accounted for within the same level of discourse. It is nonsense to leave out Revenue and simply state "– Cost = Profit." There are only two ways to increase profit: increase revenue or decrease costs. Recognizing the formula as MECE can help remind you to address both the cost and the revenue aspects in your strategy.

This list is MECE:

Spades, Diamonds, Hearts, Clubs

This list is MECE:

Winter, Spring, Summer, Fall

Each entry in the list is *mutually exclusive* of every other one. There is no overlap in their content. Winter ends on a specific day of the year, and then the next day is the start of Spring. Every date on the calendar is, with certainty, part of one and only one season. There is no card in the deck that is part Spades and part Diamonds.

The elements in the list, when taken together as a collection, entirely define the category. No item is left out, leaving an incomplete definition. Thus, the list is *collectively exhaustive*.

This is not MECE:

North, South, West

It's not collectively exhaustive. It fails to include East, and is therefore an improperly structured list.

Consider the following list:

Revenue – Cost = Profit. Free Cash Flow.

This is not MECE because "free cash flow" is not at the same level of discourse as the other items. It is true that free cash flow is an important part of any public company's earnings statements. But that is unrelated to this equation, even though they appear to all be in the category of "stuff about money in a company." That's a weak category for a list because it's not sufficiently directed to an audience for a goal.

What about this one:

Internal Stakeholders, External Stakeholders, Development Teams

This isn't MECE because "internal" and "external" divide the world between them. Development Teams are a subcategory of Internal Stakeholders for a technology strategy.

Elements that are subcategories of other elements must not be included. Consider this list:

North, South, Southwest, East

This is not MECE because it leaves out one of the elements, West, and so is not collectively exhaustive. It also includes Southwest, which is not topologically on the same plane as the other elements. It dips into a lower level of distinction, as in the "free cash flow" example. Southwest is contained within the higher level of abstraction of South. So the elements on this list are not mutually exclusive.

These examples are straightforward (obvious) in order to illustrate the point. But they share an attribute that precious few lists in the world have: they are enums by definition. It is clear what goes on the list and what doesn't. Most things in life are not this simple.

Consider the following list of departments or job roles in a dev shop:

- Software Developers
- Architects
- Analysts

It's not exhaustive: we left out Testers, and other roles depending on your organization, such as Release Engineers, Database Administrators, Project Managers, and so on. To test if our list is MECE, we must ensure we have pushed ourselves to think of all the relevant components that make up that category.

Remember the first rule: know your audience. Your longer, more detailed lists should be kept for your private analysis to help you reach your conclusion, or reserved for lists of things to be done in the project, such as a work breakdown structure. But you don't want long lists when working with executives because they have Executive ADD. Even though you'll worry that you're leaving crucial things out, just give them the summary, but make it MECE. Then you can reveal only the headline: the impactful conclusion that makes a difference to your audience.

The Rule of Three

A good rule of thumb is to find the level of abstraction that keeps your lists in categories of three or five items. For whatever reason, people seem to more naturally understand and remember lists of three, or at the least, odd-numbered lists. Consider two movie titles: *The Good, The Bad, and The Ugly* is more memorable than *The Cook, The Thief, His Wife, and Her Lover*. Push yourself to make your lists with three to five items. Prefer lists of three or five over lists of four. You'll find this little trick helps keep your thinking quick and nimble, and it will shorten your turnaround time because your work will be closer to what you'll need to present to executives and stakeholders.

Consider this list of age groups:

- 0–5
- 6–10
- 11–15
- 16–25
- 26–35
- 36–45
- 46–54
- 55–65
- 66–75
- 76 and above

This list is technically MECE. None of the categories overlap, and the sum of the subcategories equals the whole category. It might be OK for a data scientist doing customer segmentation. But probably not even then. It's too fine-grained and low-level, so it's not very good for strategy work. You need to keep your visor higher; look more broadly to horizons to distill the few things that really make an impact and drive change. It's more analysis and art than science. So even though the list is technically correct, you will lose your audience with details like this, and you can find ways to cluster and consolidate them better, along the contours of a real difference or divergence depending on your own organization's products, services, and markets.

Let's look at a quick example of how to apply this idea of MECE lists.

Applying MECE Lists

Imagine you've been enlisted to create a recommendation to the CTO for a new database system to replace your legacy system. If you merely state the single database system you want to buy, any responsible executive will reject your recommendation as heavily biased, poorly considered, and potentially reckless.

So we want to first consider our audience, with empathy, and always ask: Who is this for, and what do they need to know either to make a decision or to do the thing in question?

Your deciding audience wants to know that they have been given a clear, thorough, thoughtful, unbiased proposal and that they are not being manipulated. In our empathy, we realize that everyone has a boss, and that no one in a company of any size just makes a decision in a vacuum. It's not the CTO's money. So your CTO must in turn answer to his bosses for the system he selects, and is accountable for its success. Your recommendation will be successful if you give your deciding audience a list of MECE lists.

But the list of database system choices is potentially in the thousands. It is impossible to include all of them, and impractical and unhelpful to include even 20 of them. Being ridiculous is not what is meant by "collectively exhaustive." So first we'll create a list of criteria to help us make our final list MECE. I include three or five factors on which you will base your selection and write those down, as they become part of your recommendation too. You're showing your audience how you came to your conclusion, just like showing the long math in school: you're not just giving the answer, but providing the steps by which you arrived at it. This helps the audience follow your story and agree with your conclusion.

Then we'll perform a survey of the landscape, including systems that meet the criteria. Include open source alternatives as well as commercial vendors. We might have a few of each. If we recommended only the one we already wanted, we would miss the chance to perform the analysis, squander an opportunity for learning that might change or augment our view, and lose confidence in our choice and ability to execute. Including only our one recommendation would certainly and immediately invite considerable skepticism and questioning about the alternatives and how we considered them.

So make a MECE list of options. The list is exhaustive according to your chosen criteria. Say you have 8 or 10 options in your list of "all the database systems considered." Say so in your recommendation. It shows you've done your homework and suggests less bias and a more data-driven, analytical approach. Then say you narrowed it down to five options to present. That list includes two you reject and state why. You have a list of three options remaining.

For each element on your list of remaining recommended vendors, create another list of lists: "advantages, disadvantages" (that's a MECE list itself). The elements in each list should be something about the technology, particularly 1) the functional requirements such as key features that distinguish it from the competition and 2) nonfunctional requirements such as performance, availability, security, and maintainability (that's a MECE list, too). Consider these systems also from the business perspective: ability to train the staff, popularity/access to future staff, ease of use, and so forth.

Then from the list of acceptable candidates, present them all, ranked as Good, Better, and Best. (The Good, Better, Best list is MECE too, because you wouldn't improve its MECE-ness by adding a "Horrible" option: the category or name of this list is the *acceptable options*, which presumably does not include "horrible, and therefore unusable ones.")

The Good option might be the one that is acceptable to you, and is low cost but not optimal. The Best one might be the most desirable but highest cost, and so on.

Organizing your list this way makes an executive feel more confident that you have an understanding of the entire landscape, aren't too biased, and show your reasoning. That makes your recommendation stronger.

The Celesital Emporium...

In 1668, English philosopher John Wilkins published a proposal for adopting a universal language as well as a universal system of measurements. In his estimation, this was an entirely rational classification system.

In 1952, Argentine poet Jorge Louis Borges published an essay titled "The Analytical Language of John Wilkins." As a critique of Wilkins's work, Borges offered the following list, in his story "The Celestial Emporium of Benevolent Knowledge," purported to have been created by a 14th-century Chinese emperor as his taxonomy for classifying the members of the animal kingdom:

1. Those that belong to the emperor
2. Embalmed ones
3. Those that are trained
4. Suckling pigs
5. Mermaids (or sirens)
6. Fabulous ones
7. Stray dogs
8. Those that are included in this classification
9. Those that tremble as if they were mad
10. Innumerable ones
11. Those drawn with a very fine camel hair brush
12. Et cetera
13. Those that have just broken the flower vase
14. Those that, at a distance, resemble flies

The list is hilarious, because it is so obviously an example of an incomplete set of sets. There's a lot left out here. Many of the categories also overlap (can a creature not be at once "fabulous" and belong to the emperor and have just broken the flower vase?). Do not all animals, at a sufficient distance, resemble flies? What belongs in "Et cetera"? Who could possibly make meaningful use of this?

Borges's point was that there is not a single, unifying, rational way to classify All The Things, that there are cultural differences that affect our views, and that ultimately such taxonomies can be shown to be arbitrary. So that's understood. The point here is that the division of animals in the "Celestial Emporium of Benevolent Knowledge" is perhaps the least-MECE list in the history of earth. Yet how many of our project and architecture lists, on further inspection, perhaps resemble it?

Getting good at quickly checking if you are thinking in lists and then making sure they're MECE has the pleasant side effect of helping build your powers of analysis. Think of MECE as a lens. Every time you make a list, immediately test if it is MECE. Use it as a heuristic device with your team: inspect your list with the team as you're meeting, be sure to ask if the current list you're working on is MECE, and then refine it. Your team may groan at first, but they will gradually start to see the value, and then they will not be able to imagine how they ever lived without it.

Make your work lists of lists, and make those lists MECE. Your recommendations have a better chance of getting accepted, supported, and executed on. And you will create more power for your organization and your team.

Logic Tree

If I had only one hour to solve a problem, I would spend up to two-thirds of that hour in attempting to define what the problem is.
—Unnamed engineering professor at Yale, via William Markle

A *Logic Tree* is sometimes called an *Issue Tree* in the world of strategy consulting. The tree branches out as a decomposition of the problem you're starting with. Collect possible root causes into groups, using the MECE technique, and then break them down into subgroups. As a technologist, analysis of this kind should be very straightforward for you.

The output of a Logic Tree exercise is a diagram. You can draw it in a mind mapping tool or presentation software. If you sketch on a whiteboard or paper for your initial draft with your team, transfer it into digital form so you can keep it in your growing Strategy Deck.

You will use Logic Trees in two ways. The first is for determining the problem. These are called *Diagnostic Logic Trees*. The second is for determining the solution set, called *Solution Logic Trees*. Either way, you're following the same method with the same type of diagram as output.

Every strategy starts with a set of problems to be solved. The strategy itself is the set of solutions to those problems. A Logic Tree is the critical starting point for any strategy. It ensures you have defined the problem correctly and helps you enumerate the best strategic solutions.

If you are not very clear on the reason for making a strategy, it will be more general work, less relevant to any audience, and less executable. So if you're asked to make a multiyear strategy, or a smaller local strategy, be certain you have alignment on what problem your strategy is meant to address before doing any other work. If you just got asked to make a strategy (as sometimes happens), be sure to ask your manager a few questions first about what problem she wants solved.

People at large organizations spend a lot of time doing hard work on poorly defined or unimportant problems. The result is useless at best, and a disaster at worst. To avoid this trap, you first must know what problem you are solving. There is no generic, cookie-cutter strategy in the world: there are frameworks to help you consider which set of actions is right for you. This one will help focus your work, make it go quicker, and make your resulting strategy more relevant and executable.

Diagnostic Logic Tree

Diagnostic Logic Trees attempt to determine the applicable subcategories of problems and a root cause. They answer the question of *why* the issue has occurred.

As you ask "why," you are using your powers of deductive reasoning, working backward from a known current state.

To reiterate, you start any strategy by first clarifying what problem you need to solve. You are then ready to create the Diagnostic Logic Tree to determine why this problem or situation is occurring.

Solution Logic Tree

Solution Logic Trees are a way of representing possible solutions or courses of action to address a problem. They answer the question of *how* to proceed. You create this kind of tree after making the Diagnostic Logic Tree.

Creating the Tree

To create the tree, you'll first conduct a diagnostic analysis and then a solution-oriented analysis. These are separate exercises. It is tempting to jump to solutions without taking the time to gain a clear understanding of the true problem.

Represent your thinking in two separate trees. You may be familiar with the Five Whys, or fishbone diagram, which is also called an

Ishikawa diagram (*http://bit.ly/2wGI5Vx*). We'll use a similar structure to create the trees.

Once you are presented with a problem, ask why that would be the case. You may quickly see several possible reasons. Write each reason as the second level of the fishbone diagram. Then ask in turn why that would be the case, and write the reasons at the next level. Do this using the MECE technique (see "MECE" on page 29). Repeat a total of five times to come up with a set of possible root causes. Now you can make a declarative statement in your Ghost Deck (see "Ghost Deck" on page 253) that this is the problem and this is the root cause. For more on Ghost Decks, see Chapter 9.

My colleague at Sabre, Justin Ricketts, likes to use the example in Figure 2-1 to help teams see how to approach a Five Whys analysis. It shows a memorable way of demonstrating how you can come to simple solutions and processes.

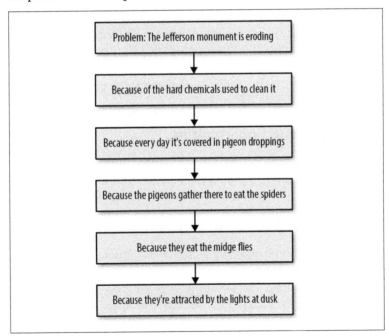

Figure 2-1. Example of Five Whys

So it turns out that the Jefferson Monument was eroding because the lights that illuminate the statue at dusk attracted tiny midge flies, which attracted spiders, which attracted pigeons, which required cleaning crews to use harsh chemical processes to continuously keep it clean.

The solution to the problem was to simply turn on the lights that illuminate the statue one hour later—saving work crews, preserving the statue, saving on electricity and bulb replacement costs, and disrupting fewer tourists who come to observe the statue—and it cost nothing and took no time to implement. Justin's illustration is a great way of showing how you can get to the root cause, but also how the solution may be easier than you'd think.

After you have determined some problems your strategy can address, and then figured out their root causes, you can start to formulate plans for addressing them through a variety of lenses and with tools we'll explore in subsequent chapters.

The other part of the strategy scoping is to consider solutions. To do this, start by imagining the ideal end state—that is, what the world looks like after the problem has been solved or no longer exists. Make that declarative statement in your Ghost Deck. Ask "how" that state could be realized by determining what the prior necessary condition would have to be to achieve it. Do this in five layers of depth, regressing closer to the current state that has the problem. This will help you plan the path forward.

Problems Versus Opportunities

Here we've focused, for the sake of brevity and convenience, on problem solving. But if you focus only on problems, the best you can do is maintain the status quo. Therefore, don't forget to focus on *opportunities* for your strategy, things that represent gains to your customers and organization that they might not be aware they need.

This requires you imagining a better world, absent any direct feedback that people are hurting without it. For example, no one in 2007 was walking around the streets feeling the pain of not having a smartphone—they didn't exist. No one had apps, and no one was sad about it. The iPhone didn't directly address a clear and present pain that consumers felt at not having apps in their lives. But the invention represented a gain for consumers, augmenting and improving their lives and giving them conveniences they hadn't thought of or knew they wanted.

Apple commonly employs this strategy of looking for customer gains, not just pains to solve. Take one of many other examples from the company: in 1998, no one was in despair or unable to be productive because their computers were only one color: boring black. But once Apple made the iMac in five colors named after fruit, the product sold like hotcakes, and is actually responsible for saving the company, bringing it out of the financial crisis created in Steve Jobs's absence. The strategy seems to have worked out OK for Apple.

Hypothesis

Let us employ the symbol 1, or unity, to represent the universe, and let us understand it as comprehending every conceivable class of objects whether actually existing or not, it being premised that the same individual may be found in more than one class, inasmuch as it may possess more than one quality in common with other individuals.
—George Boole, *The Mathematical Analysis of Logic*

A *hypothesis* is a starting point for an investigation. When you hypothesize, you make a claim about why something might be the case, based on limited data, to offer an explanation or a path forward. You wouldn't make a proposition about something you are certain of. You may not have enough evidence yet to even convince you that it's true. But making such a claim puts a stake in the ground that suggests a path for focused analysis. In philosophy of logic, a proposition takes the basic form P → Q, meaning "if P, then Q."

In your strategy work, there is no one single moment in which you declare a hypothesis. A hypothesis is a tool that gets worked into conversation, that gets used together with other tools as a helper. Unless you regularly keep company with strategy consultants, you won't often hear people say, "My hypothesis is..." (but strategy folks love the phrase). You have to recognize that when your team asks, "Why do you think this happened?" or "What's the reason for this?" you're being asked to state a hypothesis.

Consultants at Bain and McKinsey are hired at exorbitant rates to answer hard questions for CEOs. They might have an engagement to recommend whether the company should sell a certain division and exit the market or whether it should acquire a company, or they might be asked why profits are down in Europe, or what strategy the company should use to market in China. These are big, difficult, strategic questions. If they were easy to answer, there would be no need for consultants.

These consultants will spend the next six weeks to six months answering these questions. They conduct research using every available channel, run workshops with key employees, and create recommendations. Their work product is a *deck*. These decks are usually very long and dense, containing loads of graphs and charts. This deck represents the answer to the key questions that started the engagement.

McKinsey consultants famously start engagements by quickly making a hypothesis, maybe after only a few days or hours on the job at a new company. Given that there is so much on the line, they don't work at the company, they may not have prior experience in the client's industry, and they may hold an MBA but be otherwise straight out of school, this sounds preposterous. But it isn't, and here's why. They're very good at forming hypotheses, using mental models similar to what we'll discuss here.

The Five Questions

Hypothesis formulating is making a claim about the world: "this is that." Or, "the reason for X is Y." Or, "the way to make A better is to stop doing B and start doing C." I suppose you can just start making statements along these lines and call it a hypothesis. But that's not going to get anyone a strategy consulting job at McKinsey, and it's not going to serve you as a building block for your strategy.

This pattern is implied by the hypothesizing that strategy consultants do, but is not their process. So you might see very different material on this pattern in other sources. What I describe here I've adapted and customized based on my graduate studies in philosophy and what I have to put to work making successful strategies in my roles as CTO, CIO, and Chief Architect in a variety of companies.

Clinton Anderson was a Bain strategy consultant for 20 years. He once told me that his job in that time was about asking the right questions. The hard part is determining what the right questions are. Professor of Philosophy Alison Brown helped me see that in this context, hypothesizing (asking the right questions) tends to mean we start by asking these five key questions:

1. What is the conjunct of propositions that describe the problem?

2. What semantics characterize these propositions?

3. What are the possible outcomes?

4. What are the probabilities of each of these outcomes coming true?

5. What "ease and impact" scoring values suggest the right strategy?

This is our framework for asking those questions well. Let's take them in order.

1. The Conjunct of Propositions Describing the Problem

When it's time to perform an analysis, which is most of the time, we start with the first of our five questions: What is the conjunct of propositions that describe the problem?

Twentieth-century philosopher Ludwig Wittgenstein was one of the leading thinkers in propositional logic. Propositions and propositional logic are well, but not definitively, explored in his book *Tractatus Logico-Philosophicus*, which I highly recommend. Ten years earlier, in 1911, Wittgenstein's teacher Bertrand Russell wrote a paper titled "Le Réalisme Analytique" in which he describes propositions. Here we'll unpack a few simple tools from this field to aid in our analysis.

In the *Tractatus*, Wittgenstein writes that "a proposition asserts the existence of a state of affairs" (section 4.21). So when you make a proposition, you are making a claim about the world. You are characterizing something that should be able to be expressed as a truth value.

When you are presented a problem, define it as a set of *propositions*. Each proposition is connected by the *conjunct* (the logical operator AND). Within each proposition, the *variables*, or constituent names, are also linked by logical connectors, so that you can deduce the truth value of the overall formula from determining the truth or falsity of each variable.

In modal logic, a proposition is true in accordance with its being borne out by the facts. So you must collect a few data points before making a proposition. Ultimately, your hypothesis will be a list of subhypotheses, each based on an insight, which in turn are each based on a series of data points (see Figure 2-2). As we frequently hear from machine learning teams: if you think your data is clean, you haven't looked at it hard enough.

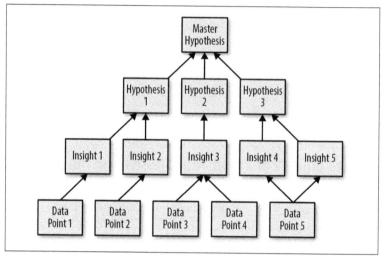

Figure 2-2. Hierarchy of data, insights, and hypotheses

Proposition P is a truth function of a set of constituent propositions if and only if you fix the truth value of P while determining the truth value of every proposition in the set. This is a cheerfully academic way of saying you have to be clear on what you are talking about: define your terms. People use "resource" to mean "compute power" or "human programmer." When you say "customer," do you mean the franchisor you are selling to or their customer? Your definition of "system" is likely too slippery to be talked about. So again, the simple solution is to define your terms.

Insights

An *insight* is when you mix your creative and intellectual labor with a set of data points to create a point of view resulting in a useful assertion. You "see into" an object of inquiry to reveal important characteristics about its nature. In regular conversation, this is required all the time—for instance, to understand the punchlines of jokes. An old Groucho Marx joke goes like this: "This morning I shot an elephant in my pajamas. How he got into my pajamas, I'll never know." Getting the joke requires us to see into the ambiguity of language, that the word "in" has multiple meanings. It can mean that Marx is wearing the pajamas, or that the elephant has found its way into Marx's pajamas, which we don't expect.

McKinsey publishes a set of its insights every year. This is a collection of conclusions and recommendations it's reached based on its surveys and independent research (the data points). You can read one at *https://mck.co/2MIY1Bs*. That document represents a rich set of examples of what we're talking about here. Let's take one example of forming an insight. The document states, "Culture is the most significant self-reported barrier to digital effectiveness." Then it presents a chart containing the top 10 factors technology executives cite as preventing them from effectively executing their digital strategies. This is not an insight, because it mixes no thought with the survey McKinsey conducted. It's just a representation of the raw findings—the data. Additional research from McKinsey indicates that several companies that have addressed their cultural problems head-on, by cutting down silos, have performed better and more quickly than competitors that have not. This is another data point. These data points are combined to reveal the insights that companies that are more willing to take risks, more responsive to customers, and more connected across diverse functions do better in the market. These insights lead to the hypothesis that executives must not ignore this fact and must not wait for their cultures to change organically, but instead must foreground and emphasize this specific kind of culture change—cutting down silos—in order to succeed at their digital strategy. *That's* making a claim, based on insights, based on data, and it recommends a course of action that is not obvious or intuitive. As you build your strategy, this is what you want to do.

Note that it's a good idea to read and cite material like McKinsey Insights reports in your Strategy Deck appendix, as part of your data point collection work, to help you reach your own insights that lead to your strategy.

Sometimes, to the untrained eye, a mere tautology can appear as an insight. A *tautology* is something that is *necessarily* true, so as to be redundant. That's not an insight. A tautology is an assertion—a proposition—that is true for every possible value of its constituent variables, so it's not useful. Nineteenth-century German philosopher Hegel refers to them as "trivially true": he's basically saying that although "A = A" is true, it reduces to making no claim, so it shouldn't be discussed like it matters—it's trivial. Sometimes people (ourselves even) speak in redundant or circular terms when trying to define a problem. The statement "all bachelors are unmarried" is necessarily true as a proposition, but only because we have redundantly reworded the definition of bachelor: we have added nothing to our understanding. Watch out for tautologies as you perform analysis work in creating a hypothesis, or a Logic Tree (see "Logic Tree" on page 37), or in many other exercises in strategy creation where you need to form a real insight about the topic at hand.

2. The Semantics Characterizing These Propositions

Now let's ask the second question in hypothesis formation: What are the semantics that characterize each of the propositions?

Here you are creating an interpretation, determining the discourse around each of these propositions. That's because, again according to Wittgenstein, the "elementary proposition consists of names. It is a nexus, a concatenation of names" (*Tractatus*, section 4.22). But your interpretation must be clearly prescribed by a *domain of discourse*. To put it more simply, the word "play" means something different to a shortstop than it does to a theater goer than it does to a violinist than it does to a femme fatale in a film noir than it does to a toddler than it does to a deconstructionist philosopher. "Gradient" means something different to a data scientist than it does to a UI designer.

As you conduct your analysis, it's powerful to realize that you are operating within a discourse, a *patois*, a learned and shared and, to some extent, private language. What are the terms you aren't sure of? What are the terms someone else might not be sure about? Your work and the spheres of technology and architecture participate in what Wittgenstein called a *language game*. We use old words in new ways, and new words in old ways, and apply a word from one realm of life to another. Words have a preponderance of meaning.

This causes confusion, missed expectations, improper specifications, and incorrect application. It's bad for software and organizations.

To sum up the point of this second of the five key questions: "stuff means stuff." Being aware of the language games in which you and your teams are working is a great step toward being clear with your language.

This allows you to be clear on your definitions of each proposition, such that you can assign quantifiers and qualifiers with more rigor.

You examine here what is believed, what is doubted, what is hoped for, and what has been invested in to determine the truth value of your proposition. For example:

- Ask yourself how biases might be entering your work. Keep a data dictionary to act as a glossary of terms if necessary. Keep your language and terms clear and precise and accurate. A common mistake here is use of the word "platform." People in tech say it so much that they think they have one just because they said it, but it often is improperly used as a synonym for "system" or "application." A true platform offers APIs that allow customers to build something new of their own on top of it. Android is a platform. Alibaba is a platform. AWS is a platform. Salesforce is a platform. Your mission-critical system might be important to your customers, and wonderful, but if people can't make new applications of their own on top of your system without talking to you, it's not a platform.

- Ask yourself what language is used that isn't clear. I have heard product managers ask teams for a "concept model." This was apparently an art term brought over from a previous employer, and might be a great idea. But no one knew what it was. Is it the same as an information architecture? A set of use cases? A set of UX wireframes? Are we telling customers that we're delivering an AI platform, but the data scientists think we're doing a few machine learning algorithms in the background? That's laudable, but different, and linguistic alignment turns out to be A Thing. You can't deliver it if you don't know what it is. Rooting out ambiguous terms will go a long way later.

3. Possible Outcomes

Our third question is, What are the possible outcomes?

Determining the possible outcomes of a decision or action is an act of imagination, and also of reasoning. You can brainstorm with your team to consider what the possible outcomes might be. Write them down into a MECE list. Keep this list around in a spreadsheet or something, because although you'll soon get started by focusing on one path, that doesn't invalidate others. You'll want to use this list for further exploration.

Brainstorming is a useful activity when organized and timeboxed. It will give you a load of sticky notes that suggest good next steps. But it's not going to draw the trajectory from here to a possible future in any sophisticated way, or help you hash through your hypothesis as a thought experiment before you go too far. For that, we'll quickly review inductive and deductive reasoning.

Inductive reasoning finds a fact (a true proposition) and generalizes from there to create a new proposition about broader circumstances. You draw conclusions based on data. The data, as true facts, offer evidence that supports a conclusion. This is what we hope to do as a necessary first step in strategy construction. This is quite useful in hypothesizing. But people fall into traps when they generalize here, and can draw incorrect conclusions. With inductive reasoning, the facts are certainly true, but the conclusion is only *probably* true. It cannot be *certainly* true. Insights are the product of inductive reasoning. It can add nuance and support to the claims you make within your strategy work if you show the probabilities. More importantly, you must be careful to not take as certainly true what is only maybe true. We see this frequently at business meetings, and we need to be able to identify when claims are being overstated so we can determine what other evidence we should collect, or take a different direction in the analysis.

Start by defining your terms and looking at the data you have, and labeling it properly. What relevant facts are there, what research can you do, what database queries can you make, what invoices can you find, what logs can you trace, who can you call up to get a report so you can start with some thread of data?

If you're considering opportunities instead of problem solving, read McKinsey Insights reports, industry articles, technology trends books, business books, *Harvard Business Review*, O'Reilly books, MIT Sloan School of Management books, and your favorite websites, and talk with your colleagues to see what you might be able to take advantage of.

Either way, it's a research problem, like in school. You're like an investigator at the scene of the crime. You need a starting point that isn't based on conjecture. You don't need the whole picture, and probably can't get it yet, if ever. So you start with something concrete to work with and take a shot at making a hypothesis quickly so you can start testing.

4. Probability of Each Outcome

The fourth question you ask in conducting an analysis regards figuring out how likely different possibilities are to occur: What are the probabilities of each of these outcomes coming true?

You don't have to be super-specific, like "the probability of hypothesis A coming true is 76%." If you feel you have enough real data and sophstication in your methods and a small enough problem set to make such a claim, knock yourself out. But I try not to talk that way. That's because in general, people whose full-time jobs it is to predict things are typically pretty bad at it. For instance, Kevin Warsh, former governor of the Federal Reserve System, recently stated at the AH&LA Forum in Virginia that the Fed accurately predicted 0 of 144 financial crises globally that resulted in a recession between 2005 and 2014. And that's kind of all the Fed does. But you can roughly assign probabilities to each of those outcomes with some kind of traffic light to represent ranges of probability such as High, Medium, or Low.

We might state our claims as "I hypothesize that our customers can increase their revenue by 40% if they use our machine learning product." Or we might say, "I hypothesize that within five years mobile phones will represent only 10% of the market and therefore we should use our technology to create a wearables product." Those are fine hypotheses, assuming we have done our homework and can show the data in a slide that helped us draw that conclusion. But one trap here is a logical fallacy called *false precision*. If we were to ask anyone on the street what the temperature of a human body is, we would likely hear "98.6 degrees." This is not as true as it suggests. The precision of this number, and the decimal place, gives the impression that it is a single number that is constant and never fluctuates within more than a tenth of a degree. Of course, human body temperatures regularly fluctuate, and depend on a great variety of factors, such that it's more accurately stated as a range (it's something like 97.5 to 99.5 degrees under normal conditions). Precise numbers make things that aren't facts look like facts. Executives don't like having expectations set for them that aren't met. We set them up for disappointment when we overstate things this way. We tend to produce numbers instead of ranges for estimates all the time. I suspect that's because we are afraid as technologists to state that we don't know something, since our whole careers are predicated not on how sociable and sporting and what snappy dressers we are, but on how smart we are. Train yourself to use ranges. Technologists commit the fallacy of false precision more than any other group of people I've seen—as much as 27.3% more.

We must not be misled by the traps of inductive reasoning. Just because we have seen something in the past does not mean it will continue.

Bertrand Russell famously and colorfully indicts inductive reasoning thusly: Imagine a turkey who is an inductive reasoner. He is fed without fail every morning of his life for years, and reasonably concludes this will continue to the point of never thinking of it, until Thanksgiving morning when his throat is cut. This is a good lesson for technology strategists and business executives alike.

And we should make another, more nuanced point. We can reason that a fair coin has a 50% probability of coming up heads when we flip it. However, upon the first flip coming up heads, we then start to assume that the next time it will come up tails. Thus has much money been lost at the roulette tables in Las Vegas. Every flip is independent of the last. It is possible that we flip a coin 76 times, and that every time it comes up heads. Of course, the probability of flipping a fair coin 76 times and its coming up heads is 1.3×10^{-23} (or 1 in 1.3 sextillion). We do not expect this to happen. But if, that having happened, we were to place a bet that the next time it would come up tails, we would be seduced into thinking that the chances of it coming up heads *yet again* must be impossibly low. But there is no "yet again" to the fair coin. Even on this 77th flip, the probability of heads remains one in two. This is debated delightfully in Tom Stoppard's play *Rosencrantz and Guildenstern Are Dead*. Upon seeing the coin flipped heads 77 times in a row, one character remarks, "A weaker man might be moved to re-examine his faith, if in nothing else at least in the law of probability." (Fun fact: Rosencrantz and Guildenstern are two minor characters from Shakespeare's play *Hamlet*.) So flipping with the same outcome 76 times in a row is an entirely different question, and different probability, than *this* discrete flip after 76 previous flips that happened to come up heads. So there are two matters, not one.

We must first understand the data without adding our assumptions, conjecture, explanations, filters, and biases to them, and make sure we're clear on what we mean. Here's an example, devious in its apparent innocence. Once when making a strategy for a company, my team needed to understand the number of customers we supported on the current hardware so we could help project costs for supporting more customers in the future, and use that as input to determine the cost differences if we migrated to the cloud. I asked the team how many customers were on the system. I was told it was about 30,000. That ballpark was good enough to start working, but as we needed to refine the business case, we thought eventually we should actually query the database. I was told it was 44,000—a difference of 47%! A short time later, I was given another number of 39,000 and then later, 34,000. This was a very straightforward question. We were all over the map. How could this be? It turned out that there were some guesses, and then some assumptions built into the queries people ran—in one case the DBA filtered by "active" customers (a perfectly reasonable assumption), which refined the query to throw out rows that hadn't been updated "recently" (whatever that means). Starting with good data and only true facts, and refining what you name things so you're clear about their status, is critical to increasing the probability of your inductions being true, relevant, useful, and important.

Bayesian probability

There is a tendency in our planning to conclude the unfamiliar with the improbable. The contingency we have not considered seriously looks strange; what looks strange is thought improbable; what is improbable need not be considered seriously.

—Nobel Prize winner Thomas Schelling

Schelling's lesson for us is to not make assumptions too quickly regarding what we find unfamiliar in the data. Unless you start conducting a data science project on your own strategy project, the probabilities you assign to your hypotheses will be more like educated guesses. Those guesses should be as free as possible of assumptions based on what is unfamiliar to you. It may be new, or it may be new to you, but that fact alone is value-neutral in terms of what strategy should be pursued.

Here's a little framework, as a set of general steps, for assigning better probabilities to your hypotheses.

Imagine that the president asks you if acquiring a certain technology company is the right thing to do, or you're weighing in at a meeting about whether we should pursue customers in South America or Europe next, or the CIO asks you to recommend whether we should build or buy a key part of the technology offering, or the CTO asks if we should use an open source or commercial database at the heart of our next product, or your manager asks why this component keeps failing on a semiregular basis. In short, something has happened to cause these questions to be posed: there's a new event requiring you to hypothesize a diagnostic explanation, offer an opportunity, or project an outcome. Let's take a semi-Bayesian approach to the case:

1. The first step here is recognizing that these are very difficult, open-ended questions, and that you are in fact being asked to hypothesize.

2. Next, based on the event, quickly develop your first hypothesis, a judgment of something that you predict might be the case based on data and insights you draw from them.

3. Then determine the probability that your hypothesis is correct, without succumbing to the fallacy of false precision.

4. To do so, first ask: What is the *prior* probability? That's X. It's the probability you would have assigned to your hypothesis coming true *before* this new event occurred, under the current circumstances. This should help separate the distinctive and relevant aspects of the situation (the signal) from the noise.

5. Now estimate the probability of this event occurring as a condition of your hypothesis being true (Y)…

6. …and of it being false (Z).

7. Assign your *posterior probability*—your revised estimate based on the fact of the event.

This technique is useful during troubleshooting, or when you're creating Logic Trees for diagnostics.

This sounds like an unrealistically laborious process to undergo, but once you get used to it, you can do it roughly in your head in a minute or two. Instead of assigning a specific numeric probability, you can use ranges and just state High, Medium, or Low.

In broader strategy discussions, I suppose you could use this as a model if the situation calls for it, but this is a level of detail that I rarely see applied. Once people know enough and are talking enough about these things to be able to do this, they start to a conversation in a new way where no one would think to ask about this kind of precision.

This is the simpler and more useful formula for how to make decisions under high levels of uncertainty:

1. Create and hold a variety of hypotheses in our heads at once.

2. Think about them probabilistically, using an informal application of the Bayesian method.

3. Update them frequently as we get new information that might be more or less consistent with each.

Deductive reasoning

Deductive reasoning is the opposite of inductive reasoning: from a general principle, you move to a specific conclusion. It asks, "If we assume the premises are true, does the conclusion logically follow?"

If the premise is true, then it should be very easy to test it, using the basic rules of logic, to determine the validity, assumptions, and contradictions that are at work in the analysis.

Our job here is to be sure that the stated principle is one that is valid enough to cause us to act on it, and determine the ways in which we must act. For example, sometimes enterprise architects publish a set of principles for the organization to follow. I've done this myself, following my TOGAF (The Open Group Architecture Framework), training many years ago. A popular principle of this kind is "Data is an asset." The point of such principles is that architects can't specify where the programmers should put every semicolon in their code, and nor should they. The principles allow that when developers are left to their own devices to make a local judgment call, they can refer to the principles to help them decide how to create this particular module in accordance with the stated architectural values. I've also heard this principle ridiculed as "meaningless" or "empty." But if such a principle is not stated, developers on a team maintaining, say, a shopping service might not siphon off the shopping data to save for later, because they've written only the code necessary to fulfill customer shopping requests. In that case, the data scientists who follow them—hoping to exercise some machine learning algorithms for better classification, customer segmentation, or a recommender system—will be out of luck. If architects publish their premises, and teams can perform a bit of deductive reasoning to form a logical conclusion to direct them in solving a local concern, the organization will be more aligned and more agile.

5. Ease and Impact Scoring

The fifth and last question in our analysis framework takes up the set of possible outcomes along with their probabilities, so assigns them a value in order to prioritize them. We ask: What "ease and impact" scoring suggests the right strategy?

We've done our homework, collected data, formed propositions as insights while recognizing the semantics at work, stated hypotheses, and assigned them probabilities, and now we've got a pretty sizable collection of possible stuff we could set the organization off to go execute. But we can't do everything at once. So we must prioritize.

To prioritize the work, we'll use a practical method.

Create a spreadsheet listing your hypotheses or other work items. Add two columns: one for ease of execution (how easy it would be to get that done) and one for impact (how much of a difference it would make to do it, how much positional advantage it would give you). Figure 2-3 presents an example.

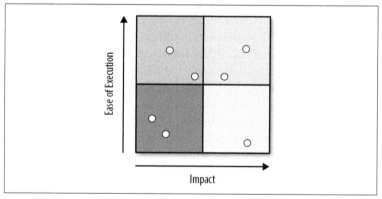

Figure 2-3. Resulting scatterplot chart of scoring your proposals on ease of execution and impact/value

Using a spreadsheet program to automatically plot these items, color four quadrants with equal areas behind the plot, like so:

- The top right are items that are relatively easier to do and have the greatest effect. Color this quadrant green. They should be prioritized first.

- The bottom left are the things that will be hard to do and make only a small advance. Color this quadrant red. They should be prioritized last.

- The top-left quadrant are things that are easiest to do but have a relatively small impact. Color this quadrant yellow. They should probably be prioritized second.

- The bottom-right quadrant are things that are hard or very time-consuming to get done, but are important to advancing your strategy. They don't represent quick wins and aren't the most important, so should likely be prioritized in a third group.

This is only a guide, not a hard-and-fast rule. It serves only as input for you to make your final determinations on what to recommend doing in what order. So it may be that there are elements from the middling quadrants that you exchange in priority, doing one or two big-ticket items instead of several easier, small ones. This is a judgment call depending on your other competing priorities, team capacity, and strategic directives from executives. The resulting chart makes a great visual for your deck, to help substantiate that you considered many alternatives, took a data-driven approach, and made your recommendations from the many available options based on what made sense.

You can use a variation on this, replacing "Impact" for "Value" and "Ease" for "Effort." While these are words a businessperson readily understands, I don't like them as much because they are not both positive axioms, so they're inverted from each other: you want more value for less effort. So "easy" is good, and "valuable/impactful" is good too. It's kind of "six of one, half a dozen of the other," as they say, but helps make the chart quick and easier for your audience to understand, which is empathetic and therefore helpful rhetorically.

Signal and Noise

We can draw a line from the Ease and Impact scatterplot to a related idea: the 80/20 rule, sometimes called the Pareto rule. An common example of this rule is that 80% of your profits come from 20% of your customers. Using the 80/20 rule as a starting point gives us a different way to filter and sort our data, hypotheses, and strategic priorities. It's an informal way of separating the signal from the noise:

Signal
> Something that points to the true state of affairs, something that represents the stuff that matters.

Noise
> Random patterns that might easily be mistaken for signal, or the sound produced by competing signals.

Business moves quickly, and we are frequently asked to make recommendations and estimates long before we feel comfortable that we have enough data, or enough understanding of the problem to do so properly. I've seen architects poring over data for many weeks on end, trying to ensure they've looked at every aspect of the problem before coming to any conclusion. They do endless prototyping and analysis for months just to determine that, yes, in fact the most popular deep learning library is the one they want to use. This doesn't work for modern business. While it seems thorough, and is perhaps well intentioned, it's bad for business and it's unnecessary. You cannot read and try out everything, and everything isn't important. As Larry Page stated, the only cost that matters is opportunity cost, so hone your intuition to make quick "good enough" conclusions, which you can carefully refine later.

There's a discussion in Nate Silver's wonderful book *The Signal and the Noise* that illustrates the point using poker. Silver discusses how "keeping the water level high" means that new players can level the playing field with very experienced, strong players by doing these things:

- Learn the hands
- Learn a rough idea of the odds
- Fold your worst hands
- Make a modest effort to consider what cards your opponents might hold

Doing only those things will substantially mitigate your losses. Because of the distribution of the cards, 80% of the time, you'll be making the same decision about your hand as the best poker players would, even though you've spent 20% of the time learning the intricacies of the game as they have.

Therefore, when wading through hypotheses to make your strategy recommendations, you can hope to make the same recommendations as the best strategists by using just a few of the most applicable patterns, identifying the most fundamental data points, and developing hypotheses that open to the biggest impact. You might come up with 67 recommendations to fix the problem. What are the 10 best, based on high impact and ease of execution? You have better hopes of getting 10 important things done in a quicker time frame, with more clarity of vision for the teams, if you can prioritize well.

Come up with a few, or several, hypotheses quickly, and pick the one that looks most promising to investigate. Your first avenue might not be right, or it may be that multiple forces are at work and there's not a clear, discrete, simple answer.

Perhaps the question posed to you as part of formulating your strategy is: How do we make higher-quality products with less defect leakage? You might hypothesize that you don't have high-quality developers because you don't pay a market rate. Alternatively, you might hypothesize that you have high-quality developers, but the code base was allowed to grow without a concomitant investment in test and deployment automation. Or perhaps you have a capable development staff and automation but don't have domain expertise, or the product management team has consistently prioritized features over nonfunctional requirements. Or management says it cares about quality, but at the end of the day, everyone is bonused on hitting the date, and ultimately that prevails at a cost to stable, maintainable software. Brainstorming for a few candidate ideas goes quickly at a whiteboard. All of these hypotheses sound reasonable, and will quickly spring to mind. They present very different strategies for correcting them, and it is not necessary that only one is the most impactful root cause.

There is an obvious challenge with starting with a hypothesis so early in your engagement. You can, almost per force, introduce a bias. That's to be assumed, and it serves to give you a scope of work to begin to gather the data and understand the relevant factors. And then you can stand back objectively and let the data speak for itself.

Revise your hypothesis if the data does not support it, and follow a different path.

Your initial hypotheses may very well be wrong. That's fine. This is about putting a stake in the ground to get a good place to start, and then coming up with more hypotheses. It's about proving something right or wrong as quickly as possible so that you can move on.

Context

Taking things out of context is another common cause for faulty reasoning, which leads to faulty conclusions, which makes for bad strategies. Unfortunately, it's all too common. We forget or forego the context in which an executive or competitor made a declaration, or the context for a managerial decision to use this vendor instead of that, or the context in which an outage occurred or a message was sent.

Recording, and making transparent, how you arrived at a conclusion will help provide context to future readers of your strategy. Indeed, many of these patterns are tools to help you build, piece by piece, a proper set of propositions to arrive at the right strategic conclusions, and happily offer a transparent trail of how you got there.

Resist the temptation to wait until you have all the data before you start. You will never have all the data. There is no such thing as "all the data." The universe is an infinite conjunct of propositions. Therefore, you must necessarily draw a line around some set of propositions that you collect together in strong relation. Then be bold and make a claim. Ask smart people you trust who aren't sycophants to argue the hypothesis.

Eventually a hypothesis will need to be tested by action. Let the impact of being wrong determine how much analysis you do before taking that action—to a point. Once you start building on your hypothesis by creating the execution plan, you will be able to tell if you're in the right ballpark.

Once you're in the ballpark, you need to perform more data gathering. This means conducting research within your company and on the web, reading industry reports, and finding anything you can to help you determine that your hypothesis is true (in the case of diagnosing problems), or probable (as in the case of imagining opportunities).

This is a simple technique, but starting with it early in your strategy engagement will help align your subsequent strategic technology choices with the business.

Objects and Relations

As Wittgenstein shows us in the *Tractatus*, the world is all that is the case. It is a collection of propositions, an infinite conjunct of lists-of-lists of objects, their attributes, and their relations to one another.

For our purposes here, let's call an object anything that is a possible focus of inquiry. It's something that we can call discrete, such that we could refer to it directly, as a sign, like a child pointing at a ball and uttering "ball!" (Yes, that's a very problematic statement in semiotics, the philosophical study of signs, but I won't fascinate you with the reasons here.)

When you conduct an analysis, determine what the objects are, how they are compositions of other objects, and where objects are finally atomic (no longer usefully divisible for your purposes).

Determine what their *necessary* relation is to other objects: that is, this object exists if and only if another object does.

What is a *necessary but not sufficient* condition? To get a job, it is a requirement (necessary) that you apply for it, but that alone is not sufficient, as you must also interview and get accepted.

What are the *contingent* relations? This object exists if and only if a given relation or attribute continues to exist.

For our purposes, there are a few different kinds of relations in the world, but surprisingly few. Let's review them, as shown in Figure 2-4, so when we're conducting research or creating our strategy, we can sort large volumes of data more quickly and reliably.

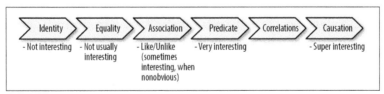

Figure 2-4. Kinds of relations, on a spectrum of interestingness

Identity

Identity says, this thing *is* that thing, in every particle: A = A. This kind of relation is a tautology and represents a thing in itself, in a vacuum. It's not interesting.

Let me take that back, just slightly. It's interesting in only one way. But it's a doozie. As astonishing as it may sound, companies tend to not know who they are. By which I mean, they don't have a clear sense of their own identity. Everyone in the organization does not have a rock-solid shared understanding of why the company exists, who its customers and partners and competitors are, or how it makes money. If I had not seen this many, many times in my career I wouldn't remark on it, because it sounds absurd. The lesson is to be sure that you do know the answer to these questions, so it can inform your strategy. It may surprise you.

Equality

Equality means the complete description of this differs in no case from the complete description of that: A = B. This kind of relation is important if you can show that two seemingly different objects reduce to the same thing, or two seemingly different courses of action actually reduce to the same effect. This is fine for informal analyses. Saying "this is that" is the stuff of metaphors and poetry. That's actually the definition of a metaphor, because it's certain that "this" is, by definition, this, and not that, upon any inspection. It turns out to be impossibly problematic, even for the smartest people in history, to properly find a good referent for "this," or "here." Nonetheless, such statements abound in conference room meetings, and can mislead us if we don't recognize them as the poetry of business that they are.

Association

Associations represent the state that two known different things offer some kind of interaction that changes them. Things are now a bit more interesting. Associations can be directional: one way or two way. Determining nonobvious associations is necessary, but not sufficient, to doing great strategy work.

Predicate

The term "predicate" is somewhat overloaded. In logic a predicate is a property or attribute of something, which is different than in grammar, where it refers to an affirming verb statement about a subject (a related idea). A predicate is an expression asserting some state of affairs. It represents something you can say about an object, something descriptive about its attributes.

In grammar and logic we can say "is a cat" is an expression. It is not a complete sentence. Likewise, "has a longer tail than" is a more complex predicate, as it presumes two variable values (the subject and the object).

The complex predicate is a statement of a relational property, an assertion that "cat" is a be-able thing and existence ("is") is a thing (sort of). Alone, it is not true or false. To determine whether a predicate is true or false, you must fill in the missing referent (the who or what that is being referred to). To say, "Mister Boy is a cat," we now have an assertion that we can test the validity of.

We write $\exists x$ to mean "there exists some x." This is a claim that x is something to be, that is capable of bearing the property of existence, which means both less and more than we tend to think. We can state "x = cat" and "B = Mister Boy," just assigning variables. We state $\exists x B x$ to mean "there exists some cat such that Mister Boy is a cat."

This may sound like I'm being overly complicated about obvious stuff, like who's this guy who doesn't know if he has a cat or not? Well, things may be in certain sets, or in multiple sets, or in no sets. Sets may be empty (have no members). Sets exist within a discourse that mediates the objects, the relations, and the sets they're part of.

Consider this proposition. Consider "everyone." We say "everyone," but we don't mean it. Do we mean all the people alive in the universe right now? Do we include Sophia the robot citizen of Saudi Arabia? Everyone who has ever lived, is now alive, and will be alive in the future? That's the MECE set translation of "everyone." So I think we don't usually mean that. We mean something more modest like "these six analysts at the customer site in this one room who used this one feature one day, but there might be more or less of them even now as we speak and they may have put someone else into some of those roles by next week."

The ∀ symbol means All The Things, everything. It means that within a domain of discourse any (all) of the members can be substituted for a variable—something is universally true within the universe of the domain.

Let x = the predicate "is in New York City."

The predicate logic expression ∀x then translates to "everything is in New York City." One challenge in everyday life as we sit around making great technology strategies is that this is a *valid* statement—not because it's the case that *everything* is in New York City (contrary to what New Yorkers may think), but because it's a *properly constructed* statement within predicate logic.

To help with this, predicate logic conveniently provides us the idea of the *domain of discourse*. Think of a domain as a set.

We'll refer to your set (your universe you're demarcating, your domain of discourse) by S. S has only one member (in set theory, and thereby in computers, we call this a *singleton*). And that member is the "Empire State Building."

The statement ∀xSx could be translated then as "for everything that is in New York City, a domain exists called the Empire State Building, and that domain, with all its universe of members, has the property of existing in New York City," which actually reduces to "everything is in New York City," which *sounds* wrong, but is not only valid (properly constructed) but *sound*—it's actually *true*. That is, it's true *in this case*, because of the demarcation of the domain of discourse—the entirety of "everything" here consists only of the one thing, the Empire State Building. It's also the precise equivalent of saying "The Empire State Building is in New York City," which is nice because it's rather exhausting talking the other way.

The lesson for both the architect and the strategist is that we have this domain today, but can we create a competitive advantage by establishing an outpost in an adjacent domain? If our domain is "hotels," an adjacent domain might be "vacation rentals" since they both have to do with travel accommodations. If our domain is publishing books, an adjacent domain might be streaming instructional videos, since they both have to do with ways of teaching. A book and a video may have very similar content ostensibly, but use very different means of production, have different audiences, and use different distribution channels. They might be one thing and they might be two separate things, depending on your purposes and where the business is going, can go, and should go.

So the architect must look at these two ideas, determine the relevant questions about what members are in each set, and check how much overlap there is. That helps you determine whether you're really talking about one thing or two things. This is important in system decomposition. The mistake I see architects make a lot, and the reason I belabor all this here, is that they don't start in this prior step: they make all manner of assumptions about the demarcation of the domain, don't look at the propositions, and don't examine the language. So they won't decompose the system properly or in a strategic way. But starting in this prior step of determining what the domain really is, and what the sets are, what each set's members are, and what the discourse is will have wonderful ramifications for the way you design the system, how extensible and performant it is, and what business strategies it enables or curtails.

Remember the Five Questions. The second question, regarding the semantics around a proposition, shows us that we are in a domain. In short: when people say "everything," they *never* mean *everything*.

To help clarify, push people to make absolute statements. If someone says, "This thing is what happens," then you can take them at their predicate logical meaning and ask, "Is that true for everyone, alive and dead, always, and in all cases, across time and all eternity?" Then they say "no." And you say, "Well, that's what you said." And they reply, "I'm so grateful to be corrected by you; that's really charming. What I meant was, that's what Sally does on Tuesdays. If it's not raining."

We Don't Know What Money Is

Why am I emphasizing this? It may seem like the furthest thing from your job, but I urge you to scrutinize your language and the language of others in order to be rigorously clear on what you mean. I belabor the point here because it's arguably the most important thing in the book. Knowing what you're talking about is almost impossible, and drawing a logical boundary around a domain is almost impossible, and saying anything articulate and meaningful about it is almost impossible. At a recent gathering of Washington, DC "luminaries," I had the good fortune to meet Kevin Warsh, former governor of the Federal Reserve System, who

---

went to MIT, graduated from Stanford, and got a JD from Harvard. He was talking to a small group about the economy—a complex language game in itself. He rattled off the top of his head 10 or 12 statistics about the state of things and concluded publicly, "The bottom line is that we don't know what inflation is. Because we don't know what money is." That is an incredibly articulate, accomplished, smart man. He wasn't joking. He meant it, and he was right.

There is a point to this perhaps surprising divergence for a business book (if that's what this is) into the details of predicate logic. Didn't expect to see any backward *E*s when you woke up this morning, did you? People have often asked me how I can be successful in technology when my degree is not in computer science. It's very easy to learn Java syntax and write flexible, maintainable software if you understand predicate logic, and it's easy to design software APIs if you understand semiotics and language games, and it's at least not as hard to make resilient and scalable architectures if you understand set theory.

It boils down to this, and if we can promise each other to remember this lesson, then I will let this go: we are making uncreditable assumptions all the time about all the things, such that we make equally uncreditable claims, such that we make bad decisions about architecture and strategy and suffer bad outcomes.

In short: saying stuff is certain when it is not certain sinks ships.

Improve your semiotics, improve your life.

Examine your objects and their relations. Make lists of their predicates. Be careful to not overstate.

To adhere to this lesson, deconstructing this a bit will help us.

Predicates are incredibly important in analysis, and are the building blocks of predicate logic and propositional logic. Predicates are the mines where most gold is hidden, and where the most miners meet their doom. In other words, the attributes of an object are more complicated than they appear, and if you get them wrong, the consequences for your analysis can be disproportionately problematic. It is deceptively difficult to list the predicates of an object.

Correlations

Two objects are correlated if a change in one will usually produce a change in the other, or if the two objects are very frequently found together. This is much the stuff of machine learning, in which algorithms execute over massive data sets to determine the algorithms that describe the data in order to make predictions. These are particularly fascinating, and must be carefully noted throughout your analysis.

Causation

The fact of this state of affairs necessarily and unequivocally causes some next state to occur. It seems obvious to suggest that if you hit a ball with a cricket bat, you caused it to sail into the air. Fair enough. In simple, direct, physical relations, it's harmless to assign causations to things, unless you're a quantum physicist. Familiar causation of this kind affords wonderful things, like ball games and rocket ships and being able to perform crucial acts like drinking coffee. It's important. But in the business world, as in the unruly sphere of human behavior, assigning causations is dangerous. It is almost never the case that there is a simple, easily explained line directly creating a new circumstance. Sigmund Freud calls things that have a preponderance of valid-sounding causes "over-determined." That is, there are too many things operating at once, all contributing in some way to producing this state of affairs to really reasonably say, "This caused that." Or worse, "This causes that" (present tense), as if it's a rule that it always happens that way. Things tend to be more nuanced, contingent, more correlated, more variously associated in a complex business and technology world than straight causation allows for. Causes tend to be a panoply of reasons, with various prior causes, operating at various intensities in various circumstances in varying frequency. If you can identify all these vectors, you might be able to find a cause. That requires careful work and a lot of description. So if you can find a true causation in your analysis, more power to you; that's fantastic: it will make your job much easier. But, you know, good luck with that. And don't blow too much time on it. Do just enough to make a useful claim without overstating, overreaching, and overestimating probabilities.

Strategic Analysis as Machine Learning

In its most basic sense, the process of machine learning (ML) has roughly the same basic construction as our analysis process as presented here. It involves hypothesizing, finding a model, and casting probabilities, much like the work of strategy consultants. Of course, as a relative of data science, it follows more or less the scientific method. Though this doesn't extend our pattern set, I thought I would draw a connection conceptually, because this connection makes the world feel richer and more delightful.

In the popular imagination, perhaps for grammatical reasons, people tend to think of "machine learning" as the machine itself learning what to do, such as what next chess move to make. But what the machine is learning is actually a function: what it's learning is what function best explains the data. A machine learning job is one that, given a mass of data, determines how to frame the data in the context of a hypothetical function (f) that would explain the data, and that hypothetical function is the thing the machine learning algorithm tries to figure out. In the simplest terms, given the data as input, use the learned function to predict the probability that the output is accurate. Stated as a function, that's:

```
Output = f(Input)
```

The job of machine learning is to determine this equation:

```
Y = f(x)
```

...where x is the input data, f is the function or model that can draw correlations and fit the data (such as the function that can draw a line through data points on a plot), and Y is the label, the predicted value the ML elects. Machine learning asks what is the right function f to give you label Y?

The process goes like this:

1. Determine your hypothesis, your question, the label you want to find.

2. Determine the data sources that can provide you a meaningful, relevant answer or context, using internal and external sources. Prepare and clean the data and impute missing values.

3. Determine the right model. In ML we ask, would this work best with linear regression, a random forest, or another model? Usually an ensemble of methods can produce the best results.

4. Fit the model.

5. Predict.

In ML, fitting the model means finding the algorithm that draws a line through the data points, the statistical function that explains the data best such that it can properly label new data. For the strategist, it means something analogous: finding the right mental model, the right systems architecture, the right recommendations and decisions across people, processes, and technology that creates the best path through the available data to the future. This involves making some predictions about what the world will look like and how you'll want to be positioned, and assigning probabilities as we've discussed.

My hope is that this correlation between our present work and our ML work is interesting to you and spurs some additional thoughts in your context. To me, the strategy process is analogous to this ML process. It works for me as a mental model, and I hope it does for you too.

Summary

The steps for forming a sound analysis include:

1. Quickly gather data to form more than one hypothesis based on the question.

2. Perform the initial analysis by asking the Five Questions, examining context, using inductive reasoning, and separating signal from noise.

3. Narrow the areas of focus by prioritizing them, scored according to ease and impact.

4. Assign probabilities to key propositions by using Bayesian probability.

5. Gather more data, test, and revise your hypotheses and analysis as necessary.

Use the MECE technique (see "MECE" on page 29) and Logic Trees (see "Logic Tree" on page 37) throughout, as applicable.

This is an iterative process (depending again on the scope of your assignment and whether you have time for more than one shot at it).

This is also what I'll call here a *fractal* process. With a fractal, each part has the same statistical character as the whole: the pattern is self-similar across any scale. It can be big, such that you're applying it across a broad question or problem with a lot of research and formal expressions of each of the items, taking hours to complete. Or it can be small: using this process on just this, another small piece of one small piece of the puzzle. A fractal is an equation that is eminently scalable. If you train yourself to think this way, using it as a default processing mechanism when people make claims to you, you'll start to do this quickly, naturally, and informally in your head, once you get really good at it.

Remember, too, that when you are given a problem to solve, you should analyze the problem and the solution separately.

Whether the scope of the strategy you are building is small and local, or broad and far-reaching, these questions and the analysis patterns presented here will help you create a great strategy. Use them all as metapatterns throughout your work, like fractals: quickly and informally in your head for small problems, and with lots of evidence, time, care, discussion, and formal recording all along the way for big problems.

In the next chapter, we dive into the patterns for creating your strategy, starting with the broadest context: that of the outside world.

CHAPTER 3

World Context

In the previous chapter, we looked at how to reason in ways that will be applicable throughout your strategy patterns work. Now, we get to the heart of the creation patterns.

The patterns presented here represent the broadest context—that of the world outside your own company. We start here to ensure your strategy work is properly grounded and that your more specific, local strategy choices consider important trends, themes, and vectors beyond the walls of your corporation, and even your industry. They'll give you more empathy and understanding with your customers. These patterns will also help shape your views to ensure the technology strategies you create are the most applicable and supportable. Additionally, presenting your homework in these patterns will show your executive team that their concerns are your concerns, giving both of you the confidence that your technology strategy is aligned with the business, and not only a shopping list of shiny objects.

While these patterns could seem distant from your comfort zone in technology, that's part of the point. People who are strategists for a living base their business decisions on this kind of work. Rooting your work in analyses of the climate and directions the broader world is taking will help make your strategy thoughtful, sound, and complete. Understanding the context and the language in which the business operates will give you a terrific boost in making your architectural recommendations best support your organization. I hesitate to say that you, as a technologist, can do very well to think like a businessperson and talk in their language. That's because, after all, if you're in a position to make strategy recommendations in your organization, I'm sorry to tell you, but you're already a businessperson.

There are four patterns we'll look at to help ferry you in your journey to the dark side of business:

- The *PESTEL* analysis is a simple framework for understanding the broad political, macroeconomic, social, and technological trends operating in the world outside. It helps give you necessary context to make your technology direction in harmony with the conditions informing your business. The work you do here can feed Scenario Planning.

- *Scenario Planning* is a fun, collaborative exercise that will help you imagine different futures so that you can plan how to encourage the happy ones and shore up against the scary ones. The work you do here can feed the Futures Funnel.

- The *Futures Funnel* is a diagram that presents in one compelling picture your conjecture of different possible ways your company's future could play out. I've found it to be a quick, easy, and provocative way to have a level-setting conversation with executives to ensure that you have the right focus and common understanding of the business vectors.

- The inverse of the Futures Funnel is *Backcasting*, in which you posit a desired future state and trace backward to the current state to see what you'd need to do to make it come true.

If you are creating a broad multiyear strategy, or need to make a presentation to your colleagues or peers in your industry about where you're headed, these patterns are quite useful.

PESTEL

The PESTEL analysis was created in 1967 by Harvard Business School professor Francis Aguilar. You use a PESTEL analysis to answer this question: What strategic direction is suggested by the current and anticipated Political, Economic, Social, Technological, Environmental, and Legal climates?

PESTEL offers a simple, memorable framework with which to analyze the key drivers of change in the context in which your business operates. It's used by "businesspeople" (of which you are one) to determine when to launch a product, when to create or update a brand, when to shore up investments in one area of the business, and when to perform organizational planning, marketing planning, and so on. Clinton Anderson, President of Sabre Hospitality and 20-year Bain consulting veteran, defined strategy to me as "the purposive allocation of resources to help achieve a certain aim." The PESTEL isn't about allocating those resources: it comes before that. It helps you see what the weather might be, so you know to pack an umbrella. It's one of the strategist's starting tools.

The PESTEL analysis is in this chapter because it isn't specific to any particular industry and is foundational. But if you're in the business of making pharmaceuticals, the aspects of the PESTEL climate you'll find relevant will differ from those of the strategist from a telecommunications company. You will create your PESTEL while viewing each category through the lens of your own industry. That is, to take one of the six PESTEL elements as an example, there's no such thing as "the economy" in a sense—that's a reification. But you can bring your comments back to the specific ways a given trend or climate within each category might impact your industry and your customers. For instance, if you're in the travel industry, fluctuating gas prices might affect your customers and your business. How will you mitigate this? If you're making software products, gas prices are likely a weakly linked relation, and therefore an unnecessary, irrelevant place to focus your economic analysis. You're not analyzing "the economy" itself—you're using the economic landscape as a context for one aspect of your business.

PESTEL Is MECE

PESTEL itself is MECE—all of the six subcategories it comprises together are on the same level of abstraction, they shouldn't overlap as you perform your analysis, and they represent a complete, good enough picture of the broader world.

Let's look at each aspect more closely by offering some examples of the types of questions you can ask. There's no formal framework within PESTEL to help you answer these questions. As an idea, it's really not much more than the acronym.

Political

How will government policy change incentives for different industries? Consider trade and taxation changes. How might terrorism and military actions impact your contracting business? Regulation in China is different than in other areas, and its firewall means you might need to create a separate copy of software. How does that change your deployment strategy? How would new government sanctions deprioritize or delay your president's interest in international expansion? If a state travel ban on Mexico is instituted, how would that modify your strategy?

Economic

Do consumers have the discretionary or disposable money to buy your leisure electronics or luxury product? What is the cost of financing to your customers who need to build an office to create space that your software helps lease? What are foreign exchange rates such that people might become less engaged in international travel, stay home, and drive more? What about unemployment levels and projections, level of GDP, and other economic trends?

For example, your research might uncover the following data points:

- Travel and tourism investment in 2016 was USD 806.5B, or 4.4% of total investment. It should rise by 4.1% in 2017, and rise by 4.5% per year over the next 10 years to USD 1.3T in 2027.

- Millennials save at a higher rate than other generations: One in six millennials has saved over $100K, and millennials save money at a rate twice that of baby boomers.

- By 2025, the eight largest cities in the world will have a total population equivalent to what the US had in the 1960s.

These are unadorned, uninterpreted facts. Once you have those data, you can put your thinking cap on, draw some conclusions, and look to gain insights about them. That might look like this:

- Fluctuations in the US dollar, Euro, and other foreign currencies can create sudden pockets of places where travel unpredictably becomes undesirable for a period of months.

- Introduction of Bitcoin and other cryptocurrencies could require additional infrastructure if it enters the mainstream for payments.

These are insights because they're making weak claims and projections about possible outcomes.

Social

What are the changing attitudes of the people who constitute your primary base of customers, vendors, partners, and employees? Consider generational trends, family trends, and educational trends. Do the differing tastes and habits of millennials cause your CEO to reconsider certain aspects of the business or create a new brand? How health-conscious are people? What are the dietary trends? Are people more active? What are the educational trends? If most people read on a cell phone, or learn through watching videos, or live with their parents until they are 30 at a far higher rate than they used to, how do you imagine your CEO will find that relevant to the business, and how might that in turn change your strategy?

Technological

This one may seem redundant for us, but it's often not. We get focused on the work at hand, and if we're heads down in a mobile tech project or a legacy migration, we may not be keeping up with the latest in IoT and artificial intelligence. Consider this as if you are not a technologist, so you can more objectively look at technology trends from a business perspective. Work to understand how broad populations (countries, generations, customer segments) are using different kinds of technology and what advances are being made in popular areas of tech. Go to meetups and tech conferences or watch them online afterward, read Forester or Gartner papers, and McKinsey Insights, and check out websites such as O'Reilly, ThoughtWorks, Tech Crunch, and others as an easy start. They publish many whitepapers you can access even if you don't have a membership.

Environmental

What are the ecological influences on your business? Are climate changes affecting your industry? How likely was it that trends toward sustainability in the consumer mindset and efforts to produce low-emission vehicles contributed to the rise of Tesla and its technology strategy with laptop batteries for electric vehicles? Are your customers or fulfillment associates and suppliers affected by the weather in ways that your products or logistics software can better support?

Legal

What laws are hotly debated recently that may change? Again, try not to think from a technologist's view, considering only things like net neutrality (though that's a good one to be aware of, especially in the internet business). What recent laws have been passed; what sanctions have been imposed on different countries? What new laws are brewing or anticipated? GDPR likely has an impact on your big data, analytics, and machine learning strategy. If you're a franchisor, the co-employment laws would make a difference to your technology strategy, so maybe don't suggest writing your own franchise employee scheduling application. Does the legalization of marijuana potentially change your business? What about antitrust laws if you're interested in a merger or acquisition?

Creating the PESTEL

Making your PESTEL document is much like writing a concise, high-level research paper at school.

First you do the research, and then you write it into a short analysis paper. The length will depend on how broad the strategy is that you're doing at this moment.

Next, you put those points into slides for your Strategy Deck. The PESTEL should go in the appendix to support the technology recommendations and claims you make in the body of the deck. People won't likely want to read it up front—they'll start skipping to the conclusion, so you may as well anticipate this and put it in the back.

Researching for PESTEL

These areas of research may be new to us as technologists.

The kind of thing you're looking for are broad statements, with data and sources, about the state of the economy and political outlook. This is how CEOs talk and will help give you the context that can inform your decisions.

Your job here is to quickly research for key stats that serve as signals, or indicators, that you can use in your Strategy Deck to ensure that you make technology decisions properly within that context and do not disregard it. CEOs and executives are interested in things like this:

- Are baby boomers living longer such that more people will be in hospitals or nursing homes for longer, and how will that change their business?
- How are people in the millennial or digital native generation using technology differently? How do their expectations, habits, lifestyles, incomes, savings, gender identities, and political attitudes differ from their parents' as they grow to become the dominant consumer base?
- Are people moving to the cities or the suburbs? What is driving that?
- What areas of the world are seeing organic (people being born) and inorganic (people moving) population growth? How does this change the languages, internationalization, and localization that they may ask you to support in your software? If you globalize, you might need a plan to roll out one continent at a time. Which ones, in which order?

Your PESTEL should include statistics to support a long-term outlook, say, two- to five-year projections. For the Political, Economic, Environmental, and Legal parts of the analysis, there are several sources you can use. Find sources in economic forum conferences, or in published research papers, or in outlooks published by McKinsey, Bain, and BCG on their website. Also look for those published as "Global Economic Outlooks" by the likes of Ernst and Young, Deloitte, Forbes, and the International Monetary Fund. For the Social outlook, you can find good sources in the International Labour Organization, Pew Research, Pew Social Trends, and SIRC.org in the UK, and check out resources such as Cognizant's Future of Work (*http://bit.ly/2wQmJps*) website. Note that many of these web searches readily produce a variety of other options depending on your needs. Because the methods and sources used vary, and because you want to make it easy to validate and look up later, don't forget to cite your source.

The PESTEL probably needs to be updated only once per year, or following some major historical or disrupting event.

Applying the PESTEL

You want to start with a PESTEL analysis early in your strategy work. Write it out as a document, preferably in a word processor first. I've found it helpful to create a scrapbook to use as a kind of "raw material dumping ground" to generate a lot of data and material quickly. Then, in a second round, you can go through and refine it, distill it down to the connected points that start to paint a picture of the landscape for you. Eventually it will become a set of slides after you have gathered your raw material. You will use it in a few different ways.

First, you'll want to have the PESTEL document yourself so you can refer back to it later as you continue applying other patterns to create your strategies. Its primary purpose is as a reference and contextual guide for you in executing the next stages of your strategy creation. Then you'll put it into slides in your Strategy Deck appendix. It will ensure you are making choices from a business perspective, and considering what executives are concerned with.

Next, you can use the PESTEL document as an independent, standalone analysis. Once you've got a draft, you can use it as a token to gain consensus from others in the business. Share it with your nontechnical colleagues in product, strategy, or sales, or with members of the executive team, and ask for feedback to see if you have considered the right things, didn't leave out anything, and are drawing conclusions that make sense to them. They may know more about this area, as technology is a small part. Validating the PESTEL up front ensures you're building on a solid foundation.

If you're creating a holistic, longer strategy (say, a one- to three-year outlook), you'll doubtless end up creating a deck to represent it. You can include these PESTEL slides in an appendix of your Strategy Deck for your executive audience so they can recognize the homework you've done. It will give you and them confidence that you are thinking from a business perspective and that your subsequent technology recommendations are therefore the right ones for them to pursue.

So the PESTEL work is in three parts:

1. Gathering the data through research while doing your best to not mix your biases and assumptions with it.
2. Stating your insights.

3. Making local recommendations based on your insights. These will roll up together to form your business strategy.

There is likely a business strategy already, created by your Chief Strategy Officer. So it's important to check in with her to make sure that you are in alignment, see things the same way, and can cross-validate your findings. Sure, you could just use her existing business strategy, but it may not be written down or accessible, and this helps you learn the language of the business and be more empathetic with the broader concerns so that your tech strategy develops more naturally from a business-oriented view. The fresh perspective will present a good opportunity for a rich conversation. Plus, it's fun.

Scenario Planning

Of the many strategies in the world, the default strategy is consistently the "Do Nothing" strategy. We don't wake up every morning and evaluate whether or not we should still live in this house, eat breakfast, and continue to have a dog. We think, "This is my life," and we continue our established routines. Maintaining the status quo—the Do Nothing strategy—is far and away the dominant strategy of people and corporations.

There are two problems with this strategy. The first is that it creates optimism bias. Worse, it deepens our belief in established and familiar patterns, enervating our ability to perceive change and anticipate the unexpected. People assume the future will look like the past—recall what happened to Russell's turkey ("4. Probability of Each Outcome" on page 49). Instead, can you ask "What if?"

Your technology strategy will be richer and more layered, and will support the business in a more relevant and powerful way. You'll choose to spend time and resources on stuff that matters more.

Scenario Planning is an an organized way of asking the question "What if—?"

Its history traces back to the 1950s at the RAND corporation, where a fellow named Herman Kahn devised the tool to test a variety of military strategies that could be employed against the Soviet Union during the Cold War. You can read more about the history of Scenario Planning in the *Harvard Business Review* (*http://bit.ly/2CvheSr*).

You may recall the movie *War Games* from the 1980s in which the computer played the game "Global Thermonuclear War" against itself (in a kind of generative adverserial neural net, I surmise) millions of times in order to determine the winning strategy (conclusion: there isn't one). This was a popular computer version of military Scenario Planning in action.

This is one basic format for conducting Scenario Planning in your organization, based on my experience several years ago with a McKinsey engagement. It starts with the consulting group conducting a lot of research and interviewing key members of the leadership team. This process takes several weeks. Then the group schedules a two- or three-day workshop for the leadership team, and gives us a presentation for an hour or so that represents its findings and hypotheses. This serves as a starting point and level setting for the exercise. Then we break into small groups, generate a bunch of scenarios, and work through a variety of them to imagine how they might play out. We then reconvene to distill the ideas down to a few that sound interesting and important. You can do this with a private voting round. Then with the remaining few, we divide into teams to figure out good arguments for why our scenario should be the one to win. The leadership takes this as input and thinks about it. As a result of this workshop, my company's leadership at the time decided to go into an adjacent line of business and buy a company.

That's the basic process you can use for Scenario Planning.

Steps for Scenario Planning

Scenario Planning is not rocket science. It's mostly about carving out the time for the leadership team to get out of daily operations and think about the future with a diverse crowd so they can gain additional perspectives on how well they are positioned in the market, what competitors or substitutes might be coming for them, and what opportunities they have to grow the business.

To get into a bit more detail, you can create a map. Pick one of the scenarios you've imagined, even if it's a "weak signal." You'll need a basic shared understanding of a barrier for plausibility. Imagine what three possible impacts of that would be. Then do the same for each of *those* impacts to create a set of second-order impacts that result from the first. You're projecting the weak signals out into the future to come up eventually with a tree of how things play out in the world, using your PESTEL (see "PESTEL" on page 70) as a backdrop. In our logical architecture of the pattern catalog, this pattern operates in the sphere of the world, so you don't want to confine yourself to only your industry. You're on the plane of global, large-scale trends. There's also nothing here specific to technology.

During the workshop you want to:

- Review all the trends out in the world that could affect your company's business. You can get this from your PESTEL. Look at different geographies, different industries. Consider how different trends might disrupt, reroute, or otherwise hurt your business. This is an intelligence-gathering exercise. Define a strategic problem on this basis. It should come in the form of a sentence such as "Should we pursue an alternate growth strategy?"

- Create a list of the trends with your estimation of the impact.

- Build the scenarios together as a list. This is not something you delegate to others. Given their daily book of work, more junior folks may not be able to raise their visors enough to see far. Don't allow yourselves to succumb to group think, or to avoid alternatives that are plausible, but less so, in favor of the most likely or dramatic one.

- Assess the impact of each scenario. Develop alternate paths for each as in a Logic Tree (see "Logic Tree" on page 37). Do not give too much weight to things that seem very improbable. If that sounds counterintuitive, it is not uncommon for teams to get bogged down trying to suss out details or estimate probabilities for scenarios and impacts that are largely unknown. Just give it a tag and move on. You can do this more easily by assigning different levels of uncertainty, relative to the other items instead of something like a raw score.

If you're not the CEO, then pulling together the top 10 or 12 leaders in the company to run this workshop will be a challenge. Putting three McKinsey consultants in a room for a month to do research and dream up hypotheses will run you around $500,000. If this isn't in your budget, you can hold 50,000 bake sales to raise the money, hire a cheaper firm, or just do it yourself. For our purposes, we'll treat it this way. But this isn't one you do alone. Put together a half-day workshop. Invite the clever people, making sure that it's a diverse audience of cultural and work-role backgrounds. Then brainstorm for a bit and follow the preceding outline.

I recommend you do a poor man's version of the initial "imagining the future" deck by bringing in experts from various parts of the business and technology to create and present their own short deck on their vision of the future. Having directors put this together is a wonderful way to invite them into the leadership team, and give them a place to shine. This has the added benefit of giving you a good sense of who the go-getters on your team might be, who the next leaders might be.

Look for the weak but plausible signals you hear from them. Then use inductive reasoning to forecast each of the weak signal's impacts. You're not picking your favorite, or one that you want to see happen. You're forecasting the future. If it calls for rain, you gotta say it's going to rain, even if you wanted to go to the beach.

If you're in a legacy company that has a cash cow and isn't the most innovative, this could be the workshop that saves your company and helps point it to the future.

The value of Scenario Planning is real, but indirect. Use the results not so much in their own right—no one is going to look at the poster boards afterward—but rather capture them into a set of slides, which again you can put in your Strategy Deck appendix or just save to refer to as you conduct your technology strategy. It's perfect homework to feed a Futures Funnel (see "Futures Funnel" on page 80) and a Backcasting (see "Backcasting" on page 83).

That said, Scenario Planning does create value in these ways:

- It exercises your imaginative muscles.
- It helps you to perceive change and be agile in adapting to it.
- It gives your team a (fair) perception that your company is thinking ahead and thinking objectively in order to plan properly to take advantage of opportunities and stave off adversaries.

Futures Funnel

The Futures Funnel pattern is closely related to Scenario Planning (see "Scenario Planning" on page 77), and is really just a visual representation of the final, distilled outcome of that work. It's a fun and compelling view that is useful for busy executives. You need to be able to fit it on a single slide, as shown in Figure 3-1.

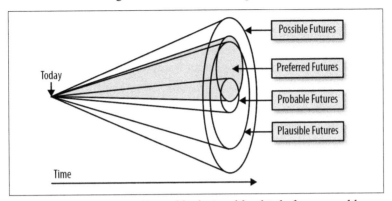

Figure 3-1. Your Futures Funnel looks just like this before you add your descriptions

The funnel in the picture acts like a Venn diagram, of course. Think of each of the circles at the end of the funnel as a set. Your Futures Funnel will look just like this. Literally just plunk this down into your deck, with the addition of only one thing: a brief description of each of the four futures.

The widest set is all the things that could happen, the *possible* futures: any future can eventuate only if it's possible.

Within that, it gets slightly more complicated. The next smallest subset is the *plausible* realm. This is the set of things that are more reasonable to expect to happen. It's possible that a giant lizard rises up from the ocean and squashes Portland, but it's not plausible. We don't think about the ones that aren't plausible too much.

You'll notice there is one key difference between this and Scenario Planning. Here you are adding the value judgment of the *preferred* future. These are the things you want to happen. This, sadly, is the tiniest little port for us to try to land. It stretches across things that are plausible and probable and preferred, which is great, and things that are preferred but silly.

Next there are the probable outcomes. This is the set of things likely to happen, some of which we want, and some of which we don't. Both areas are the place to focus. To help you think deeper about the preferred and plausible outcomes, and the preferred and probable outcomes, I refer you to the Backcasting pattern (see "Backcasting" on page 83).

Ignore any thought of what's preferred but not plausible: this is the realm of fantasies. I suppose you could win the lottery, which might be preferred, but it's not reasonable to suppose that you will, and there's not much to be done about it anyway, so there's no point in thinking about it.

But how do you come up with the material here? I suppose you could just put your thinking cap on, sit down, and invent what all the possible, plausible, probable, and preferred futures are going to be. And if you're a futurist and can do that, that's terrific. But if that's not working for you, Table 3-1 shows a little framework to help you as you consider what this set of possible futures might be.

Table 3-1. Considered futures framework

Internal	Conceptual	External
Financial, organizational resources	Correlations	Potential futures
Current and roadmap architecture	Causal chains	Expected customer behaviors
Current and roadmap product portfolio		Expected competitor behaviors

To help you fill these out, I recommend you use some other relevant patterns here: the SWOT analysis (see "SWOT" on page 87) and Porter's Five Forces pattern (see "Porter's Five Forces" on page 89). Those will really help jump-start your Futures Funnel.

Beyond its role as representing the outcome of a sophisticated Scenario Planning exercise, a second use of the Futures Funnel is to act as a substitute for Scenario Planning. If you have very little time to turn something in, or you are not working on a strategy of broad scope at this point, just do a Futures Funnel instead. It acts as a less rigorous (not at all rigorous, but that's fine for many situations), mini–Scenario Planning exercise. Used this way, instead of the expensive multiday workshop, you implement it by just sitting alone in a room, thinking about what might happen, what's plausible, what's probable, and what's likely. And then write it down and ship it.

Backcasting

We know what forecasting is: you start in the present and try to look into the future and imagine what it will be like. *Backcasting* is the opposite: you state your desired vision of the future as if it's already happened, and then work backward to imagine the practices, policies, programs, tools, training, and people who worked in concert in a hypothetical past (which takes place in the future) to get you there.

It's a wonderful tool.

In any forecast (or backcast), there are two kinds of variables: dependent and independent. The values of dependent variables can be known only on the basis of the values of the independent variables. *Dependent variables* are the unknowns, the moving parts that you want to ascribe an outcome to in order to engineer a strategy toward making that outcome more probable. *Independent* variables are controlled by the strategist, and make up the levers that you can pull to try to change your outcome. Figure 3-2 shows the process.

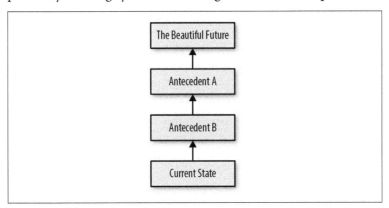

Figure 3-2. The backcasting process

Necessary but Not Sufficient != Sufficient but Not Necessary

Be careful when assigning causation, as we discussed in Chapter 2. It seems reasonable to say "a necessary condition of having a baby is being pregnant." But this is obviously false. So as always with antecedents in backcasting, and root cause analysis in diagnostics, beware of assumptions and biases creeping in.

Here are the steps in the backcasting process:

1. With your architecture, strategy, and product teams together, create a simple vision of the Beautiful Future. Do not give consideration to today's circumstances, or how achievable it might be, just where you want to be. Don't edit yourself. This should be a concrete image, or a metric goal such that you can determine very decidedly whether you have achieved it or not. For example, it could be fairly direct, like "All our software releases are on time," or "No customer finds a bug before we do," or "Defects have been reduced to six sigma levels." Those may not seem like the realm of the strategist, but they are the realm of the CTO and development executives. And often you'll have "get well" strategies. But these are examples. A more complex future vision might be about a legacy system replacement with a new, modern system. How does the team know when they're done? How about "when they cut the power cord on the existing legacy system." That's an image, it's concrete, and you can quickly see how a whole lot of things would need to have happened before that moment.

2. Hypothesize the immediately prior necessary state: those things that have to happen before the next moment can happen are called *antecedents*. They are the necessary condition for the next state to obtain. This is shown in Figure 3-2.

3. Then, once you have hypothesized the array of antecedents to the end state, you repeat the process to hypothesize the antecedent to that antecedent and so on, until you work your way back to the current state.

   The current state is also called the *status quo*. It's Latin for "the state in which" we find ourselves today. It's the set of present affairs across people, process, and technology.

   When you are performing this tracing back, keep in mind what would have to change with people, processes, and technology in each of the three steps. You cannot typically change one of those elements without incurring at least some impact on the others. Thinking of only one of these categories will result in myopia, and a failed strategy.

4. Next, consider the consequent. A basic statement in propositional logic has three parts: the hypothesis, the consequent, and the logical connector between the two. It looks like this:

$$P \Rightarrow Q$$

and means, "If P, then Q."

What you're looking for here is that true premises can never produce a false consequence, which means it's logically *valid*. But a hypothesis is a premise, not a statement of fact. So it's easy to get into trouble and assign as consequents things that don't follow.

The consequent does not necessarily mean the consequence as it does colloquially, as in, "This directly causes that." The consequent here *should be* the logical conclusion that necessarily follows, as an implication, as in "If Mister Boy is a cat, Mister Boy is a mammal." As we've been cautioning, people in business meetings are not typically rigorous about this sort of reasoning. It is tempting to say, "If Mister Boy is a cat, Mister Boy is adorable," but this is not a necessary consequent.

Worse, there are many absurd-sounding statements that are logically valid, but still nonsense, because you're dealing with a hypothetical proposition. For example:

If pigs can fly, then I should wash my car on Tuesday.

Once you have worked out your vision, your antecedents, and your consequents, use your powers of analysis as described in Chapter 2) in probability assignment to tag each antecedent hypothesis with a probability, given the current state. If you're pressed for time, you can guess. But going through the exercise and sketching it out as shown will point you to a set of conclusions about actions to take. Then you can prioritize them and get them in a project plan.

Summary

When creating a broad, multiyear strategy, you can apply these patterns in the order they are presented, starting with analysis: first consider MECE and create a Logic Tree (both described in Chapter 2), and create a set of hypotheses. Then, write your PESTEL analysis (see "PESTEL" on page 70) and conduct a Scenario Planning exercise (see "Scenario Planning" on page 77). You can then create your Futures Funnel (see "Futures Funnel" on page 80) diagram and perform a Backcasting (see "Backcasting" on page 83). That will then likely cause you to refine your analyses.

Of course, if you're making a more specific, localized strategy for, say, changing out your database vendor, you can take the PESTEL analysis, for example, more lightly, or skip these, and move on to the next set of patterns: those for understanding the context of your industry.

CHAPTER 4

Industry Context

You can't just ask customers what they want and then try to give that to them. By the time you get it built, they'll want something new.
—Steve Jobs

In this chapter, we review three patterns useful in understanding the industry that your company operates in:

- SWOT
- Porter's Five Forces
- Ansoff Growth Matrix

Even if you have not been explicitly asked to perform an industry analysis and are only making a local architecture, I encourage you to quickly consider your project through these lenses, as they will improve your design's extensibility and fitness to purpose.

SWOT

You may have used a SWOT analysis. Because they're simpler and quicker to create than other patterns in this book, they are more popularly known. We can cover this quickly.

SWOT is an acronym for Strengths, Weaknesses, Opportunities, and Threats. It gives you a view of these in a single slide.

You can conduct a SWOT analysis in three easy steps:

1. Conduct interviews with people at different levels in the organization and in different departments and roles. Ask them what they think your strengths are as an organization; what gives you competitive advantage; what people, process, and technology you have that makes a difference and helps you win in the market. Then ask them what your weaknesses are in people, process, and technology within the organization. Ask them what they see as new, different, innovative things the organization could be doing and where there is an underserved market, stubborn competitor that perhaps you could topple, or similar business you can serve.

2. Record their responses in a list organized into those four categories, with tags for "internal" (forces within your organization), and "external" (forces outside your organization). Reduce the list into the most important elements, removing duplicates and overly anecdotal or biased items.

3. Transfer the lists into a slide that looks like Figure 4-1.

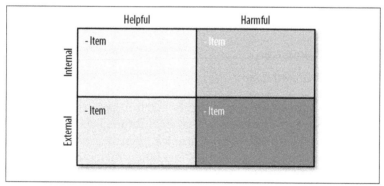

Figure 4-1. Strengths, Weaknesses, Opportunities, Threats

These ideas are organized through two lenses, or across two axes: placement and potential. Placement is either inside your company or outside it. Potential refers to whether it's harmful or helpful.

Strengths
These are internal, helpful things.

Weaknesses
These are the internal, harmful things.

Opportunities

These are external things that can potentially help you if you can figure out how to prioritize and take advantage of them.

Threats

These are external things that you can't control and must survey, understand, and determine how to shore up a defense for.

You can exercise the most control over internal things, so these are generally good places to start. Getting your own house in order is frequently easier and far more beneficial than always eyeing the competition and praying it doesn't rain.

The SWOT can become part of your overall Strategy Deck to communicate with executives, and is most useful as material to focus and provide drivers for your architecture decisions.

Recall you can apply this and many other patterns in a variety of situations:

- As a new person in an organization, you can do a SWOT analysis less formally and for your own understanding of the business, and to help you know where to focus.
- When you're creating an evolution of a legacy system, SWOT can help you plan the architecture and the accompanying product.
- You can use SWOT when creating a departmental strategy.
- When planning partner business updates or key customer meetings or large customer pursuits, SWOT can help you plan selling points, key differentiators, and responses to complaints and concerns.
- SWOT analysis can help you create a long-term broad-based technology strategy across your whole organization.

Porter's Five Forces

Michael Porter attended Princeton and then Harvard, and is a professor in Harvard's School of Business. He founded The Monitor Group, which was later sold to Deloitte. He is widely considered one of the most prominent thinkers in the theory of management. He developed the Five Forces model in 1980 to help companies understand the different kinds of pressures that bear down on business so they can create and maintain competitive advantage. The forces he identifies are shown in Figure 4-2.

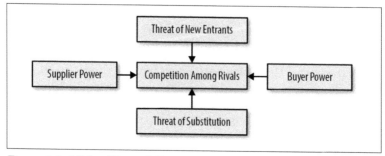

Figure 4-2. Michael Porter's Five Forces

Let's review each force.

Threat of New Entrants

This is the set of risks presented by new competitors entering your market. Google entered the search market in 1998, upsetting the then-dominant Yahoo! Amazon entered the brick-and-mortar retail grocery market with its acquisition of Whole Foods, creating a challenge for Sprouts and similar outlets.

The most attractive market segment is one in which entry barriers are high and exit barriers are low. High barriers to entry also tend to make exit more difficult. The airline industry has an incredibly high barrier to entry, since by definition you need to buy or otherwise have access to an airplane to fly people around in, you've got to get a variety of deals to land those planes at many airports, and there are serious regulatory hurdles to contend with.

You may have assets of your own in the form of patents and rights that can prevent others from entering your market. But beware of relying too heavily on this. The New York City taxi companies had a barrier to new entrants in the form of expensive medallions issued by the Taxi and Limousine Commissions. The gig economy upended this.

There are several other factors to consider:

- Switching cost: how hard is it for your customers to leave your service and use a competitor's?

- Access to key distribution channels
- Government polices and regulations
- Capital requirements and total costs
- Economies of scale that can be realized
- Product differentiation
- Customer loyalty to established brands and brand equity
- Industry profitability

You can see how nearly all of these factors work against the airline industry, as an example. If an industry has high margins, such as the software industry, it becomes attractive to startups.

Ease of Substitution

A substitute product uses a different technology to try to solve the same economic need. Examples include meat, poultry, fish, and tofu, which can substitute for one another. Many landlines have been substituted with cell phones. This one is interesting because it seems like they're both phones. But the threat came from outside the traditional phone industry—Apple wasn't in the landline business and made a better landline that people switched to. So ask yourself how easy it is and what the main candidates would be for someone to stop using your product because of a substitution.

Factors to consider include:

- Perceived level of product differentiation.
- Number of substitute products available in the market.
- Availability of close substitute. The Netflix engineering teams foregrounded the creation of APIs, as did Amazon, to make their products more ubiquitous and easy to access, and to mitigate against new devices or channels that could give audiences different content.
- The general propensity to substitute. If you sell enterprise accounting or resource planning software systems, the propensity of middle-aged executives to change their multimillion-dollar operational software is typically low. Teenagers, on the other hand, eagerly search out substitutes for any current fashion or means of social connection.

- Relative price of the substitute (consider the Canon and Xerox example in Chapter 1).
- Switching costs buyers will incur.

Far fewer people buy desktop computers than did 10 and 20 years ago due to the advent of the powerful laptop, the smartphone, and a variety of internet-connected devices.

Bargaining Power of Customers

How much power do your customers have in the relationship? What is the degree to which they can influence or dramatically change your business? Factors include:

- Degree of dependency upon existing distribution channels, and number of available alternative channels
- How differentiated the products in the space are
- Bargaining leverage, particularly in industries with high fixed costs
- Buyer switching costs
- Buyer information availability and customer education on the products
- Availability of existing substitute products
- Buyer price sensitivity

Bargaining Power of Suppliers

Suppliers are the organizations that provide your company with the raw materials, components, labor, and services so that you can create your product. Suppliers can wield considerable power, depending on the dynamics of the industry, particularly where there are few substitutes, and the resources or talents are unique.

In the software business, there are really two primary suppliers. You need storage and compute (some kind of data center) and you need software developers. Your "supply" in this case is people. You can hire them, grow them as interns, get a bunch at once through an acquisition, outsource, hire agencies, and use consultants. Currently, much AI work requires PhDs in math or computer science, and the supply falls far short of the demand across not only the software industry, but all industries as they seek further automation and competitive advantage. As a result, they command incredibly high salaries, and can pick from an array of potential employers. As suppliers, these developers wield considerable power.

Factors to consider include:

- Employee solidarity and labor unions
- Level of differentiation between alternate sources
- Impact of inputs on cost and differentiation
- Potential substitutes
- Strength of distribution channel
- Ratio of supplier concentration to firm concentration
- Supplier options to serve other companies

The software industry doesn't really have labor unions. But in California, anyone with the job title of "engineer" is required to make a state-governed minimum salary. Of course, many firms pay higher than this, but it is a form of supplier power.

Related to differentiation levels across sources is the idea of the "10X programmer"—the special talent so skilled and knowledgeable that they can do the work of 10 regular programmers. Whether such a unicorn really exists at such a level is perhaps debatable, but it is crystal clear that not all programmers are created equally, any more than all basketball players are created equally. The more your technology stack is a commodity, the less differentiation there will be.

Consider the following talent life cycle.

In an emerging technology, where there are innovations springing up and relatively few pioneers on the planet who have even done this cutting-edge thing, and others in the same industry have yet to even hear of it, there is incredible talent differentiation.

Eventually word gets out, people get excited, and the clever people start learning this new technology and how to apply it. There is still considerable differentiation, but mostly because while the supplier pool has grown, there is a wide gap between "I've done it before" and "I just heard of it." There are still precious few experienced practitioners, there is fierce competition to attract them, they do their own startups, and they command high salaries.

If there's enough application and profit in it, eventually many technologists arrive on the scene, companies arise to teach it, and innovators profit by making it accessible to less schooled and less experienced practitioners. The sillier startups start failing, the hype cycle settles, and people see the tech's true utility and where to apply it.

Eventually, however, when the tech becomes very widespread, it becomes like a commodity relative to its use value, where there is precious little differentiation. The price for this talent goes way down, and it becomes rather easy for employers to substitute one developer for another. This is where, say, Java is today: high demand, but everyone's sort of just expected to know it and there's little wringing of hands in executive suites about whether they'll be able to find Java talent.

Then the tech becomes all but entirely automated away. People used to have whole jobs where they only had to type HTML because the web seemed like magic. Now only robots make HTML; it's not a job for people anymore.

Industry Rivalry

Industry rivalry is about how the public perceives a product and distinguishes it from that of the competitors. A business must be aware of its competitors' marketing strategy and pricing and also be reactive to any changes made. Considerations here include:

- Sustainable competitive advantage through innovation
- Powerful competitive strategy
- Competition between online and offline companies
- Level of advertising expense
- Firm concentration ratio
- Degree of transparency

Applying the Five Forces

Using the Five Forces is about thinking of your company in a holistic way and doing the research—getting the data—to create insights about what's happening to your company.

This is a very powerful tool for the technologist. That's because while every businessperson knows about Porter's Five Forces, their familiarity with it may mean that it isn't written down in a formal way. If it is, and you can access it, fantastic. But what I've mostly seen is that this is the very job of the business folks—to know these things, keep them in their heads, and make decisions accordingly. So, in addition to helping you learn about your business, ask smart questions, and instigate interesting conversations among your peers, you've got another reason to use the Five Forces. The business folks who have to do this kind of analysis quickly and in their heads, and just maintain the knowledge and make slight adjustments to their outlooks as they read headlines, have likely not seen the business from your perspective, through the lens of technology. Prepare your thoughts with this framework specifically in terms of how it applies to your technology, your software product portfolio, and your organization.

Here are four easy steps for putting the Five Forces to work:

1. In your scrapbook deck, or your burgeoning Ghost Deck (see "Ghost Deck" on page 253), for your strategy work, make a slide for each force, and list how, in your view, the company is positioned within it.

2. Make your claim regarding how an aspect of your proposed technology solution or direction supports or defends against each force. How do these circumstances change what you had previously thought your technology strategy should be? How do they expand it?

3. Tag each threat with a traffic light: state in red, yellow, and green if the threat seems high, medium, or low.

4. In a conclusion slide, make succinct recommendations regarding how you as a technologist think you can best position against each force.

Ansoff Growth Matrix

The Ansoff Growth Matrix (AGM) was first published in the *Harvard Business Review* in 1957 by H. Igor Ansoff. In his article "Strategies for Diversification," Ansoff illuminated the need for product managers, marketers, and executives to think about the potential avenues and risks of growth, and gave us a rule-of-thumb type of guide for so doing.

The Ansoff Growth Matrix looks like Figure 4-3.

Figure 4-3. The Ansoff Growth Matrix

It's about four different ways you can grow the business. Here's how to read it:

Market penetration strategy

In the bottom left is the set of products that you have currently and the current markets in which they're selling. With these products, you're trying as a product manager to figure out how to gain market share. This is the easiest avenue, since you have confidence in your existing products and can build on word of mouth to get more customers like the kind. Can you acquire a competing company in the same field to gain more customers like the kind you already have? Can you introduce a loyalty scheme or otherwise create some stickiness? How do you ramp up your sales force?

Market development strategy

Moving up, develop new markets to sell your existing products in. This means that you don't necessarily have to change the products but instead sell them to a different kind of customer as a substitute for existing products in those markets, or begin selling in new countries, which may mean you have to adapt them. This is what Canon did when it figured out how to make copiers priced low enough that the company could sell to individuals and small businesses, who were previously neglected. The menu items and labels and even the names of products sometimes need to change. You may have to consider what additional special features to offer to cater to the new market.

Product development strategy
Create new products in current markets. Can you create additions to your technology, building a platform or ecosystem? Amazon Web Services, for example, frequently adds new capabilities to extend the product set it offers to the same set of customers.

Diversification strategy
Develop new products in new markets. This is quite risky and expensive. The benefit to considering diversification, just as in your personal financial portfolio, is that you minimize any negative impacts in changing tides.

The AGM will likely be one of the more distant models for you as a technology strategist, so I won't belabor it further, but it's good to realize that your product counterparts and marketers may be thinking this way, and you can understand your portfolio better through such a lens.

As with many of the models in this pattern catalog, you can extend the AGM to consider not only your business and technology strategies, but your personal career strategy for growth and development as well.

Summary

This chapter introduced a few patterns to help you analyze your particular industry so that your tech strategy can take it into account. These included the SWOT pattern (see "SWOT" on page 87), Porter's Five Forces (see "Porter's Five Forces" on page 89), and the Ansoff Growth Matrix (see "Ansoff Growth Matrix" on page 95).

In the next chapter, we will drill down to the corporate level. The patterns there will help you understand how to create a strategy informed by your corporate position.

CHAPTER 5

Corporate Context

In this chapter, we look at the patterns that operate internally within the sphere of your own company. There are more patterns in the corporate sphere than in the others, as the work of your technology strategy is primarily centered on how to position your company for competitive advantage. They are:

- Stakeholder Alignment
- RACI
- Life-Cycle Stage
- Value Chain
- Growth-Share Matrix
- Core/Innovation Wave
- Investment Map

Stakeholder Alignment

> *Strategy without tactics is the longest route to victory. Tactics without strategy is the noise before defeat.*
> —Sun Tzu

The way to be successful in a company is to do something that matters to someone who matters. To test the validity of this assertion, consider the alternatives.

The first is for you to spend time doing stuff that doesn't matter to the people who matter. If the work you're doing does not matter to the executive leadership in your company, you face a choice. On one hand, you can get on board with something that does matter to them. Drop what you're doing and find a different team, a different role, or a different project that does matter to them; or redefine what you're doing so that it fits better with the stated direction and values. On the other hand, some soul searching may reveal that your passion for that misaligned project or process is so consuming, persistent, and fierce that you simply do not want to give it up. In that case, you must convince the executive leadership that it must change, or you can leave the company for one that shares your passion or start your own.

Projects that don't matter to the people who matter are misaligned. These projects will keep you employed for a short time perhaps, but they are not likely to complete, and will not advance your organization or your career. Eventually, someone will ask about that little project line item on a budget spreadsheet. If no one in the conference room knows what it is or why we're doing it or who the customer is, it will be sidelined and cancelled. Being on the team of misaligned projects wastes the time and resources of both you and the organization.

The second alternative is to do stuff that does matter, but only to people who are not the leaders. The leaders set the strategy—the technical and business direction—and expect it to be executed.

In both of these scenarios—even if your personal contribution is strong, and you show up every day with conviction and do your best —if your project is misaligned, it will be cancelled. If somehow you and your team do cross the finish line with a misaligned project, that day will see your meagerest rejoicing,[1] as it will highlight something that was previously thriving only because it was under the radar. If you are associated with projects that don't matter to people who matter, it dramatically lessens your own chances of being viewed as a strategic, go-getting up-and-comer in the organization.

---

1 This phrase is from "Something Identifies You" by Peruvian poet César Vallejo (*http:// bit.ly/2QaA18p*): "Something separates you from the one who remains with you, and it is your common slavery to depart: thus, your meagerest rejoicing."

The impact to the company is that resources are hidden or misspent, delaying the chance to complete the strategic projects.

If your organization has a proliferation of projects that don't matter to the people who matter, it must gain alignment so can spend its resources working on stuff that does matter. Organizations that cannot do this fail.

Therefore, you must be sure that you have the support of the most powerful leader you can. The most technical or highest-ranking leader in your organization will likely be the CTO or CIO, or in smaller organizations, the VP of IT. It goes without saying that there is no meaningful technology strategy without their support. However, their support alone is not enough. You must also have the highest-level executive's support, or the probability is high that your strategy will stagnate and suffer. It is the noise before defeat.

In my view, the best leaders and the best-led organizations are sharply focused on strategy, and the projects they fund and the customers and partnerships they pursue all logically follow as consequents from this strategy.

Yet not every leader recognizes the centrality of strategy. Your president or EVP or SVP may change direction quickly, without notice, chasing any dollar waved in front of him for any customer or attractive project that comes along. He may have an unhealthy relationship with partners, vendors, or customers, resulting in an inability to see himself as master of his own fate. He may simply lack the focus and tenacity to stick to a plan that spans longer than a quarter. These are very difficult working conditions for the strategically minded architect.

Executives in some organizations may ignore or even show outright contempt for strategy. They proudly act on instinct and inspiration, and consider any strategy as the work of bureaucrats or dreamers disconnected from the real world, or as something quaint and cute that best belongs on the shelf to collect dust with the rest of the stuffed animals. People can enjoy the freewheeling lifestyle and moderate success that sometimes accompany this mode, but this is not how market leaders are typically made.

Alternatively, your executive leaders may not have quite such an adversarial view, but still may not understand the importance of your technology strategy. But regardless of what it is, you must understand your highest leader's view on strategy. This is the only way to know where you're starting from. Typically, leaders will readily sort themselves into strategic, or something else. That "something else" will lurk in the guise of "intuitive" or "deal-driven" or "operational" or too busy to think about the future. If your CEO or business unit president or Chief Whatever Officer is not interested or well versed in strategy, you can still be successful, but will have a longer, harder road ahead of you. If this person shows outright contempt for strategy, my estimation of the probability of your success is low. In that case, my recommendation is that you put down this book, stop caring about strategy, and ride the roller coaster until it goes off the rails, or, if you find yourself now inspired and steadfast in the joys and fruits of strategy, find a more clueful organization to work for.

It may also be the case that your leadership understands well enough that it must have a strategy, and you have simply been tasked with creating or contributing to your organization's technology strategy. That's a fortuitous first step, and saves you the work of convincing them that strategy matters. That's a hard row to hoe.

Determining Stakeholders

If you want to get something meaningful done, you must first understand the organization chart. To do so, start at the top. Find out who is the CEO, and your business unit president. Ultimately, your strategy must matter to these people, or it will fail.

Stakeholders in What?

All this stakeholder business is more about who has an interest in the project that will result from your strategy. It's not about the stakeholders in the process of creating the strategy documents. But use it as applicable.

You must know who reports to whom so you can make smart decisions about who to communicate with and include in your strategy creation project. To gain support for your strategy, you must have alignment from only three groups of people:

- The people who will pay for it and stand on a stage and tell others that it's important (your leaders, the executive team).

- The people who will execute it, and need to understand it well enough to care about it and execute it properly (your teams, the individual contributors doing the work).
- The people who will ignore or undermine it if their views, aspirations, and concerns aren't represented (your peers).

Therefore, you must have a 360-degree view of the organization. This will help you understand how your organization works, aspects of the process of getting things on the Roadmap and funded, where bottlenecks might be, and more.

Determining Drivers

Once you have examined the org chart, determine what leaders at the VP, Senior Director, and/or Director level matter in terms of your strategy.

These people will be inside your technology organization, but you must also take into account those in other organizations within your company. If the operations or "run" team is under a different leader, identify key leaders here. You must consider product management, sales and account management, the legal team, project management, and the HR team. Your strategy will not be the right strategy, and will not be supported or effective, if you do not consult key leaders in these organizations.

Similarly, you should expand the circle and consider those outside your company entirely. Depending on your business, it is likely a good idea to consult with key customers and important franchisees, and gain an understanding of what plans and views your vendors and suppliers have.

While you must understand these fundamentals, it is not necessary or practical to consult everyone. Don't do this. It will take inordinate time, and likely result in something that looks like it was designed by a committee, whereby everything is watered-down and compromised to such an extent that it is drained of all meaning. If you find that your strategy contains any platitudes that might make good candidates to be printed on a T-shirt or chiseled in the lobby's marble floor, this is a sign that you have gone too far. If you are not making statements that someone could reasonably argue with, you are not making a meaningful or impactful statement—you're not making a choice and putting a stake in the ground to forge a new future.

Who stands out as powerful on this team? While most leaders will at least try to make it appear that they love all their children equally, in reality they do not. Based on their background and proclivities, where they are trying to take the company, the problems and opportunities they face, or the tenure of the members of their executive team, the CFO may exercise far more power than the head of sales, or vice versa. The mergers and acquisition (M&A) team may be two people languishing with no funding to buy anything and therefore little of consequence to do. If the prevailing view is that it is too risky, error-prone, and lengthy to build many things from the ground up, and the strategy is to acquire the best and integrate them, then the M&A team at a conglomerate might be very large and well funded (read: powerful) and busy buying another company every week. In such a case, it is important to consult this team, as their input matters more, and your strategy should reflect that.

If your business unit president cares about the sales team more than anything else, you must include relevant messages for your sales team, and give them a script to talk to customers with. If your CEO seems to listen most closely to her CMO, and you frequently see them on stage together, it would be wise to consult them both and see what materials they have that you can start with.

Reaching out to these extended members of the leadership team for their input has the additional benefit of making them aware of your strategy.

Stakeholder List

Once you have considered all the different teams and leaders just discussed, you might find your list is surprisingly long. You will not be able to keep it in your head.

Therefore, keep your list of the key stakeholders in a list. Make a simple spreadsheet with columns for:

- Name
- Title
- Organization
- Contact information

If it seems that the stakeholders are too obvious, or that there are too few to bother making such a list, you have not dug deep enough.

Expect that the list will contain 10–30 names, depending of course on the size and nature of your organization.

Creating the list is simple. It will serve as a building block for other useful documents, such as the Stakeholder Matrix (see "Stakeholder Matrix" on page 105) and the RACI chart (see "RACI" on page 108).

You will also need it for later, in architecture documents, town hall invite lists, invite lists for steering committees, and more.

Stakeholder Matrix

Different stakeholders have different roles within your strategy project. The frequency and type of interaction you have with each of them depends on the nature and focus of your strategy. Consider your work from their point of view. Is their support important to its success? Do they have knowledge or expertise that could improve, refine, and strengthen your strategy? How much will your strategy change their processes or daily work once implemented?

Once you have your stakeholder list, add two columns to it:

- Influence
- Impact

Influence refers to how important this person's support is. What is her ability to change your direction, impose new priorities, dictate critical aspects, ensure your funding, or otherwise determine constraints for your technology strategy? It's the degree to which she can impact your strategy.

Impact, on the other hand, refers to the degree to which your strategy, as it becomes realized, will impact her. For example, your strategy will have a high impact on the developers now using an aging technology stack if you're proposing to consolidate on a single modern toolset. If you are introducing a services strategy, you must be closely engaged with the product management team. If your strategy involves outsourcing nondifferentiating systems to vendors, this may impact sales and HR. Of course, these are simply examples and depend on what your company does.

Now that you have these two additional columns, use them to score each stakeholder on a scale of 1 to 5 for his or her influence and impact.

Generating 2×2 Matrices

We'll do a lot of generating 2×2 matrices, the four-quadrant charts that plot values to help drive decision making. The basic process is that you enter the values in Excel, create a bubble chart, and then color the backgrounds to create the quadrants.

See *http://bit.ly/2MlCIpr* for a tutorial or download my template from *http://www.aletheastudio.com*.

You can now use the scores to plot your stakeholders on a 2×2 chart with influence on the y-axis and impact on the x-axis. It contains four quadrants, as shown in Figure 5-1:

Monitor
    Those who are relevant enough to make the list, but have comparatively low scores for both influence and impact.

Maintain confidence
    Those who have high scores for influence but low scores for impact.

Keep informed
    Those who have low scores for influence but high scores for impact.

Collaborate
    Those who have high scores in both influence and impact.

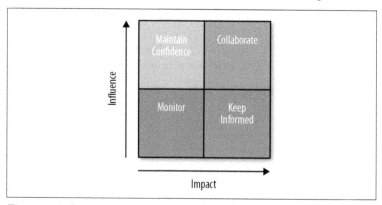

Figure 5-1. Once your matrix is complete, the names will appear in the quadrants

Here is how you work with the stakeholders represented in each quadrant:

Monitor

Ask them on a regular basis about changes in their worlds and what they see coming, and note what might inform your work. Check in with them occasionally and informally regarding your progress. Broader understanding of what you are doing and why will create additional groundswells of support that may be handy later.

Maintain confidence

Invite them to executive steering committees for your technology strategy. Send them reports on your activities. Be sure they understand your milestones and know how you are doing with respect to achieving those. Ensure they understand and approve your metrics for success. Ask about trends or insights they have that might modify your strategy. Follow up on their continued buy-in on the Roadmap. Discuss your progress and funding regularly in some detail in one-on-one meetings.

Keep informed

Include them in an email distribution offering occasional updates on the strategy. Invite them to broad forums such as a town hall where you are presenting an update. Talk with them about work they might have to prepare, such as communications, trainings, deck updates in their departments, or other materials they might have to create as your strategy progresses. Go to their department meetings to present specifically to their team. Discuss the strategy and progress with them at cocktail parties.

Collaborate

Actively work with these people on a regular basis in full partnership to co-create the ideas and execution plans within your strategy.

Now you've got a strong understanding and representation of the organization. You may need to update this from time to time as people come and go, get promoted, and change positions, depending on the length of your project. But now you are well prepared to quickly get things done in parallel threads.

RACI

Now that you have created your Stakeholder List (see "Stakeholder List" on page 104) and Stakeholder Matrix (see "Stakeholder Matrix" on page 105), you have the raw material for helping you collaborate and communicate about your technology strategy project.

RACI is an acronym originating at the Project Management Institute (PMI). It stands for Responsible, Accountable, Consulted, Informed. These are classifications for the participants in your project.

We make a separate document for the RACI instead of just adding to the Stakeholder Matrix. That's because though there will be some overlap, these lists tend to have different people on them.

List broad categories of work down the lefthand side:

Responsible
> These people do the hands-on work to complete this task. Depending on the nature of the items in your work list, this can be any level of title.

Accountable
> These people are answerable to executives for this item being delivered on time with appropriate fitness and quality. May be a VP or director.

Consulted
> These are subject matter experts on some aspect of the system. They are not directly on the hook for doing the work. They may make local decisions or certain aspects that you seek them out for. They'll give advice such that their ideas will change your work, the design, or otherwise modify your strategy. Identifying the right Cs on a project is the difference between a lot of buy-in and a robust product, and something more tepid. If you're making new software, you should likely consult the CISO's office.

Informed
> This is a one-way street. You update these people on project status, and they don't have a say or a recommendation about the work you're doing and can't change it. This category might include the VP of tax so that he's aware of your project and can look you up when it's time to determine if he can apply for an R&D tax credit.

In the column headers across the top of the RACI spreadsheet, list who is involved in the project in each of these four ways. To complete the spreadsheet, enter an *R*, *A*, *C*, or *I* at the cell intersecting which person is assigned that role for that item. Not all of the cells will be filled in. For each work item, you must have exactly one person assigned as accountable for each item. For the other items, at least one person must be assigned to each of the four roles. Typically, there are one or more responsible people, several consulted, and several informed. The completed RACI document looks like Figure 5-2.

	Jeff	Michael	Reto	YOU	Alex	Anna	Bill	Cindy	Felix	Fred	Hans	John	Livio	Luc	Marco	Paul	Peter	Sue	Ted	Tim
Planning/Schedule	R	A	I	C				C												Q
Risk Management		I	I	Q					A								R			
Quality Management			R	C					R											A
Procurement				R		Q			R								R			A
1. Specifications Listing								A	R								R			R
2. Site Requirements	C	A	R	Q						R										
3. Call for Tenders			Q	A	R	C				R							R			R
4. Budget Approval				A	Q					R						R				R
5. Contract Negotiations			A			Q	R	R									R			

R - Responsible (works on, A - Accountable, C - Consulted, I - Informed, Q - Quality Reviewer

Figure 5-2. A typical RACI spreadsheet (source: Wikipedia)

The primary mistake I see people make in RACIs is the temptation to assign multiple people as accountable for a given item. Because the accountable person is typically a VP, or someone with the power to stop or change the definition of that item, or to build the team involved, she must have decision-making authority, and her boss must have the convenience of going to one leader capable of creating the outcome and reporting on progress. Yet assigning multiple accounting parties seems to happen every time people start to make a RACI. Still, you must force yourself and the team to pick only one accountable person for each item. It is tempting to do otherwise because it seems democratic, and multiple stakeholders may have a vested interest in the outcome, or a team may be shared. But it's likely a sign that you have not defined the task properly. Inspect the task with the team to see if it needs to be recast or split. If upon inspection it truly is the proper definition and level of granularity, and two leaders still seem right, pick the one who has the most control or vested interest in the outcome of that item.

Horizontal Headers

Excel has a feature that every project manager knows, but technologists might not: you can turn your header text horizontal to save space. This little trick compacts your RACI and makes it more readable.

RACIs are very valuable and often underused. On the surface, technologists might view them as too obvious or superfluous to bother creating. They might dismiss the RACI as busy work that doesn't matter. If you find yourself tempted to do so, I urge you to reconsider and to take the time to create the RACI. You can often get it done in a short time, and you will refer to and refine it throughout your project as things become clearer.

The RACI clarifies the first two of the following key aspects of any project (the last two are represented in the vision and the project plan):

- What are we doing?
- Who is doing it?
- When must we do it?
- Why are we doing it?

That's going a long way for very little investment.

Alignment Meetings

You can use the RACI and the Stakeholder Matrix in a variety of ways. You'll be surprised how often you return to them and refine them as your project progresses. Their uses include:

- Performing work streams or creating work breakdown structures
- Creating the project plan, Roadmap, and backlog
- Structuring town halls in which you announce the strategy and provide periodic updates
- Populating invite lists to executive steering committee meetings
- Informing working group meetings for a specific subset of your project

- Providing customer forum updates
- Delivering business updates with vendors and partners
- Conducting one-on-one meetings with stakeholders

There are numerous variations on RACI, including one from Bain called RAPID. If you feel something's missing, or are fascinated by the subject, you can read more about it on wikipedia (*http://bit.ly/2MEluTq*).

Life Cycle Stage

Companies, like living creatures, have a life cycle. They're created, they grow, they enter maturity, they decline, and eventually they reach the end of life. Every company that exists is at some point within this life cycle.

Companies, like people, stay in these different stages for different periods of time. It's important for you to know at what stage your company currently is, how long it has been there, and how long you estimate it's likely to stay there before moving to the next.

The reason this matters is that there are typically different levels of value associated with companies at different points in their life cycle. That sense of value creates a level of willingness to pursue innovation. This is typically very high in the beginning of a company's life, when it's trying to create a new product and gain market share or create a market. It's usually more cautioned and considered in mature companies, and all but absent in companies in decline. Knowing the stage you're in gives you a sense of how much work you'll have to do to get something done. It also gives you some guidance on what your tech strategy should be about.

Determining your company's current stage is easy. If you're in a public company, you can read the 10-K report. This report is required by the Securities and Exchange Commission and details the financial performance and the outlook for future earning prospects. There are quarterly earnings statements posted, and quarterly earnings calls that anyone can listen to or read transcripts of. This gives you a good idea of where your company might be. What you're looking for are specific revenue numbers. Figure 5-3 illustrates the basic flow of each stage, but it's just for rough guidance.

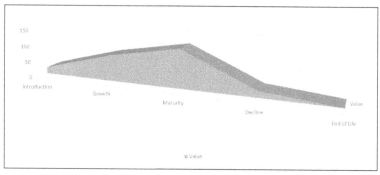

Figure 5-3. Life cycle value stages

The following are some basic guidelines; these are in no way hard-and-fast rules. Companies have hiccups and turnaround efforts, change how they report revenue, and so forth. So you can't just read one number and know the answer. Longstanding companies can enter dark periods and then get a leader with a different vision and create renewed energy, introduce a great new product, and emerge successfully. So anything goes, but let's look at some broad categories as a guide:

- If your company made 5–8% more revenue than it did last year, you may be in a mature company. These companies tend to be well established. They may have long-term customer contracts. They may have saturated market, having sold their flagship product so well that now there's no one left to sell it to. That means the business will be looking for alternate growth strategies. Its sales pipeline may be dry, and so it may be looking for greater share of *wallet*—the business term for how much money you're getting from a customer versus your competitors or other vendors. The company may be looking for ways to cross-sell. In that case, a tech strategy that foregrounds platforms or focuses on stickiness, or quick-win add-ons to the existing product, could be relevant and lucrative.

- If your company made 8–15%, look at its revenues from the previous years. This could be strong growth, or a sign of slowing down, depending on the charts. This will likely be a soul-searching strategy season for your company in which it must figure out carefully how to position itself for sustained growth. Expect a pivot of some kind, and be sure to stay close to your executives to know how this should inform your technology plans. Expect fluidity and volatility, and ensure your tech strategy aligns with this pivot by focusing on agility in the system, such as microservices or improved Agile development methods.

- If the company made 20% or more, it's likely in growth mode. Your strategy might focus on getting to market quickly and strengthening your core. If you have deadbeat products that aren't performing, do you resurrect them or kill them off? Explore this further in the Core/Innovation Wave pattern (see "Core/Innovation Wave" on page 126).

- A company whose revenues are on a continuous downward trend, or which is growing at 0–5%, is likely in the declining side of maturity. Employees tend to expect a 3% raise every year just for showing up. If your company is growing at 3%, and a primary cost driver is labor, it's not growing at all. Ask why this is happening. Look at what in your tech product portfolio you can repurpose quickly. To know how to focus your strategy in this case really requires careful planning, and using more of the patterns here to create a more holistic strategy will be important. It will also be important to focus your strategy on cutting costs. However, you must consider how your strategy will positively impact both top-line revenue and bottom-line costs.

Companies with negative revenue growth tend to go into a spiral: they have to cut costs to make up for missing revenue, which leaves no money to innovate, which makes them lose more customers and more revenue. This is a tough one.

If you're in a private company, leaders tend to be tight-lipped about the financial performance of the company, and it can be difficult to determine what stage you're in. Consider how long you've been in business, ask some executives if they'll divulge the revenue numbers, especially in comparison with recent years, and have them characterize it.

This is a simple pattern: you determine the life cycle stage your company's in, and then use the preceding guide to informally consider how should shape your insights and hypotheses. These are some relevant questions you could consider at different stages of the life cycle:

Introduction

Can you expand from one key customer to other customers in the same market? How can you properly time your investments in help so you can grow rapidly without overinvesting? How can you get your name out there and acquire more customers? This is survival mode, and you are all about revenue.

Growth

Here the concerns shift a bit. To grow substantially, you'll be considering expansions. New market, new products, new customers. This means you'll need to consider automation strategies, but balance that investment as more opportunities and customer feedback change your product. Do you need to update your product to include more internationalization or localization features? How are you examining your processes for efficiency? How do decisions get made now? Is the culture getting away from you? How can you deal with the fact that "what got you here won't necessarily get you there"? How can you reuse certain aspects of the business? Have you mastered your product quality? It's not only about revenue now, but about cost management as well.

Maturity

At this point, a company has significant market share, is a known leader in some area, enjoys recurring revenues from its scaled business model, and can reasonably manage costs. That means it has a target on its back, and a set of existential questions before it: How can it expand into other markets in order to diversify its kingdom? It will have taken some time to reach this stage, and the world has been changing. What are the environmental threats as suggested by a PESTEL (see "PESTEL" on page 70)? What substitutes might be introduced, even by a company with no direct aim of toppling you? What competitors are squarely aiming for you and your customers, and what are their methods, and what threats do they present as suggested by the Five Forces (as described in "Porter's Five Forces" on page 89)? How do you stay relevant? Your processes are all in place; your employees, suppliers, and customers have all come to expect certain things; and yet you must in a sense reinvent yourself without losing your ground, to prepare for continued growth and defend against the threats.

Mature Tech Companies

We have seen IBM and Microsoft go through the maturity stage and wrestle with these existential questions. They tend to challenge prior assumptions and find a way to incorporate, or sublate, two seemingly opposing terms. IBM's stronghold in the mainframe market started to loosen when the availability of cheap, commodity servers and the attendant possibilities for automation meant that software designers could rethink terms like resilience and distributed systems. IBM had to reinvent itself as a services company. Microsoft in recent years has come to offer Linux products—something absolutely unthinkable in the early part of this century.

Companies can potentially stay at this stage indefinitely, as long as they are sharply focused on operational management. But they won't grow without doing something different.

Decline

Companies do not have to decline, though of course most do eventually. The companies that cannot find a successful answer to these existential questions of reinvention will enter a death spiral of cost management, which prevents research and development and innovation, which precipitates stagnation and irrelevance, which continues the vicious cycle.

Growth for Growth's Sake

For what it's worth, since we're trying to be rigorous about challenging our assumptions, companies are not *required* to grow beyond a self-sustaining size. There is no law to that effect. Of course, such a statement is anathema, if not downright blasphemy, to typical corporate dicta in the US, whereby growth for growth's sake is a wholly unchallenged assumption. This is typically because outside investors want to see a better return for their money and create this pressure. But consider for a moment the oldest companies in the world that still are in business today. Many of them were started 1,000 years ago, with the oldest continuously operating business having started in Japan in the year 587: nearly *1,500 years ago*. There are nearly 5,600 companies in the world older than 200 years. Of those, fully 60% are Japanese—four times as much as the second-place country, Germany. And Japan is home to more than 21,000 companies older than 100 years—more than any other country. Of course, most of these oldest companies are in industries that have continuously served humanity's unalienable needs, making some form of food, drink, or hotel accommodations. But it's also interesting to note that 90% of the companies on the list have fewer than 300 employees.

When companies try to grow at all costs, they can enter into markets whose forces they don't understand, try to appeal to customers they don't understand, and start doing things they aren't good at. Growth is obviously important to investors. I hope they'll let you pursue it in a sustainable fashion.

This analysis is but one input of many we're discussing to help direct how your strategy should be focused, or at least what it should take into account; that's all.

Value Chain

Competitive advantage cannot be understood by looking at a firm as a whole. It stems from the many discrete activities a firm performs in designing, producing, marketing, delivering, and supporting its product. Each of these activities can contribute to a firm's relative cost position and create a basis for differentiation.
—Michael Porter

In 1985, Michael Porter, whom you met earlier as the father of the Five Forces, wrote a book called *Competitive Advantage: Creating and Sustaining Superior Performance*, as a follow-up to his 1980 book, *Competitive Strategy: Techniques for Analyzing Industries and Competitors* (both from Free Press). Both books became classics within management circles and offered a new framework called the Value Chain.

One purpose of the Value Chain is to help you understand where your bread is buttered. That is, it divides the world into value creation and support to illuminate where value is created and where it isn't. You should be crystal clear on what your company does to create value, what products they sell, and to whom. If this sounds too obvious to say, it's surprising how this is not always clear, especially depending on your products and industry.

Let's look at the framework itself, shown in Figure 5-4.

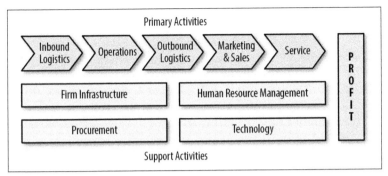

Figure 5-4. Porter's Value Chain

The image envisions a company as a series of inputs, a transformation at each step, and subsequent outputs along the chain that work together to provide value and realize profit. Let's unpack each of the five major activities leading to profits:

Inbound logistics
   Receiving raw materials from suppliers to the plant

Operations
   Transforming the raw materials into valuable products

Outbound logistics
   Getting the products from the plant to market

Marketing and sales
   Getting the products from the market into customers' hands

Service
   Repairing or correcting or improving the products after they've been purchased

You examine each point in the chain to find opportunities for improvement and deliver the maximum value for the minimum cost, and in so doing create a competitive advantage. Businesspeople are used to doing this sort of thing. But if you as a technologist approach your architectures with this in mind, you can create more value for your company.

Maximizing Efficiency

Here are some *efficiency* questions you might ask yourself:

- In your software product development, can you reduce debilitating technical debt? Getting some of the cruft out of the way can improve time to market and time to value, as well as reduce what (at software companies, anyway) often amounts to 80% or more of the cost of doing business: human labor.

- Are there parts of the code or systems architecture you can rework to reduce the server cost? We've all seen inefficient, long-running jobs and carelessly written or poor-quality code that spawns a million network messages when smarter code could accomplish the same work more efficiently. I've seen code on distributed systems get rewritten and double the throughput on half the servers with a lower network bill. These can be hard to measure based on your tools, but subject matter experts who know the system well will likely have an idea of where to start to sniff out such areas.

- What are current manual processes that could be automated to reduce the turnaround time, improve quality, or save on human labor that can be used for more creative purposes?

- Can you use free, open source software in certain places, replacing costly enterprise contracts with their attendant 20% or 22% annual maintenance fees? Or can you use free versions of commercial software such as MailChimp and Google Analytics?

- Can you digitize outbound logistics with digitized training or delivery methods? Can you improve tracking and customer transparency? Can you create automated agents or assistants to bring more transparency or put more power in the hands of customers?

- Can you reduce travel costs through digital or virtual applications, or free applications such as Skype, Hangouts, or FaceTime?

- Can you reduce service costs and turnaround by designing and architecting your products in a more modular way, like Canon did?

- Does this step truly add in your value proposition and market differentiation? If so, keep it in-house and become expert at it. If not, consider outsourcing or contracting. (For more on this difference, see the "Core/Innovation Wave" on page 126.)

- Can you separate true needs at each step versus perceived needs? Sometimes inefficiencies leak in because "that's how we've always done it." Are there "entitlements" that have built up over time as what were once nice-to-haves became expectations, resulting in false requirements?

- Can you use the cloud or Software as a Service in new ways? If you migrate to the cloud, can you foreground automation to turn servers on and off, particularly in nonproduction environments, so that you aren't paying for what you're not using? Can you be sensitive to transferring capital expenditures (capex) to operational expenditures (opex)?

- Are there places where process participants can collaborate better, or collapse several steps into a few?

- Are there redundant or legacy versions of products you can consolidate or kill off and offer lagging customers an alternative?

- Can you organize your applications into services to reduce the likelihood of redundant, inefficient code?

Maximizing value

Similarly, at each point there are some value-related questions you can ask, based on the type of value that technologists can offer:

Sustain the value
Running current business operations, and providing the systems, applications, plumbing as requested. There's value in email and office software that we surely would feel if it left us. But the problem is that this is where we typically focus, and no one cares about it until it breaks. This is the preventative and regular maintenance category.

Maximize value
Finding places to create value in current systems; doing the same things better.

Discover value
> Inventing new things of value. Can we provide new markets, new products, new channels? Can we discover Post-it notes in the lab while trying to do something else?

As usual, the way to approach this is by making a terrific analysis list as described in Chapter 2.

Supporting Functions

There are *supporting* activities as well—those necessary evils for a company of any size, like HR and the IT folks. Porter leaves out some obvious things, such as Legal, which could be a sizable, or at least powerful, portion of your company and even have some non-trivial impact on the Value Chain (I can think of a few large enterprise software companies for whom this is true. Some even make money suing their own sales reps.) So this kind of diagram sort of fails our prized MECE test (see "MECE" on page 29), but we can let that go.

The supporting functions, since they do not directly create value or competitive advantage, are more frequent candidates for cost-cutting measures than value-maximizing measures. For instance, look at how you can automate or outsource tax preparation and invoicing. Check with your legal team about upcoming contract renewals to see if there are less expensive but still effective options.

Get Real

Once I made a technology proposal to the company president. She is a very smart woman, and before becoming president was the CFO. As I pitched my technology strategy to her, I pointed out that by taking one of my recommendations, the company would save half a million dollars. She asked how. I replied that with the proposed automation, the work that was done by 10 people today could be done by 6, with better quality. I was proud that I had done some quick third-grade math and been so thoughtful as to foreground the financial aspect that she cared about over the technology. But her response was something I'll never forget: "Which four people are you going to fire today?" I said I hadn't thought of that and didn't want to fire anyone—they were all good, capable people and could do other things. She said, "Fine, but you can't say 'cost savings' since they're still on the payroll. There's maybe some bene-

---

fit here, but it's not cost savings. Fix your deck." That was a good lesson.

Applying the Value Chain

A second purpose of the Value Chain is to help provide you a handy list of each of the key processes to check to determine where you can create more value, gain higher margin, create a differentiating advantage, and cut costs.

Here's how I suggest using it:

- Treat it as a high-level checklist to establish a baseline understanding of what your business unit does, as a reminder to yourself to not leave any of these process points unaddressed in your technology strategy. Of course, depending on the challenge you've been posed, certain areas will be more or less relevant.

- Determine the owners or some knowledgeable, communicative person within each of these areas to determine how it works, where it sees advantage, and where it needs help. Consider each in terms of people, process, and technology.

- Consider and identify specific ways that your technology strategy can directly improve costs, improve margins, or add to profitability for each of the points in the process. Map technology recommendations to each.

You may wonder about technology being relegated to a support function. In 1985, the web didn't yet exist, so we can still interpret the Value Chain chart pictured earlier as relevant today. In a software product company, we can think of operations as the function that makes the product, with technology still existing as it does on Porter's chart as a support function in the form of the back office and plumbing.

Revenue diversity

But the larger the company, the more diverse it will be, and it will have its hands in many cookie jars, making money in a variety of ways—even within a single division. We all are familiar with Pepsi, and think of it as a soft drink maker. It's easy to assume all the money comes from Pepsi cola. But the company also owns Tropicana and Gatorade and partners to sell the ready-to-drink beverages you buy from Starbucks (which, by the way, owns a record label), and Lipton tea, and Stolichnaya vodka. Yet, in the last decade, despite how Pepsi might be thought of in the popular imagination, beverages accounted for only 50% of PepsiCo's revenues. Pepsi also owns Quaker Oats (which also sells Rice-a-Roni and Cap'n Crunch), has had numerous restaurant chains like California Pizza Kitchen, and acquired Wilson Sporting Goods equipment company in 1970, and even owned North American Van Lines.

Did you ever see the movies *Stripes*, *Ghostbusters*, *Karate Kid*, or *Tootsie* in the 1980s? They were produced by Columbia Pictures in the five-year period that the movie studio was owned and run by none other than…the Coca-Cola Company.

The candy company Mars ran a company called Chappell Brothers. You may not have heard of them: they make dog food. But that shouldn't be surprising given that Nestle, whom you probably think of as a chocolate bar company, owns Purina, one of the largest pet food manufacturers in the world, and has a significant stake in L'Oreal, the makeup company. In fact, Nestle has over *8,000* brands.

What about Proctor & Gamble? In 2014 it announced that it was selling off 100 brands in order to focus on its remaining 65 brands, which represented 95% of the company's profit. That's a lot of brands, and a lot of money concentrated in only 39% of the company (recall the Pareto rule from Chapter 2).

But such revenue diversity is not the sole domain of conglomerates. We think of hotels as selling hotel rooms. While of course that's true, most higher-end hotels typically make only half their money on selling hotel rooms, with the rest coming from restaurants, meeting rooms, convention fees, tee times, spas, and the like. Many hotels in Las Vegas sell the room for very cheap or even give it away for free, because the bulk of their revenue comes from gambling.

And these things change and shift with differences in consumer trends and competitive forces. According to a Bank of America report, in 1990 nearly 65% of revenue in Las Vegas came from gambling. Twenty years later, a Business Insider article reported that (*https://read.bi/2MEvKuU*) 65% of its revenue came from nongaming sources, such as shopping and restaurants.

Companies enter joint ventures, partnerships, agreements, and licensing arrangements. If you think you know how you get paid in your company, I urge you to investigate and dig deeper to really find out all the sources of revenue. Only then can you understand all the sources of value creation in your company and how to account for them in a supporting architecture. You might build a set of different microservices or design a data model differently if you understand these aspects of your business.

Then there's the other side of the coin: things companies do strategically but that don't have clear revenue streams yet. These can matter tremendously. At the recent O'Reilly Artificial Intelligence conference in New York City, a Google executive stated quite plainly, "Google is an AI company, full stop." We think of Google as making money through selling ads (since even in recent years that's where $80 billion of its revenue comes from, with all its other products and businesses generating only $10 billion altogether). Of course there is a plan there, and it's holistic. All those other businesses feed Google the data it needs for its current and future AI work. Waymo, the division within Google for autonomous vehicles, is projected to add as much as $40 billion to Google's top line by 2025.

So companies are more diverse than they may at first appear, and place a number of bets—some of which they expect to pay off long-term, and some more near-term. Understanding the ecosystem within the Value Chain is helpful to the business-minded architect. I once created an architecture that probably wasn't the optimal design for a particular system, because I was too focused on the technology and thought of one company in particular as a big competitor. That was true, but unbeknownst to me, that company was also our partner in a joint venture arrangement little known outside the executive team. Had I been aware, I would have made different technology choices. Since then, I do my best to know where our bread is buttered and make the architecture decisions and technology strategies accordingly.

The Value Chain is intended to be used within a single business unit or division, to keep things coherent. But you can also apply it within a department, depending on the level of analysis you're performing and for what purpose. But Porter's statement from the epigraph at the beginning of this pattern doesn't preclude us from using the Value Chain breakdown at the global level, the industry level, the corporate level, or the department level. We are not business professors. People get entire PhDs on the idea of Value Chains. People can get incredibly nerdy about this stuff. If you want to be nerdy about

Value Chains, you're welcome to read Porter's 600-page book and its companion volume, which is a slimmer 400 pages. For us, it's just a picture. And that's just fine. We needn't adhere to the strict dicta around the use of a tool like this. Think of it instead as a good reminder of all the different areas of your division to tour. Your strategies will be more holistic, more pertinent, and more impactful if you are sharply focused on real business problems and creating value, and see many opportunities to do so.

Getting your baseline metrics

One final but critical point: you need to get a sense of the relevant costs in each of these areas. Take a baseline and know where you're starting from. That way, after your new solution is implemented, you'll be able to measure and demonstrate the costs reduction you created. This will be an important metric to have in your back pocket, not only so that you understand how effective your solutions were, but so that management knows that too.

The Process Posture Map (see "Process Posture Map" on page 138) will help you with the Value Chain.

Growth-Share Matrix

The Growth-Share Matrix is also known as the "BCG Box." It was created by Bruce Henderson in 1970 for the Boston Consulting Group. It was intended as a tool to help companies analyze and manage their portfolios. Its purpose is to help companies allocate resources.

Here are the four quadrants. Depending on the size of your company, this matrix can be used to view products in your portfolio or entire business units:

Cash cows

> These have low growth but high market share. These are your successful, mature products in an established industry and mature market. You milk them for the cash they consistently bring, and they're fantastic because they don't cost much to keep running. You don't want to invest much in these products, because the opportunity for further growth is limited if the market is not growing. You won't see a great return on additional money, even though these products are cherished. These parts

of the business tend to be used to fund innovations or startup areas in the business.

Question marks

These are the problem children. The market is growing, but this product has low market share. These are typically young products or startups. You must ask why they are not more successful. Do they just need more time, is the market too crowded, has a competitor gained on you with better features or stability, are customers not interested in your product, or have substitutes emerged? The job here is to determine how to turn them into stars by getting more share. This usually requires big investments and can be a tough decision. If after years of investing they can't grow, they become dogs. So these are the ones to focus your analysis on.

Stars

These products enjoy high market growth and high market share. They're big and getting bigger. These are where you invest and protect. But continuing growth requires continuing capital investment. Your hope is that you can dominate the market and these become cash cows.

Dogs

These products have low market growth and low market share. Stop investing and retire them.

The Growth-Share Matrix is shown in Figure 5-5.

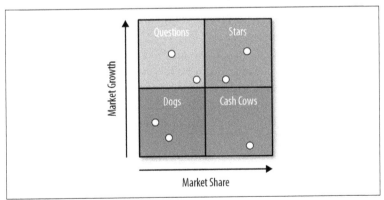

Figure 5-5. The Growth-Share Matrix

Generating the Growth-Share 2×2

You should just keep a template around for making these since you'll do it with some frequency. That's because executives and business strategy consultants simply *adore* these kinds of four-quadrant overlays on scatterplots. If you are attacked by a wild strategy consultant, do not run: simply show him a PowerPoint slide with a 2×2 matrix on it, and he will be instantly absorbed and begin looking for holes to poke in it, giving you time to escape. (See the note in "Stakeholder Matrix" on page 105 for a quick way to generate the 2×2 for this and similar matrices).

You can use this matrix in your portfolio planning and strategy season exercises. You should at the least be aligned with the strategy team on the placement of the applications. Do not make grandiose plans to make a lot of upgrades and feature enhancements in dogs.

The Growth-Share Matrix is a very familiar tool to many businesspeople. If you don't spend too much time on it or treat it too seriously, it makes a nifty way to visualize where to focus your time and attention in a product management Roadmap.

Core/Innovation Wave

As shocking as it may be to hear, people don't always automatically agree on what projects to fund and how much to fund them. Arriving at the answers for what systems, products, and projects to fund; what features to pursue; and how much of the pie each item should get is hard to determine and can be highly contentious. These matters are debated by product management, product development, architecture, strategy, IT, business operations, and finance, of course with a breezy executive dropping an occasional bomb on the proceedings on the order of, "Oh, didn't I tell you? The leadership team just decided to move all the operations to the moon. Can you redo everything with that in mind?"

The process is sometimes fraught with ego and emotion. Worse, it's played as a zero-sum game: if you get that $10 million, then that's $10 million less for my project.

To create a modicum of order, the strategist will look for a list (or better, a 2×2 grid) to diffuse the intensity and bring data to bear. Enter the Core/Innovation Wave. This tool was shown to me by Sabre Hospitality Chief Strategist Balaji Krishnamurthy.

This pattern is useful if you're considering a set of future projects, and you aren't sure which ones to pursue or ask for funding for. Sometimes you want to get a quick idea of how complex it might be to do something. If it's far from your core business or most mission-critical systems, then it may be something you're not mature in, don't understand well, and will need more time or more funding to pursue properly. This is even more true if the project you're considering represents creating something entirely new to the world or to your organization.

During strategy season in late spring, you can use the Core/Innovation Wave as a planning tool to assist you in envisioning where the applications in your portfolio lie with respect to two key vectors: *proximity to the core* and *innovation* (see Figure 5-6). It's useful in conjunction with an Ansoff Growth Matrix (see "Growth-Share Matrix" on page 124) and an Investment Map (see "Investment Map" on page 130) and Application Portfolio Management (see "Application Portfolio Management" on page 146).

Proximity to the core refers to how close this proposed project, acquisition, product, or feature is to your main business or your key applications. Proximity to the core means how mission-critical the application is to your division and your customers. How much revenue is generated by each application today, and how much revenue is expected to be generated? How much other stuff does it enable? The ones with the most are your core products.

The x-axis is *Innovation*: Does this feature already exist entirely, or a little bit but it needs modification, or not at all? How differentiating is it with respect to enabling your future? Like babies, innovative young projects need far more nurturing than they can give in return. Moreover, you will have a harder time reaching new customers, accessing new markets, and doing things differently.

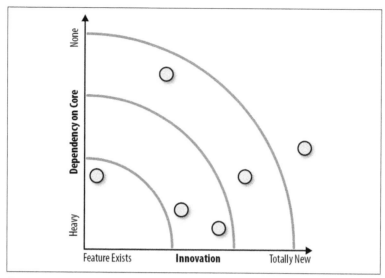

Figure 5-6. Core/Innovation Wave

To use the tool, get a list of your applications, the companies you're considering acquiring, or the projects you're considering asking the board for funding to do. In the figure, the dots represent the scatterplot for each application or proposed product or proposed acquisition or activity. Consider them across these two axes.

You can use a chart such as this to score each item as shown earlier. When you're done, layer over the waves to tag the priority level of the funding each should get, with a bias toward those in the upper right: these are the ones that are most innovative and closest to the core of your business.

The "waves" are meant to help you sort out your bubbles into general categories. For things that are close to the core and not innovative, you likely have many maintenance teams already working on them. You can staff those differently than innovative work that has little customer-facing, revenue-generating impact. You will need to fund that to ensure proper maintenance. The risk profiles are different, and the pioneering mindset, attitude, and maturity and talent of the individuals needed will be different.

You can also use this to help visualize a timeline projection, to help the executive and your teams talk with customers and present to their management. What work you will do in the next year? Next two or three years? It helps them start to conceptualize what the opportunity size might be, and why they should care.

Used in an executive slide, this chart can provide a wonderful opportunity for them to ask questions, understand broader strategic alignment, and see where your Roadmap is headed. You can show a set of pursuits you want to make in acquiring new technology companies to add to your platform.

It's easy to get this done quickly, and use that as input to a more detailed Roadmap planning session with development management.

Note that you don't have to use this tool only in strategy season once a year for big budget asks. The Wave also helps you sort other aspects of how to staff projects, and how much architectural attention to give them. You can use it just within your architecture team to determine where, and how extensively, you need to write architecture definition documents (see "Architecture Definition" on page 235) to support dev teams, or otherwise make specifications about toolsets and understand the emerging tech.

You can also use it within a project team. As with many patterns here, you can consider this a fractal, and use it to help prioritize the work of your Roadmap within a single project or system. When you're triaging features, which happens frequently, this can help you assign management or other oversight of the work, and determine places where you can try out new technologies or may need more time (if something is innovative and close to the core).

As management, you may look at items that are very innovative and see if you can carve out 5–10% of the team for some R&D work, and not load them up with commitments on the daily Roadmap. Otherwise, don't expect the items to get addressed.

Don't use this pattern on its own. Use it in conjunction with the Growth-Share Matrix and Investment Map. The Wave alone won't make any decisions for you. But it will help frame the conversation as you have the budget planning and trade-off discussions, and will help you communicate easily to executives within the deck you're building.

Investment Map

You can't do everything at once, and you can't invest equally in All The Things. You must prioritize.

The Investment Map isn't so much about money as offering a simple lens for the executive to view, in a quick and easy way, her portfolio of applications plotted against how you are thinking of planning the next year or so of work. It marries your current application set along with your emerging, innovative ideas for where you think the Roadmap should go. It will spur terrific conversations between product management, strategy, product development, and architecture about where your tech organization's focus should be.

The purpose of the Investment Map is to help you temper and balance the exciting, cool things that you want to do, the level of difficulty and preparedness you'll need to pull them off, how ready you hypothesize (see "Hypothesis" on page 41) the market is to receive them, and how big the barriers might be.

Here's the process to create the map:

1. In a spreadsheet, list the items in your portfolio and list the ideas you have for work you want to do to create new products, enhance existing ones, or try a new technology. This could include major architectural changes to key systems that might require a project to complete.

2. Score them according to the two key vectors: how difficult will it be to do that item, and how ready, right now, are your current customers and the market you're serving in general?

3. Generate the 2×2 matrix and label the quadrants.

4. Use it as input to team conversations, Roadmap planning, budgeting, and prioritizing.

5. Add it to a slide in your burgeoning Strategy Deck.

The result of this exercise will look like Figure 5-7.

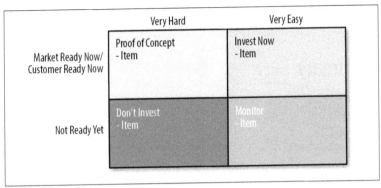

Figure 5-7. The Investment Map

The first vector is how hard or easy something will be to do (which can include its novelty, risk, complexity, level of effort, budget requirement, number of critical unknowns, and so forth).

The second vector is how ready your customers are to receive it. For example, years ago a number of the big hotel chains wanted to add digital keys that could be sent to guests' mobile phones on check-in. There were two barriers: the guests weren't ready, and their franchising customers weren't ready. There were some startups that offered this tech. But it was new, so it didn't work perfectly. If a game on your phone doesn't work, you can just turn it off. If you can't get into your hotel room, that's a bigger problem. Market research revealed that there weren't enough people with smartphones—sure, tech company executives all had them as early adopters and could afford them. Even today, only 75% of Americans have a smartphone of any kind. But nearly everyone has to stay in hotels, and phones run out of juice, so you'd need the regular door lock anyway, which is expensive to hoteliers. So the idea, even though it was a good one and continues to trickle into the market today, was incredibly slow to catch on. A sizeable, pioneering investment here would have been a mistake, as neat as the idea was.

The Investment Map works great in concert with Growth-Share Matrix/BCG Box and the Core/Innovation Wave. You want to consider these during strategy season, and budget season, and Roadmap planning season. You might update this twice per year.

I won't belabor this tool further since it's not likely going to be used every day, and by now generating 2×2 matrices should be old hat for you. It's just a handy, easy way to help drive general direction for both your current portfolio and future-oriented ideas.

Summary

In this chapter, we reviewed several patterns at the corporate or business unit level:

- Stakeholder Alignment (see "Stakeholder Alignment" on page 99)
- RACI (see "RACI" on page 108)
- Life Cycle Stage (see "Life Cycle Stage" on page 111)
- Value Chain (see "Value Chain" on page 116)
- Growth-Share Matrix (see "Growth-Share Matrix" on page 124)
- Core/Innovation Wave (see "Core/Innovation Wave" on page 126)
- Investment Map (see "Investment Map" on page 130)

In the next chapter, we'll examine just a few quick patterns with a tighter focus: the departmental or organizational level within your company.

CHAPTER 6

Department Context

This short chapter catalogs the patterns you can use within a department mental level.

Principles, Practices, Tools

This pattern helps you organize your thoughts, and consider the department holistically in the following situations:

- Aligning teams around a vision, especially a new direction
- Setting up a new department
- Creating a new structure within your department
- Creating a new methodology
- Introducing a new process or changing an existing one
- Developing an enterprise architecture
- Creating a "get well" plan
- Creating a Roadmap for a turnaround or change management plan
- Creating an efficiency plan or streamlining activities
- Choosing a toolset
- Making a build/buy/partner decision
- Aligning around a platform
- Devising a portfolio management plan

Its purpose is to help you and your teams get a clear picture of how your department works and to show them how their daily work supports the vision.

This pattern helps you create alignment in your department by showing the linkage between the principles you have, the practices you have, and the tools you employ. It helps you create a unified and efficient department because you are drawing a connection between these three things. That means first that you must have each of them in place.

Principles

A *principle* is a proposition (as we saw in Chapter 2). It serves as the foundation for a system of beliefs. As propositions, principles are abstract, but they should precipitate actions on the part of your teams that support them. Presumably, the principles are subsets or decompositions of your overarching corporate vision. If they're not, your teams and department will suffer from a lack of alignment. You'll be doing stuff that doesn't matter. This is mistaking activity for progress.

The Open Group Architecture Framework (TOGAF), which was my architecture training and certification many years ago, publishes an in-depth way of approaching technology principles (*http://bit.ly/ 2Buottr*). You can take a shortcut and read Digital Principles (*http:// bit.ly/2BtQ5ib*) or IBM's old published principles (*https://ibm.co/ 2wbWoRG*).

Here is a set of principles that I've used in the past that you can adopt and adapt or use as a jumping-off point for creating your own:

- Primacy of principles
- Portfolio of development work aligned with strategy-driven architecture
- Compliance with laws, regulations, and standards
- Primacy of security, stability, and quality
- Management of technical diversity
- Data as an asset

- Getting value from data and services portfolio requires stewardship
- Software solutions created as public, scalable, open, interoperable, loosely coupled, governed services
- Design for failure
- Global cloud

Once you have stated your principles, unpack them to explain further what you mean. Stating "Global cloud" is not going to drive an ounce of change in your organization. So explain it further in more technical terms to folks who have a chance of finding practical avenues into actual projects, like this (as an example):

> Services and applications of the platform should be built ready to run in the cloud and take advantage of such features as autoscaling and other auxiliary components while maintaining portability within the application structure.
>
> Services should externalize configurations to account for such portability.
>
> Infrastructure as code should be employed.
>
> Services must expect to be deployed globally across multiple cloud data centers, and thus should externalize their localized values and internationalizeable application qualities. They should be stateless, and their data should be partitioned to account for multiple concurrent global deployments routed to geo-specific customer groups.

These start you down a path of creating a set of practices that derive from the propositions, are actionable, and are embodied by the principles. For example, from the preceding text, we can see that we need a few practices to realize that principle. Examples might include:

- Infrastructure as code
- Continuous integration/continuous delivery pipelines
- Service design review and governance

First we'll need to pick one or more cloud providers and state what we're using. Let's say we're going to use AWS. We can then make that statement.

We can also see what tools we might take advantage of to help realize the practice. GruntWorks, for example, could be used to support the infrastructure-as-code practice. Or you could decide to build this yourself using Python and CloudFormation. That choice might depend on other principles, or the outcome of a simple Build/Buy analysis, which will mostly reduce to this: build the things that are competitive differentiators for you and buy ones that aren't.

These should give you an idea of what principles look like and how to write them so you can come up with your own:

Practices

These are the things people do on a daily basis. They are the processes, they way you get stuff done, the manner in which the principles are realized in your daily work. These might be things like DevOps or infrastructure as code or chaos engineering.

Tools

These are the specific instances of software applications that teams use as part of carrying out the practices. These should not be abstract but rather concrete, actual tools that force you to make a selection. "TensorFlow" or "Ansible" or "Log4J" or "Kafka" is the level of the values in your tools list.

It's really important to think in terms of principles, practices, and tools. If you don't, you'll have less efficiency, less clarity, and less harmony. And you'll have a collection of diverse overlapping tools and less alignment between people's daily work and the strategic vision. Many shops are just collections of tools. The tools support the practices; the practices realize the principles.

Here you're looking for three things:

- Missing elements, or logical gaps
- Mismatches
- Opportunities for improvement or upgrade

The Process Posture Map gives you a picture of either 1) elements of your current state that need to be supported or revised or 2) a practical map of how everything in your enterprise architecture will work together. So you can use this map as a diagnostic or alignment tool for the current state, or as an image of the Beautiful Future, an aspirational vision.

Example: NASA Strategy

For a good example of a CIO's strategy report that is driven by vision > mission > strategic principles > goals > outcomes, check out the NASA CIO's official strategy plan (*https://go.nasa.gov/2oH83EN*).

NASA is a government body and this plan is a public document, so it's a bit different than what I discuss in this book. But it's a textbook example of published principles (see "Principles" on page 134), clearly aligned business and IT goals, explicit IT goals, and so forth. If you think principles are too abstract to matter, note that while the NASA CIO states several of them, he does not state "innovation" as a principle, but instead states "secure," "integrated," and "cost-effective." That would drive certain decision criteria and adoption practices for sure.

So this is a great document in terms of making the process clear. Within a business setting, however, it's less likely that long-form written documents such as this would be the preferred format. I'm not sure how many businesspeople read strategies like the one from NASA, and it's a bit more old-fashioned than many tech companies would want to see—NASA has no competitors in a sense, and is a government agency. It's clear to me that publishing a five-year tech strategy in a tech company is only for full-on bureaucrats; it's the kind of thing that's irrelevant before it hits the streets. So we try to make ours more modular and easier to update on occasion, and keep the horizon tighter. But sometimes you're doing a turnaround job modernizing legacy systems, and those are the kinds of internal things that will take three to five years, depending on the damage. I just point out this NASA one because it is texbook, and you can take it under advisement. Alternate perspectives help you shape a rich strategy.

Current and Future Model

There are whole books, fields of study, and certificates on Six Sigma, process improvement, efficiency experts, process mapping, process automation, and the like. If you have the time and inclination to learn more about those areas, that's terrific. I recognize that those are important to really helping drive process change.

But for an architect, or for a Strategy Deck, you can get 80% of the way there with 20% of the work. People feel the pain every day of what's broken. You learn about DevOps, or site reliability engineering, or data science, and have an idea those might help you transform from your current state to a better one.

There are three things you can do to help you do "process optimization lite":

1. Examine the technology landscape for trends in new practices.
2. Make a Process Posture Map for your current state practices.
3. Make a Current State and Future State Operating Model.

You can include in your Strategy Deck something that helps your managers or leadership team understand the current state for what it is and see where you want to go within a new operating model.

Process Posture Map

The first step in a Process Posture Map is listing your processes in a pretty and organized way within a slide deck. Figure 6-1 shows an organized example of four main categories, with their processes under each.

Then assess the processes in your own mind and validate your thinking by talking with others to assign the process a posture. Assign one of the following five tags to each process:

Start	We do not do this in a meaningful or established way as an organization, but should define how we want to do this and begin to implement that.
Continue	This capability may require the normal continuous improvements of the local leaders but is generally is on track.
Invest	We have a nascent activity here that may have strong roots or certain strong practices and potential, and we would realize gains if we focused and grew the capability.
Assess	We have an ostensible capability here, but it should be examined for efficiency improvements in some areas.
Revise	This is clearly an ailing or weak capability that must be overhauled.

As an example, your Posture Process Map might look like Figure 6-2.

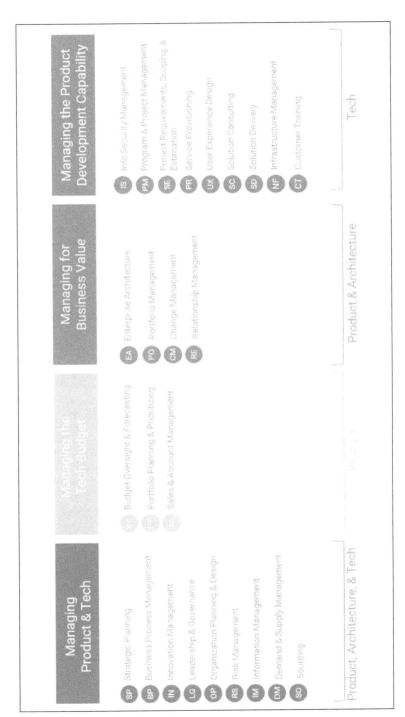

Figure 6-1. Organized list of processes

Managing for Business Value	goal	value	action
EA Enterprise Architecture	aims to deliver an overarching approach within which the tech function can design, deploy, and execute the organization's business strategy. Aims to identify new technologies that can deliver business value to the organization and assists from the intersection of business and tech	helps determine how the organization can most effectively plan the use of technology to achieve its current and future objectives. enables the organization to investigate how best to use new technologies and usage models to deliver business value.	invest
PO Portfolio Management	aims to monitor and report on the status of an investment portfolio of IT programs	helps ensure that the status of programs is closely tracked to support early identification of potential issues and to minimize program delivery conflicts	cont
CM Change Management	aims to forecast, plan through, conduct resources, communicate through challenges arising from tech & product change initiatives	realize and sustain the business benefits from change initiatives and ensure proper levels of monitoring, communication up and down the organization, proper expectations on scope & dates to realize the maximum business value	revise
RE Relationship Management	ensure that associates and long-term interactions between the IT function and other business units foster business awareness, mutually align interests, and help minimize issues of conflict	enhances goodwill, trust, and confidence between the IT function and the rest of the business.	assess

Figure 6-2. Initial Posture Process Map

What we've done here is divide the world into MECE categories (see "MECE" on page 29). This figure represents the set of processes within the category of "Managing for Business Value." We then can make a list of each business process within that. We state the goal of the business process and the value it brings. This acts as a definition of terms and allows you to see what your organization does. You might also add a column for the business process owner if there is one. If not, that might be a sign that you need some additional maturity in that process. Finally, we have the "Action" column. Using values from the table, state your recommended action.

At this point, you will have essentially created a slate of work. You will have a list of all your processes, shared definitions, and some of them that you need to go fix. Of course, process reengineering is an entire field of its own that is beyond this book's scope, but what you can do with this is consider the following:

- How mature are your processes in general? Do you have a lot with the "start" tag, which indicates that you aren't doing that process at all yet? Maybe you don't do change management or service governance in any kind of formal or explicit way and you can see benefit in instituting such a process.

- How extensive is the damage? Do you have a lot of processes with a "revise" tag?

- Recall Michael Porter's Value Chain (see "Value Chain" on page 116)—a purposeful network of business processes that, when designed together, cumulatively transform a set of inputs into an output of greater value to customers and deliver it to them. How well do these processes work together? As a collective set, are they MECE?

The point is that now you have the basis for a conversation. On your own you won't go off and just start reengineering all the weaker processes. But you can understand how much others agree with your assessments, and gain another perspective that helps focus your strategy in the areas most beneficial to your business.

Again, process reengineering is a vast field, and we can't cover everything here. If you have the budget and inclination, you can hire a firm to examine all your processes and rework them. If you need to or want to do it yourself, I recommend getting familiar with Lean Six Sigma, which is the most widely accepted, popular, and rigorous method for process reengineering. You can start with the *Six Sigma Handbook* by Pyzdek and Keller (McGraw-Hill)—it's accessible, practical, and comprehensive, and it gives you some tools to help make your "poor person's process reengineering" more rigorous and standard. And, if you get super-excited about this stuff, it will help you get a Green Belt or Black Belt certification. My custom approach to this is called Scalable Business Machines, which we cover in Chapter 7.

Current and Future State Operating Model

Next, create a simple slide that looks something like Figure 6-3. This model helps your teams see where they are (recall the "this is water" joke from "This Is Water" on page 15) and where your department needs to go. You can then have managers figure out how to draw the connections themselves for how to change the current state into the future state. You made the vision; now let them put together what exactly needs to change to get you there. They should come back with proposals with concrete actions (using an RACI as described in "RACI" on page 108) and then you can track progress.

Now you have a few slides to include in your Strategy Deck to make sure you've covered people, process, and technology altogether and are making the right recommendations so they support and enhance each other.

After you've created your Process Posture Map, and made a slide for your Current and Future State Operating Model process, you can drill down by making a current and future model slide, and then further by making a Sankey diagram representing your principles, practices, and tools.

The Principles, Practices, Tools Sankey Diagram

A Sankey diagram is a way of showing how energy flows in a system: what direction and in what magnitude. I've adopted Sankeys to show myself and my teams that our principles all had at least some practices to realize them and those practices were all realized by one or more tools.

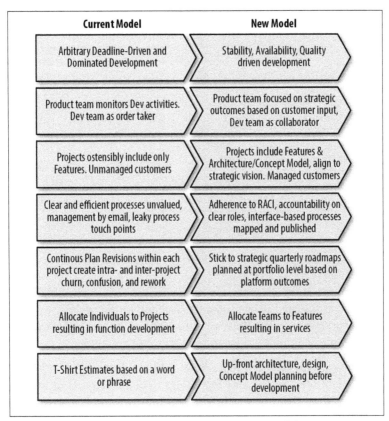

Current Model	New Model
Arbitrary Deadline-Driven and Dominated Development	Stability, Availability, Quality driven development
Product team monitors Dev activities. Dev team as order taker	Product team focused on strategic outcomes based on customer input, Dev team as collaborator
Projects ostensibly include only Features. Unmanaged customers	Projects include Features & Architecture/Concept Model, align to strategic vision. Managed customers
Clear and efficient processes unvalued, management by email, leaky process touch points	Adherence to RACI, accountability on clear roles, interface-based processes mapped and published
Continous Plan Revisions within each project create intra- and inter-project churn, confusion, and rework	Stick to strategic quarterly roadmaps planned at portfolio level based on platform outcomes
Allocate Individuals to Projects resulting in function development	Allocate Teams to Features resulting in services
T-Shirt Estimates based on a word or phrase	Up-front architecture, design, Concept Model planning before development

Figure 6-3. Current and Future State Operating Model

Using the diagram is fun, makes a neat visual to share with teams, and is a good way of checking the holistic integrity of the departmental system you are creating. If you have some principles with no practices supporting them, they are just abstract platitudes. You need to either give up the pipe dream that the item's actually a principle of yours, or go create a process that is capable of realizing it.

You can generate your own Sankey diagram with a free online tool called SankeyMATIC (*http://sankeymatic.com*). It's great. You enter your plain-text list of principles, practices, tools, and their magnitudes, and click a button. The diagrams it produces look like Figure 6-4 (it's just a snippet).

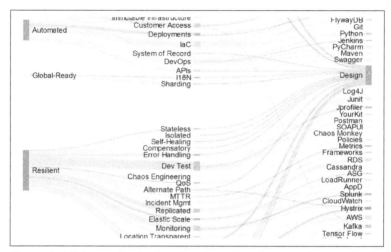

Figure 6-4. Snippet of a Sankey showing principles, practices, and tools

You can see in the diagram how we have defined some principles, on the left: Automated, Global-Ready, Resilient. In the middle, we show which practices realize those principles. Then on the right, we have the list of actual tools we use to support those practices.

So when we say we want to be more resilient as an organization, it's not a platitude: we do many real things to be more resilient, such as have a strong dev test practice. To make sure we are in fact doing dev testing and to set an expectation with developers about what tools they should use to keep us efficient, and to check that these elements all work together, we can see that in support of the dev test practice, we use the tools JUnit, JProfiler, YourKit, Postman, and SOAP UI.

You can also make Sankey diagrams easily in R for the more programmatically inclined. They're a slick way to be sure you have all three factors working together and to what extent.

Business Process Mapping

Business Process Model Notation (BPMN) 2.0 is a standard notation created by the Object Management Group for representing business processes. As you look at your challenging processes—the ones you want to improve—I encourage you to find someone on the team who is interested in this sort of thing and have him map out the current state process. Then examine it together with the team. Then, together, map a better future state process.

It's not hard to do, but like drawing UML diagrams, it is sort of detailed, and you want to get the notation right. You can read the (very long) spec at *http://www.omg.org/bpmn*. Read books and get tools from various vendors (*https://bpmn.io* offers many wonderful examples, and Visio and LucidChart work well) to help you draw proper BPMN diagrams. Figure 6-5 shows an example.

You and your team likely have a pretty good idea where the headaches are. Pick a few of the processes, chart them on an ease and impact 2×2 matrix and pick a few to tackle. With a few smart gogetters on your team and some proclivity for lifelong learning, you might get 80% of what a process expert would in 20% of the time and money.

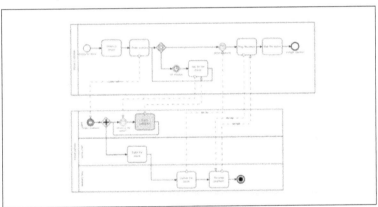

Figure 6-5. Example BPMN diagram

The Law of the Product of Probabilities

The *law of the product of probabilities*, or the *product rule*, is useful when you are examining your processes and practices for improvement. In the field of probability studies, particularly in genetics and biology, the *product rule* states that the probability of two or more events occurring together is the *product* of their independent probability of occurring. If you have two events in a process, each with a 50% chance of happening, the law of probabilities suggests that the chance of them happening together within a given instance of the execution of some process is 25% (because .5 x .5 = .25).

The trap is that we tend to take the optimization levels in each step in the process together as an average instead of as their product. It's a very different picture, and a critical distinction when you're considering how optimal your overall process is.

This is useful when we're optimizing processes, because we tend to think things are better than they are as a result of thinking in averages rather than products. So it's a good reminder that, unfortunately, we usually have further to go than we think.

We can think of the optimal scores as whatever metric we're measuring at that point in the process. For example, you might have a deployment process or a software methodology, and you can arrive at metrics such as defect leakage or technical debt. Note that what we're talking about here are independent variables within the same instance of a process. We're not talking about repeated executions of the same step in different instances.

Here's an example. Imagine you have a five-step process that you want to optimize, and you determine that at each step you have 80%, 85%, 90%, 85%, and 90% optima. It looks like you have a score of 86% overall, taken as an average. When taken as a product, however, the total optimization of the *overall* process is 47%: a very different picture.

More on Probabilities

It's far beyond what's necessary for our purposes (remember the logical fallacy of false precision), but if you're interested in this topic, there's a good overview on event probabilities at the Yale website (*http://bit.ly/2PqeEiP*).

Taken together, the Process Posture Map, the Current and Future State Operating Model chart, and the Sankey diagram of your Principles, Practices, and Tools give you a significant Roadmap, viewed through different lenses, for your organizational strategy—which your technology goals must align to.

Application Portfolio Management

The idea behind Application Portfolio Management (APM) was borrowed from the world of financial portfolio management, and originated in the mid-1970s in a *Harvard Business Review* article. With APM, you view your applications altogether and apply a cost-benefits analysis in order to determine how to best rationalize and plan the portfolio comprehensively. In this way, APM provides a key practice for the strategic enterprise architect.

A purposeful APM exercise will help you answer the following questions:

- Does your application portfolio properly support the current and stated future aims of the business?
- Are you devoting enough resources to your strategic applications?
- Are you providing too much financial support to noncritical applications? Can you release some of that support to better fund and position critical applications?
- Are you wasting money on legacy applications of low business value?
- How can you plan future application consolidation or rationalization?
- Can you reduce overall IT cost by changing the way you support certain applications?
- What risks do you have in the portfolio? Where should you focus thought and design effort?

Once you've done the APM exercise, you'll have a map to help you:

- Identify and eliminate redundant and unused applications.
- Consolidate similar applications into a single new application.
- Retire older and more expensive-to-maintain applications.
- Determine which data flows through which applications to optimize security controls.

Here's an overview of how to approach your APM work and implement this pattern:

1. List the known business goals.
2. List your technological goals.

3. List your applications altogether, and the owners in business and tech.

4. Apply the APM rubric to the application list to cluster them according to business and technology attributes.

5. Evaluate and list strategies for each application.

The result of the APM exercise will be a strongly coherent view of your total application portfolio that illustrates how well-aligned it is with the business goals, offering you insight into what your strategic plans should be to rationalize and optimize the portfolio. It gives you a view into what applications are at risk, which should be divested or retired, and which should be invested in and grown. It suggests a path for applying the skill sets of your teams to make them more efficient.

The output of this exercise will be a spreadsheet in which you do your APM work, and then a deck into which you transfer your findings. The spreadsheet will store your rubric of questions, the answers for each application, and the graphs you generate. It is the keeper of your "long math," showing how you arrived at your recommendations and substantiating the claims you'll make in your deck for how to move forward. You then use the deck to review with stakeholders and align on your plans.

This process involves the following steps:

1. As you start the work, be sure that you first agree on your business goals and the list of applications. It's amazing how people don't mean the same thing or that mature tech companies don't have a clear and commonly defined set of SKUs. This will help guarantee that alignment.

2. Once you've defined the list of applications that everyone can agree on (this is what the salespeople actually sell, this is what the IT teams actually maintain, this is what business operations actually budget and report on, etc.), then you want to make sure that you have the list of the proper owners for each system. You'll need to consult with these people later when it's time to negotiate the plans for their applications.

3. Next you establish a set of questions that you can ask about each application in order to establish its posture with respect to risk and alignment. The questions are divided into business and

technology categories. They aren't open-ended, but rather should have a numeric score attached to them, such as 1–5. Each should be weighted by its relative importance. You'll use these scores to generate a scatterplot and make it into a 2×2 matrix as we've done before. That picture can then be used as a cornerstone of your resulting APM deck with your recommendations. The resulting bubble chart looks something like Figure 6-6.

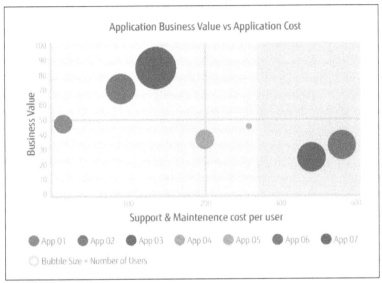

Figure 6-6. The resulting APM bubble chart

The questions or assessment attributes on which you will evaluate each application should be tailored to your environment. But in general, they'll focus on these ideas:

- What is the business value versus costs to maintain the application?
- What is the expected future business value or goals for the application?
- What are the skills required to maintain and grow the application in the future, and how well positioned are we for such support?
- What is the application health level, and what risk does that pose to the business?

- How ready is the application to undergo certain known or postulated initiatives, such as a move to the cloud or legacy transformation?

I'll offer a set of questions or desired attributes in a moment that you can use to help you get started, but you'll likely want to customize them for your organization and purposes.

Planning with Asset Classes

The APM is typically employed in organizations with too many applications to keep in your head at once, and where different knowledgeable, rational people might disagree on what the real boundaries of the different systems might be. If you have only six or eight technology products you're doing an APM for, it's probably overkill and doesn't make sense.

But if you have a large, diverse, mature organization under your span of control, you might have a portfolio of 50 or 80 or 150 applications. In these cases, an APM is essential, and you may want to go an extra step and assign each application in the portfolio to an *asset class*.

An asset class is nothing more than a label from the following taxonomy, which you can use as a guide to suggest how to plan for the future of the applications in each category. These are presented in order of their presumed strategic value:

Strategic
> Consider an application strategic if it represents a competitive advantage to your company, has many customers, is expected to grow, or is a competitive necessity. In these cases, you want to ensure it has strong market positioning, you're applying your most innovative thinkers to it, and you're focused on how to add value and create a diverse, rich platform around it.

Informational
> If an application is informational, your most likely course of action will be to ensure it's providing the most reliable data in the quickest way, that it enjoys a comprehensive data set, that it has a short turnaround time to get the data to support timely decision making, and that the data is properly surfaced where people need to see it.

Transactional

These tend to be the backbone of business, whether they are customer-facing or internal. There are only a few, clear things to do with transactional applications: to lower costs and improve throughput, ensure good-enough stability without overinvesting, and promote legacy modernization.

Infrastructure

If your team is a central organization providing infrastructure services to the rest of the business, your aim is to provide the quickest, most reliable support to the teams making the customer-facing, revenue-generating applications. Note the power of the asset classes: at AWS, compute and storage in the form of S3 or EC2 are not in the infrastructure: they are strategic, because they are competing diligently with other cloud companies. Unless you're in the cloud provider business, it's pretty certain that storage and compute for you belong to infrastructure. All too often, infrastructure teams get caught up in a "gatekeeper" mentality, rather than serving their internal customers with an enabling attitude. The thing to do with infrastructure is reduce costs to the business units, allow optimal business flexibility and choice to best serve customers, and provide some standardization. All too often, this standardization is interpreted by those in central infrastructure teams with a warden's mentality—that is, as a means of keeping all the business unit prisoners in line. This is the opposite of what they should be doing. Standardization is intended to make it easier for the business units to count on something, to train and skill up appropriately, and to build their stacks on. If the infrastructure teams can provide and even create real value, that's fantastic. Overindexing on standardization for its own sake to the detriment of customers is missing the point at best and an abuse of power at worst.

Capability Mapping

Depending on the current purpose of your APM exercise, you may want to take some additional time to create a capability mapping. This means listing out the applications that participate in a process or provide a business capability.

If an application supports more than one business capability, you will likely need to decompose it into modules or logical groups within that application to state which supports what capability.

Business and Technology Attributes

The core of the APM pattern (as I like to use it) is a spreadsheet (see Figure 6-7). Here you write the attributes you desire across the business and technology vectors; score each application against those attributes, multiplying for assigned weights; and then get a score for each vector for each application. That offers a quick way to reference what you should do with each one.

	A	B	C	D	E	F	G
			Weight	Control	Application 1	Application 2	Application 3
1	Predicted Quadrant				Stabilize/Replace	Retire	Retire
2	Total Cost of Ownership (in millions)				0.45	0.35	1.4
3	**Technical Risks**						
3.a	Application code adheres to standards/strategy	4	3	1	0	0
3.b	Infrastructure adheres to standards/strategy	4	3	1	1	1
3.c	Data adheres to Info Mgmt Architecture	2	3	2	0	1
3.d	Application architecture is modular	3	3	1	0	1
3.e	Appropriate fault tolerance architecture for application	4	3	1	0	0
3.e	Completeness of monitoring/management	2	3	1	1	0
3.f	Completeness of automated testing	2	3	1	0	0
3.g	Automated provisioning/deployment	3	3	1	0	0
3.h	Completeness of training and documentation	2	3	1	2	0
3.i	Completeness of Security Implementation	2	3	2	1	1
3.j	Technology foundation will be relevant in 3 years	1	3	1	0	0
3.k	Application requires a sustainable skill set	3	3	2	0	0
3.l	Core application is stable and meets SLAs	3	3	1	2	3
3.m	Integrations are stable and meet SLAs	2	3	1	2	3
	Technical Risk Score		111	44	22	26
4	**Business Value**						
4.a	Application is a strategic differentiator	2	3	3	0	0
4.b	Application strategy is well-defined, consistent	2	3	2	0	2
4.c	Application is mission critical	1	3	3	3	1

Figure 6-7. List of attributes with each application and the resulting recommendation

Here's a set of technology attributes you can use to consider the level of technical risk each application poses. But of course feel free to modify it and add your own to best suit your purposes:

- Application code adheres to standards/strategy.
- Infrastructure adheres to standards/strategy.
- Data adheres to information management architecture.
- Application architecture is modular.
- There is an appropriate fault-tolerance architecture for application.

- Monitoring/management is complete.
- Automated testing is complete.
- Provisioning/deployment is automated.
- Training and documentation are complete.
- Security implementation is complete.
- Technology foundation will be relevant in three years.
- Application requires a sustainable skill set.
- Core application is stable and meets SLAs.
- Integrations are stable and meet SLAs.

These are focused on a legacy application portfolio with an aim toward rationalization. Using these will help you arrive at an overall recommendation.

Here are some business attributes you might consider:

- Application is a strategic differentiator.
- Application strategy is well defined, consistent.
- Application is mission-critical.
- System outage creates high customer impact.
- System outage creates high corporate impact.
- Application features align with current business needs.
- Application features align with future business needs.
- Ability to quickly add features to the system.
- Clear governance steers the application.
- Enhancement efforts are historically accurate.
- Business process is efficient with no processes defined to work around technical issues.

List these in your spreadsheet and do the math to score each application. The data page of your workbook should be constructed like Figure 6-8.

Application	Predicted Quadrant	Cost of Ownership (M)	Tech Risk Score	Business Value Score
Application 1	Stabilize/Replace	0.45	44	50
Application 2	Retire	0.35	22	20
Application 3	Retire	1.4	26	25
Application 4	Stabilize/Replace	0.31	31	42
Application 5	Stabilize/Replace	0.04	32	50
Application 6	Grow	1.01	88	38
Application 7	Grow	0.03	79	65

Figure 6-8. The data summary page of the APM spreadsheet

The data summary allows you to take a snapshot to put into your recommendation deck or the appendix of your Strategy Deck. It shows the long math that gives executives and yourself confidence that you aren't just making stuff up, but have a measured, objective approach to portfolio management.

In the Quadrant column, you'll assign one of four labels, depending on where each application lands in one of four quadrants in a 2×2 chart that looks like Figure 6-9.

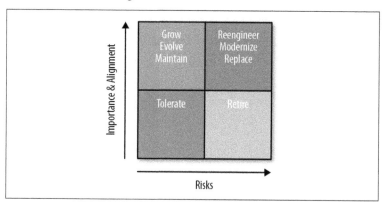

Figure 6-9. The APM application assessment quadrant

After scoring your applications according to their attributes for importance and alignment to the business, you can chart them from a spreadsheet into a scatterplot and see where they land within this 2×2 matrix. Each quadrant suggests a different posture for each application and an attendant direction to take with them:

Grow/evolve/maintain

These are your highly aligned, strategically important, and low-risk applications. Assess their costs to be sure those are optimal and have not become bloated over the years. The risks, technical debt, and technology implementation are well positioned. Assess your investment plans with these applications to ensure you're providing the right level to grow them, focusing on customer features, innovation, broader market applicability. Maintain them at high levels and support them with disciplined, strong staff and leaders who can act as operators.

Tolerate

These are your low-value/low-alignment and low-risk applications. They exist for some reason, to fulfill some purpose, but they don't represent your future. You need to keep them around. Staff them with more entry-level people. Evaluate their costs to minimize them. You really don't want too many applications in this quadrant, or it's a sign of stagnation overall. Figure out what you want to do with these applications in the future. They aren't a high priority, but you don't want stuff staying in this quadrant forever either. Nudge them toward consolidation with other applications in the growth category; or figure out if you can nudge them toward the Retire quadrant, and get rid of them by changing a process or eliminating the related low-importance process; or outsource them.

Retire

These have low business alignment with high technical debt or risk to the business. The costs to keep them around may far outweigh their value to the business. These require you to make a hard call, because invariably there are nice people associated with these languishing applications, and some middle manager fearing for the future who will campaign to save these. But they're almost certainly not worth it and no longer relevant. See if there is any function here worth saving that you can consolidate into another application, and scrap the rest and move on.

Reengineer/modernize/replace

These are the problem children, the question marks (see "Growth-Share Matrix" on page 124). They have both high business alignment and strategic importance, but have been mismanaged and allowed to devolve into a high-risk state of considerable technical debt. These are your workhorse applications that are crucial to your business, but that have unfortunately been "stewarded" by a revolving door of leaders who were interested only in short-term gains, investing in features and not architecture. Or they may have been underinvested by executives who mistook them too early for a cash cow, found themselves strapped for cash for long periods, or somehow deluded themselves into thinking that their sports car never needs a tune-up, new belts, an oil change, and tire replacement. You have another tough decision to make with these, and the outcome is hard to achieve, the planning complex, and the work long and hard. But it must be done because these are strategic applications that are important to the business. Their features are not inappropriate: they do what they're supposed to. But they won't scale in the current architecture to grow the business. Or they're out of headroom. Or hasty decisions or full-on kicking the can down the road means they're on an incredibly expensive and proprietary database platform. They need serious attention. So you must make a further business assessment and have many stakeholder conversations here to determine which quadrant to nudge them into: Can you replace them entirely with a new greenfield system, putting them in the Grow quadrant? That's an expensive proposition and risky in itself, and you're almost certain to incur the wrath of business or product managers who then worry about competing in the market since they won't be getting customer-facing features while you overhaul the internals. Or do you modernize them piece by piece, service-enable them, move them to the cloud, and get them off TPF and onto a modern platform? That's an even slower process, and potentially a death by a thousand cuts that you may not have time for.

This is the heart of the result of the APM work. But the APM in itself does nothing. It gives you a current state assessment, and then it is up to you to bring those findings before other stakeholders and use it as the start of some crucial conversations. It's one easy-to-reference input into your overall strategy. You'll need to pick based on the outcome of the APM what projects it suggests, and in what priority you should do them. Moreover, this approach to APM is helpful because it will give you a handy reference guide as you plan and prioritize the particular hot spots within each application. This could help you not only in long-term planning, but in quick-win, local remediation efforts as well.

Project Heat Map

When you come into a new organization, you will discover various projects under way. You may wish to apply the same general kinds of ideas from our APM to determine the value and alignment of these projects to evaluate their future. This idea is very similar to the Investment Map (see "Investment Map" on page 130), but with a finer grain and focus on projects. It's simple. First, list the projects. Next, determine their net value to the business based on standard metrics such as internal rate of return (IRR) or anticipated return on investment (ROI). Then, examine the quality of the project based on metrics such as the technology employed, the capabilities it provides, and whether the costs are in line and the timeline is on track. Finally, you can plot them in a heat map. Figure 6-10 shows an example of your results.

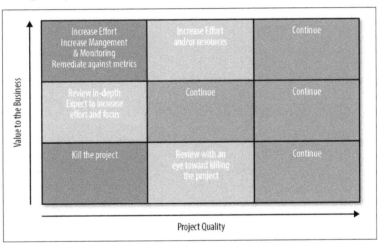

Figure 6-10. Project heat map

This heat map is clear. If the project is of low quality and low business value, kill it. If it's of high quality, stay with it. If there are question marks on the project, then the recommended actions to take are shown within the heat map, depending on where each project lands. The recommendations and colors stay the same across any given use of the heat map.

Use the APM deck to consult with key leaders in business and tech to form investment plans. It can be used well alongside the Investment Map and Process Posture assessments (see "Process Posture

Map" on page 138) as you gather material for your Strategy Deck or an Ask Deck (see "Ask Deck" on page 256).

If you have further interest in this subject, you can check out the website of NASA's Office of the CIO (*https://go.nasa.gov/2BwI3Fl*) to see how it presents its applications with APM.

Summary

This brings our technology strategy creation patterns catalog to a close. You now have a wealth of frameworks that you can use in concert to create a comprehensive and long-term strategy, or that you can use individually for more local strategic decision points and solutions of a smaller scope.

In the next part, you'll see how you can communicate what you've constructed in a compelling way that helps realize your plans and architectural direction.

PART III

Communicating the Strategy

In Part II, we examined a catalog of patterns to help you create your strategy. In this part, we'll look at how to take the strategy you've created and communicate it in a compelling way to a variety of audiences in order to achieve your aims. The 20 communication patterns in this part are represented in Figure III-1.

There are patterns for the approach we take to the work as a mental model. These are the most abstract, and represent a unique take on how to think about your work, but also feature many practical tips you incorporate into your daily work to make you more successful. Finally, we'll look at frameworks for putting together the decks in which you will keep your strategy and make executive requests.

All of the creation and communication patterns taken together represent a holistic, unified framework of templates you can use to create the substance of your technology strategy and successfully roll it out.

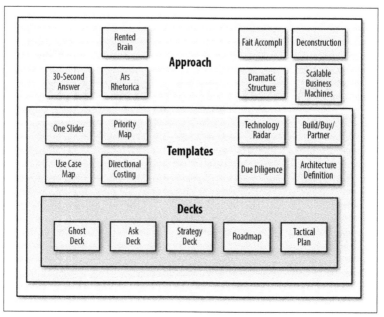

Figure III-1. The logical architecture of the patterns for communicating strategy

CHAPTER 7

Approach Patterns

Here we introduce the world of the communication-oriented patterns. You might think of this chapter as analogous to Chapter 2, where I discussed analysis. It contains the underpinnings for communicating in a variety of business settings to help you accomplish your goals.

These are the patterns we examine in this chapter:

- 30-Second Answer
- Rented Brain
- Ars Rhetorica
- Fait Accompli

30-Second Answer

Executives are busy and need to synthesize a lot of diverse data points quickly. They ask technologists questions because they have something else in mind. They need to know things directionally more than in great detail. When they ask you a question, give them an answer that takes less than 30 seconds and has structure:

1. Map an outline of three bullet points in your head, and then give the executives the simple, declarative, definitive answer.

2. Add your three reasons or characterizations with your three bullet points also as high-level declarative statements. Picture a

single slide, with one headline that is your answer, and three supporting points written in big, 30-point font.

3. Stop talking and let the executive proceed. They will either make a decision, or follow up on the points they are interested in if they want more information.

Here's a secret: nobody knows what to do. The boss is a person with children and a sick parent and nagging concerns about who will win the pennant and what's for dinner and the possible emptiness of existence—like everyone else.

Here's another secret. We hear about "busy executives" and think, well, we're pretty busy too. And so we all are. But the following secret is maybe the most practically useful thing in this book for you to know: the boss has to pee.

The boss has 19 meetings per day. She is late to every one of them, not because she's disorganized, but because it's impossible to be on time. She as a thousand mouths to feed. She has calls with the office in Singapore and lunch with a customer. She has to deal with the fallout of a security breach and is trying to hire a key salesperson that could turn things around. She has coordinations and skip levels and shifts gears constantly. I mean this quite literally: she doesn't have time for a two-minute break. People are talking to her constantly. She can't walk down the hall with a moment to think. She sleeps in hotel rooms more than her own bed. She goes to exotic locations like Paris, Tokyo, London, Berlin, Brussels, Sydney, New York, and Wichita, places we all dream of going—and she never sees anything except the four off-white walls of a windowless conference room before being whisked back onto the red-eye flight home. If you fail to recognize this, and give long-winded, equivocal answers in which you dissertate on the myriad possibilities in an open-ended fashion to show how smart you are, because it's a rare and exciting and somewhat scary moment to have the boss ask you something and you feel (rightly) that you're on an audition, you have blown it. Because in this short time that the boss is trying to listen to you, and she needs to know the answer. And if she hasn't had a break for six hours, you are trying her patience in ways that can't be spoken.

It's an old saw that the architect's answer to everything is, "It depends." This isn't a good answer. We get it that stuff is complex, abstract, ambiguous, and risky. That's why we get to have jobs as intellectual laborers, to sort these things out. Instead, give executives the three headlines and let them "drill down" or "double-click" into one they may want to hear more about.

This takes some training. Here's an example. Say you run into the SVP of Development in the hallway and he asks you, "Should we delay the deployment one week in order to fix these two issues or not?" He's in information-gathering mode, collecting data points. He will ask five other people and make a call. So your response might be something like this: "Yes. We should delay one week. First, our customers are heading into the peak season, so we'll have fewer opportunities to make changes. Second, the load test results are inconclusive. Third, it's Memorial Day weekend coming up, and we may not have the full team in support."

The boss may then ask to drill down, saying, "Tell me more about what's wrong with the load tests." Or he may say, "Got it, thanks," and move on. Either way, you did your job, and he's happy. Of course, being able to do speak in this way requires a bit of discipline, and empathy, and knowing your book of business. It gets easier with practice and the confidence that leaving out details is actually helpful. Say the three critical things and then stop. Here's how to think about framing your answers. The boss almost always wants to know one of these things:

- What is the project status?
- Do they need to do anything to help, or has the team got it?
- What is your recommendation on a particular proposed action?

Seeing into the boss's question to consider which of these things he's probably asking is a fairly reliable way to frame your answers.

The 30-second answer is helpful and polite and shows that you understand (empathize with) the boss's concerns.

Rented Brain

Duff McDonald, author of *The Firm: The Story of McKinsey and Its Secret Influence on American Business* (Simon & Schuster), drew this connection in 2013: more than 70 past and present CEOs of Fortune 500 companies were McKinsey alumni. In 2011, more than 150 McKinsey alumni were running companies with more than $1 billion in annual sales. The McKinsey consultant's chances of becoming a Fortune 500 CEO are the best in the world, and more than three times better than the second-place company, Deloitte.

They go to the best schools, often paying expensive fees to take training courses to help them study just to interview for internships, and compete for few spots in the most well-known firms. They spend their time analyzing data and advising CEOs and other executives in large corporations who can afford their hefty fees. They see into many companies in many industries across the world. They have access to enormous databases with company data from which to draw their insights, access to templates and techniques that are well tested, and access to thousands of colleagues all doing the same thing.

Strategy consultants are sometimes called "Rented Brains." They get invited in, they get asked hard questions, and then they research and put together a deck with their recommendations.

Early in my career, I worked for a very successful multibillion-dollar retail company that is number one at what it does. Its top executives loathed consultants. It was an ethos of the company. A story circulated that once upon a time a new vice president had been hired into the company. The venerable, smart, dedicated, generous, and kind CEO asked the VP for a plan in his area. Some time later, the VP returned to the CEO and stated that his plan was to hire consultants from a fancy consulting company to come in and make the recommendation. The CEO replied cheerfully, "That sounds terrific. Let's do that. So then is this your resignation? Because now I can't think of what I need *you* for." The VP got the message, did his own homework, and made the plan that he was accountable for. And he and the CEO lived together happily ever after, and everyone became rich. I think literally every employee at this 12,000-person company knew this story of the idiotic VP who doesn't think it's his job to know his own book of business. It was legend and lore; and the message was clear: 1) never hire consultants at this company, or recommend to because they couldn't possibly care about and know our business the way we do, in such deep detail. And 2) care about and know about our business deeply: you're part of the family, and we'll all be fine.

Working for an incredibly successful company—whose owner was the richest man in the state, with happy employees who stay working there for decades, and that had such an ethos—made a big impression on me. I also had contempt for business consultants, and for companies who hired them. Because I thought it meant three things:

- It shows mismanagement on the part of the executive who hires them, because it means he has not built his own leadership team, and has not properly developed his people to care about the company and know their book of business. They don't know how to do research, make a plan, and get something done.

- Even if the first is false, and the team is every bit as prepared as "big four" consultants to make a good plan, but the leader still thinks he needs the consultants, it can be for only one reason: *he does not trust his team to be objective and give him the hard facts.* He has built a team of sycophants, yes-men, wishy-washies with no point of view at best, or political social climbers or outright liars at worst. It means the leader has failed in his crucial, central role as Chief Culture Officer. Especially since, as we learned earlier from Peter Drucker, culture eats strategy for breakfast.

- The first job of a consultant is to get the next job. They make recommendations solving one problem in a way that creates a new, bigger problem requiring more time and fees to help solve.

The Smartest Guys in the Room

Between May of 2000 and December of 2001, Jeff Skilling was CEO of Enron. In that time, he had more than 20 meetings with McKinsey consultants. Skilling himself was an ex-McKinsey consultant. As he was driving Enron into the ground, the firm was paid more than $10 million in consulting fees. The scandals also brought its complicit auditor, Arthur Andersen, down with it, not to mention wiping out the pensions of thousands of workers who were innocent of the accounting frauds going on. One side effect of this scandal was that it caused the Senate to introduce the Sarbanes-Oxley Act in 2002 to protect shareholders by improving the accuracy and reliability of corporate public accounting. The decline of Enron under such manipulation is well portrayed in the engaging 2005 documentary film *Enron: The Smartest Guys in the Room.*

Consultants have directly contributed to tremendous success, but also the most colossal and scandalous failures in American business over decades. But that's just like most leaders. Business is complex, there are a lot of people involved in successes and failures, and there's a lot of rolling of the dice and hoping for the best. My role here is not to glorify and rave about some magic of these firms, or to impugn and condemn them. They do a particular thing and have some tools that, in the right hands, can be helpful.

Consultants can be a wonderful benefit to your team, and can advise companies very well in areas where they can't be experts. This pattern isn't to tell you to hire consultants or not to hire them. It's to remark on one mental shift in your own attitude that can be helpful to you and your organization.

The good leader constantly asks her team for the bad news. Help your team feel comfortable at saying what's wrong. If you fly off the handle and freak out every time someone tells you the hardware is delayed two weeks, you are teaching them to hide things from you. They come to decide that while you may eventually find out about the delays, it won't be from them, by which point it's too late for you to help.

Here's the principle of this pattern. Every day when you go into work, pretend you don't work at your company. Pretend you are a hired consultant, a Rented Brain, who is absolutely comfortable telling the bad news, making the hard call, saying what truly needs to be said, exposing the elephant in the room. You're clear. Because as a Rented Brain, you understand well that it's your job to know your book of business, and you're perfectly comfortable giving the boss your honest, best recommendation, even if it's not what he wants to hear, or doesn't put his prior decisions in the best light. Act as if you were a consultant who was not only free, but actually required to say what needed to be said, and not just maintaining the status quo or going along to get along. This mental shift isn't that hard to do, since you're already exchanging your intellectual labor for a salary anyway.

Put a simpler way: speak truth to power. Tell powerful people what they need to hear, not what they want to hear. You'll be seen as (and actually be) honest, forthright, forthcoming, objective, strong, confident, and smart. These are cherished, and rare, qualities.

If your boss is a nut job who hates hearing the truth, can't stomach bad news, or can't hear that he might not be perfect, just get another gig. It's over anyway.

Ars Rhetorica

You can use facts and logic and data and be right, and still lose.

When you are making a deck to recommend a strategy or technology architecture, you need a way to structure your arguments so that your audience approves them. Remember the secret to happiness: figuring out what you want (that's the first part of the book) and then learning how to ask for it (that's this part).

When you make a strategic recommendation, you need to be right about the best course of action. If you have followed the patterns in the first part of the book, you will be. So here we'll assume your claims make sense and are valid and have some data to substantiate them.

Around the year 350 BC, Aristotle finished a treatise called *Ars Rhetorica*, Latin usually translated as "The Art of Rhetoric" or "On Rhetoric." In this book, Aristotle positions rhetoric firmly alongside logic as one of the three key concerns of philosophy (the third being dialectic). His purpose is to illustrate how you can use debate and persuasion to get people to see things your way—not by using omission or manipulation, but in a logical and ethical manner.

According to Aristotle, to make a truly persuasive argument, include three key elements:

- Logical arguments (*logos*)
- Ethical arguments (*ethos*)
- Emotional arguments (*pathos*)

You won't be able to convince all the people all the time, but this gives you better odds. Let's look at each element.

With logical arguments, you persuade your audience based on logical conclusions stemming from facts.

To make a logical argument, show charts, graphs, and numeric data points, and illustrate in a direct line how they support your claims by using the elements of analysis we covered earlier. These might include:

- Using inductive and deductive reasoning, syllogisms
- Stating your hypotheses and the reasons for it

- Stating your method to proceed in proving your hypotheses
- Stating the metrics you'll use to measure your progress and how you'll source them
- Probabilities and ranges, confidence levels

Ethical arguments originate in the notion that we are easily persuaded by people we trust. We scrutinize their arguments less. We take them on their word as an authority and assign them credibility based on who they are, their expertise in a related field, their work history, and so on. In fact, an ethical appeal was the centerpiece of a popular TV ad in the 1980s: "When EF Hutton talks, people listen." If Jeff Dean said something about the future of AI, we would listen. If Warren Buffet even looks at the market funny, the Dow Jones goes berserk.

Be careful here not to misstep into some of the logical fallacies outlined next. It's easy to do that because while someone's background as an airplane pilot is impressive and laudable, that doesn't necessarily mean that person knows much about business leadership.

Ethical appeals can be valid, and citing research from noted authorities on different facets is a key ingredient to a successful argument. In fact, Aristotle's ethos-based rhetorical appeal forms the basis of the Google's PageRank algorithm (*http://bit.ly/2Pw9BNT*).

Emotional arguments persuade your audience by swaying their emotions, stirring them to righteous anger or disgust at the enemy, winning their hearts with rousing and exciting talk. We see this all the time in political speeches. These are actually important in business because if people don't feel personally invested and committed to your cause, they won't perform as well. But if you try to get millions of dollars out of the CIO based on emotional appeals, don't expect a check anytime soon. You can pull this lever more in town halls and 20-minute speeches, with demos that are intended to induce "ooohhhs and ahhhhs" from your audience.

These three types of arguments should be used all together, depending on the setting and what you're doing.

Note that overuse or improper use of emotional appeals is considered a logical fallacy too (see the next section). The more scientific- and business-minded among us tend to see through these arguments quickly.

Logical Fallacies

Earlier we showed several things you can do to help make a valid, reasoned, logical argument. Some arguments look logical, but are actually invalid or false pretenses to logic. These are called *logical fallacies* and must be avoided. They use irrelevant points and contortions to make their claims, and will undermine your own persuasiveness. There are dozens of them, and they are particularly perilous because they are so commonly employed in standard discourse.

Learning how to spot logical fallacies when others try to pass them off as logical arguments, whether intentionally or not, is an important aspect of doing good work. We see politicians using them all the time. Let's look at a few of the most popularly used fallacies.

Ad hominem

Latin for "against the man," the ad hominem fallacy attacks a person's background, physical traits, personality, irrelevant habits, race, religion, sexual orientation, or other personal attribute in order to suggest that their point or work is suspect, indefensible, or irrelevant. Examples of the kinds of horrible things that get said all the time that have no place in our work:

- What would she know about technology? Her degree is in philosophy!
- Don't hire anyone from that company—they're all corrupt.
- Well, you can't trust anything that guy says; he's a lefty.
- People of his religion are just concerned with making money.
- He's no fun at parties. He wouldn't make a good manager.
- As a woman, she would probably be great in HR or marketing.
- You know that guy's a liar: he's a lawyer!

This one is sometimes called "poisoning the well."

Affirming the consequent

In the logical statement "If P, then Q," the antecedent is P, and the consequent is Q. In the statement, "If today is Tuesday, then I have a committee meeting," the consequent is "I have a committee meeting." To *affirm the consequent* is to claim that the consequent is true.

When you commit the fallacy of affirming the consequent, you make an assertion, and by concluding that the consequent is true, you then also conclude that the antecedent is true. But logic doesn't let us do that. The fallacy takes the form: "If P, then Q. Q. Therefore, P." We do this a lot in technology, in our panic to find solutions to problems while troubleshooting.

Example:

- If the virus-scanning software runs too long, the application server will stop. The application server has stopped. Therefore, the virus-scanning software ran too long again.

Blind authority

The inverse of the ad hominem fallacy is the *blind authority fallacy*, which is equally common, especially in business. It states, "A is the ultimate authority. A made claim B. Therefore, claim B is true." It mistakes a military leader, business leader, or impressive corporation as a sufficient condition or valid and sound premise unto itself. This is false. The businessperson's version of this is to cite someone's title as the reason they are right. We sometimes see this referred to as the HIPPO: the Highest Paid Person's Opinion. The technologist's version of this is to substitute "big important tech company" as "ultimate authority." Examples:

- Programmers at Amazon open-source their software, so we should too.
- Google is putting AI at the heart of its strategy, so we should too.
- Facebook doesn't use the cloud—it uses its own data centers, so we should too.
- The CTO said we should should run all the servers out of his basement. That's why it was right for me to pack them up and move them there.
- The CEO said we should use mark-to-market accounting, so we know it's a best practice.

In technology we go crazy with the blind authority fallacy. Luckily, it's easy to spot and dismiss.

Blinding with science

We see the *blinding with science* fallacy in tech a lot. Smug technologists who just want to get their way try to bore their executive business leaders by dumping tons of only marginally relevant data on them to make them "cry uncle," or try to give the impression that they're such authorities that you should just go with their conclusion. To commit this fallacy, overuse acronyms, drop names, and refer constantly to arcane and highly technical-sounding things. Be suspicious if you hear something akin to this in a meeting:

- The X-86 Xeon double-cores their dev ports because their hyperthreading has a 2.11 rating but they have an in-bloom filter, which, in version 9.8.1 finally, uses Merkle Trees so we'll get the best results. You should spend five million dollars on those servers.

Developers do this a lot by digging into arcane details of their favorite JavaScript frameworks and claiming that we have to then switch everything to their flavor of the month. Pharmaceutical companies sometimes talk like this publicly in their advertisements. When someone starts talking like this, and I don't know for sure a) what all the things they are talking about are, and b) that those things are all both true and relevant, I get very suspicious that they're trying to manipulate me into doing what they want, regardless of its true importance or validity, by blinding me with science. These same people commonly also employ, and are themselves the frequent victims of, the blind authority fallacy.

Here's the antidote: immediately divest your authority on the matter, but become incredibly interested in the details, effectively taking the fallacy committer at her word. In this way, you can be completely polite yet entirely disarm the committer. Say, "Can you explain that to me? I don't know what an X-86 hyperthreaded dev port is. Why is that important to our throughput issue?" Another version of this, put more bluntly, is "Explain it to me like I'm 10." Maybe her conclusion is sound and you should in fact buy her favorite server. But now you'll know.

Hasty generalization

Sometimes called "converse accident," the *hasty generalization* is a common fallacy for inductive reasoners to misstep into. It is very common for technologists as well, who look at data and are frequently pressed to give answers before having enough time to collect relevant samples. Hasty generalization means making an unjustified conclusion based on very limited data, an anomaly, one special example, or biased evidence. You can recognize this fallacy because it always proceeds from the particular to the general. Examples:

- There are three rows in the database with bad data. Our programmers are so sloppy.

- Suzy is a really good programmer. Technologists are always so smart.

- *Robin:* I guess you can never trust a woman.
  Batman: You've made a hasty generalization, Robin. It's a bad habit to get into. (*Batman* television series, 1966)

Petitio principii

Commonly referred to as "begging the question," *petitio principii* is one of the scariest, most damaging forms of fallacy, for two reasons: first, it's so common, and second, people can do this without realizing they're doing it, and think they're being perfectly reasonable. It's a method of using as your evidence for a claim simply a restatement, or rewording, of that same claim. It takes the logical form $P \Rightarrow P'$ (where P' is merely a rephrasing of P). It's a fallacy because the conclusion does not logically follow from the premise. Here are some examples:

- "All men are rational, so Charles is rational." We forgot to say that Charles is a cat.

- "Effective learning occurs during short study periods because your study time is not wasted in longer stretches of drudgery." (Jeremy Bentham)

- "To allow every man an unbounded freedom of speech, must always be, on the whole, advantageous to the State; for it is highly conducive to the interest of the community, that each individual should enjoy a liberty perfectly unlimited of expressing his sentiments." (Douglas Walton, *Argumentation*)

This is often called "circular reasoning," like "P, therefore P," or more subtly, "A, therefore B, and B, therefore A." Hardcore logicians will take issue with my saying this, because they'll make finer distinctions, but it's close enough for our purposes. The way to defeat this fallacy is to ask for evidence, upon which the committer will likely restate the premise, and you've got him.

Post hoc, ergo propter hoc

Post hoc, ergo propter hoc is often shortened to simply *post hoc*. The full phrase is Latin for "after this, therefore because of this." It looks like this: "P happened. Then Q happened. Therefore, P caused Q." We do this in troubleshooting a lot: "I upgraded the Java version on the server. An hour later, the server went down. Therefore, upgrading Java made the server go down." I have seen this kind of logic employed countless times at 2 a.m. on crit-sit calls. It's a tempting conclusion to draw because the first thing we want to isolate is what changed. But it's a fallacy. All that you've done here is identify a potential candidate to investigate. Which is a laudable and necessary thing to do in troubleshooting. Just don't make too many assumptions based on it.

There are many more logical fallacies (a frightening number, actually—it's amazing anything works at all given how frail our arguments can be), and many good books devoted entirely to the subject. A really fun read on logical fallacy is called *How to Win Any Argument: The Use and Abuse of Logic* by Madsen Pirie (A & C Black). But being armed with these popular ones should go a long way.

In this pattern, we've covered the three elements of a strong argument: the logical, ethical, and pathetic appeals. These are called "appeals," because you're appealing to that faculty or aspect of your audience. To be truly persuasive, your arguments, your public rallying toward a vision, and your decks should contain elements of all three.

You can read a more in-depth discussion in Book II of Aristotle's original text (*http://bit.ly/2Pt7Hh1*).

Fait Accompli

When the good leader's work is done, his aims fulfilled, the people will all say, "We did this ourselves."
—Lao Tzu

The term *fait accompli* is French for "an accomplished fact," as in a "done deal." It refers to something that has been decided or happened before those affected have a chance to hear about it or reverse it.

After you've done the work of crafting a strategy with tools we discuss here, you will be faced with a meeting to present your findings to the board of directors, the senior leaders in your department, or some other deciding managerial body, depending on your place in the organization and the scope of your work. This pattern is about how you handle that meeting. You can have the greatest strategy in the world, but if you let this meeting get away from you, you can really damage and dilute the chances for your good work to thrive.

Facing a Cold Audience

This pattern is about making sure you don't go in to present to a cold audience. By "cold audience," I don't mean necessarily one that's adversarial or defensive, but rather one that you have not prepped, and does not have at least some idea of what you're going to say.

The naïve approach is to come to the meeting and unveil your work to a cold audience. You've scheduled the meeting, people show up wondering what you're going to show them, you present your strategy, and you ask if there are any questions. In such a forum, with a cold audience, you will be lucky to get past the third slide.

What is most likely to happen is that the managers, directors, VPs, senior executives, or whatever level of folks are in this audience will completely reroute the conversation away from what you're presenting. It won't be on purpose, they won't mean to, and the origins of where you lost them will be hard to trace. But an argument over some tangential matter will ignite, or you will get tremendous focus of a very aggressive nature. People will launch damning questions, puzzle out loud, or otherwise attack the work.

You will be left standing there, having presented a small portion of your ideas, with no one seeming to care about it or a palpable sense of confusion about what you're trying to do and why. Because the presentation erupted into a bunch of side conversations with people not paying attention or performing an outright mutiny on the ideas, it gets rejected either explicitly or implicitly, with people not wanting to hurt your feelings or be the shark at the meeting, but ultimately you've not moved them or changed their minds or gotten them on board with your plans.

This is a failure, and you don't usually get another shot at it. This can be incredibly frustrating for you, and prevent the organization from moving ahead with your great ideas. Why would this happen? There are a few, marginally related reasons.

Anytime you're presenting in a work forum like this, people have only one question in their minds: What's in it for me? They immediately start calculating. How does this message affect me, my teams, and my chances for success; encroach on my territory; or signal the coming of some change that I might find incredibly disturbing or rife with opportunity?

There's a cliché we often hear in business: people do not like change. We've all heard this. But it's not quite true. What it really means, or should mean, is that people don't like change that is *imposed* on them. We might be perfectly happy to change jobs, get a new haircut, or move to the Smoky Mountains. People are fine with change and they do it all the time. But we would not be happy changing in any of those ways if someone else *forced* us to do it without asking us, without consulting us, or without recognizing that we have some vested interest. We can make all kinds of changes all the time, with great enthusiasm, even as a work force within a big software company. But not if we aren't included.

Here's the mistake we made in our meeting: we didn't include the audience in our process, or at the least given them a heads up and taken some input. When you go to a meeting and some director unveils her new "strategy" and you're not sure why you're at that meeting, what the outcome is supposed to be, who she thinks she's talking to, what's going to be decided, and worse, those proposals tend to get undermined explicitly or politely disregarded.

The Meeting Before

What you need is a *fait accompli*. Put simply, you have the meeting before the meeting, in a bunch of little meetings, to line everyone up. Then the big meeting where everyone is *ostensibly* there to hear your message and accept it is more or less over before it starts, with people by and large on board, because their buy-in happened already: it's a fait accompli.

You need to have the meeting with each of the key stakeholders, individually, before the meeting, to get them on board separately. Then, when the big day comes, it's just a show about nothing, which is perfect, because you've already made everyone the ally of your proposal. The best outcome at the big meeting is that nothing much happens. No one is caught off guard, no one is challenged and gets defensive, no one is confused about what's happening, there are no hecklers taking everyone down a rabbit hole with their one weird line of reasoning, everyone nods in agreement, and you get a yes because you've already gotten one from everyone privately beforehand. With each audience member feeling separately in concert with your proposal, there's nothing to discuss, your stuff gets approved with little fanfare, and you get your bag of money to go change the world.

In essence, you need to suck the drama out of your own meeting, before it happens, so no one else can add their drama and undermine your work. If you don't do this, some person who is the most threatened, or whose perspective you have least considered or cared for, will act like a heckler at a comedy show. And if that person has any power or respect from the others in the room, human animal nature will be to spot the weakness, see that things are going south, and pile on. And then you're sunk.

So instead of relishing the drama of such a meeting, you have several little informal meetings with the key stakeholders. These can be short.

It is very hard work to put together a smart strategy for a changing and complex business. It can take many weeks. After toiling away, alone in a room, thinking, reading, and working hard, you might find it incredibly tempting to come to the reveal meeting in the manner of an artist or a showman, excited about your ideas. That's natural. But it's not strategic. We see Steve Jobs and his attendant deification, and it's tempting to want to emulate these kinds of dramatic unveilings. But unless you're Steve Jobs, this is probably not a great approach. As the business cliché goes, you want to be positioned not as the "sage on the stage," but the "guide at their side." When you're the genius who went to the mountaintop, did a yoga pose, and had the gods reveal unto you the One True Light and the Way about what your technology strategy should be, and now you've come back to the commoners to spread your gospel, don't expect much support.

So here's how to implement the Fait Accompli pattern, in a few easy steps:

1. Look at your Stakeholder Matrix (see "Stakeholder Matrix" on page 105) and RACI (see "RACI" on page 108) and make the list of whom to invite to the big proposal meeting.

2. Determine the list of who the *key* stakeholders are—the people with the most clout. Determine who is most *affected* by your proposal, who has the most to lose by it, and whose daily lives your proposal would disrupt the most. Carefully consider on this list the people who don't like you, aren't automatically on board with your ideas, grumble no matter what, showboat at meetings, and make everything about them. Try to see yourself as they would, as that external imposer. If you show up to announce that everyone's getting a new haircut and moving to Milan, expect a violent and quick uprising. This will happen even if everyone in the room wants to move to Milan.

3. Interview these people individually, tell them what you're thinking, and ask if it makes sense to them, what you're not considering, how it can be improved, and what ideas they are working on that might be incorporated. Take the notes with gratitude and make places for them in your work.

4. Then, like a salesperson, ask them bluntly, "If we incorporate these changes, does this direction make sense to you? Is this something you can support?" Recognizing later that they already have signaled their clear approval to you, they'll be loath to reverse that publicly at the big meeting.

5. Go to your big meeting with the clearly stated agenda that you're making your proposal or stating your new direction. Once there, make sure that you reference the stakeholders' work, credit their ideas, and thank them for their contribution. This is not only honest and proper, but has the pleasant side effect of creating an echo chamber of support in the room. You're implicitly telling the other bosses in the room: "Betty Boss contributed this idea, so this proposal is partly hers too. So you can't attack this without also attacking Betty Boss," which they will be much more hesitant to do.

Your strategy will get approved, and you will have made a fait accompli of the proposal. Nicely done.

This pattern is not about manipulation. It is about empathy and truly strengthening your work in a material way. There is also an awareness of some of the quirks of human behavior in business settings that don't have to be allowed to run rampant.

Managerial and executive types do not like surprises. Ever. And they definitely don't like their authority undermined or ignored. But if you line them up privately before the meeting so they can make valid and important points that you can consider, work into your proposal, and credit them with, and give them a chance to get their voice heard and state their frustrations or concerns, all will go well. You won't be surprised, they won't be surprised, and your proposal will actually be better, more relevant, and more impactful with the multitude of voices with different perspectives taken into account.

When this pattern is most deftly executed, people don't have an experience of approving your work at all: they think you are merely representing *them* and simply relaying the strategy we all know is right. They will think, "We did it ourselves."

Strategy is the art of creating power. If you don't give them power, they will take yours.

Dramatic Structure

If in the first act you have hung a pistol on the wall, then in the follow-
ing act it should be fired. Otherwise don't put it there.
  —Anton Chekov

The good ended happily, and the bad unhappily. That is what Fiction
means.
  —Oscar Wilde

The Dramatic Structure pattern is applicable when it's time to structure your Ask Deck (see "Ask Deck" on page 256). When you make a
deck, you need to be very clear on who your audience is and what
you want them to do. The best way to get them to agree to your
plans is to engage them according to the three forms of rhetoric, or
persuasive speaking, that you learned in "Ars Rhetorica" on page
167. You can engage them on an emotional level, not by making
baldly emotional (pathos) appeals as politicians so frequently do
(because this is business), but by weaving it into the way you structure your deck.

The structure of most movies, plays, and television shows has
changed little since Aristotle first identified the optimal dramatic
structure in his work *The Poetics*, some 2,400 years ago. That work is
wide-ranging, and we'll pick up only a few relevant cues here.

Our culture reuses structures and stories a lot. The popular Disney
movie *The Lion King* is simply a retelling of Shakespeare's *Hamlet*,
but with cartoon lions, as is the goofy comedy *Strange Brew*, but
with drunk Canadians. That's not so much because we're not imaginative, but because certain things work. We find novel ways to apply
the same story or the same structure. There are approximately 10
gazillion blues and folk songs with an E-flat, A-flat, B-flat chord pro-
gression. It works. So what can we learn from this?

Consider the following. It's the basic plot structure of the standard
Hollywood movie, dramatic literature, novels, and TV shows across
all media, all genres, and all eras:

1. In the beginning, we see the status quo. This is "the way things
   are today." We understand the main characters in their normal
   setting. They get breakfast, take the kids to school, are stymied
   in traffic on the freeway. The guards stand watch at the gates,

just like every night. We have established the normal routines. This is this family, and these are the things they do. Everything's fine.

2. But then one day…there's an Event. This is called the "inciting incident." There is a rupture in the status quo: the first earthquake tremors ripple through San Andreas, the bad boy comes to town, the ghost of Hamlet's father appears to tell his son he was murdered, the hotel appears to be haunted, we learn of the inexorable pull of Willy Wonka's golden tickets.

3. Now there's a problem. We can't possibly just maintain the status quo. Nothing can ever be the same again. The stormtroopers killed our family. Our lives have been spun in a different, unanticipated direction. We have no choice but to embrace our new fate, accept the challenge we never wanted, learn the ways of The Force, and become the hero we were meant to be, however reluctant or scared we are to do so, even with all the things we must leave behind.

4. The hero battles the villain (Darth Vader, Voldemort, the Nazis, alcoholism, the tornado, the Mean Girls, the aliens). The odds seem insurmountable. We look for escape, and just when we think we've found a way out, we're crushed again. We are now in the depths of despair. But in our resourcefulness and ingenuity and spunkiness, we see a tiny spark of hope: the dim possibility of a way forward. But we're exhausted. If only we could muster an ounce of energy. We are visited by our teacher, a sage, a master, a ghost, or an angel that reminds us of our fortitude, and that despite the odds, we must go on.

5. The hero defeats the villain, the enemy is banished, the reluctant sweethearts get married, and we're safe again. Even in tragedies where the hero dies, the conflict is resolved, and the world is now free to enter the New Normal. We resume the status quo, but now things are different, and we'll all adapt to this new state of affairs, accepting and beginning our new routines undisturbed.

Just about every story in our culture that isn't a wacky fringe arthouse experiment (and even some of those) follows this structure. Across the wide range of apparently really different shows, whether it's *The Godfather*, *The Wizard of Oz*, *Willy Wonka and the Chocolate Factory*, *The Shining*, *Silkwood*, *Star Wars*, or *Superman*, this is the foundation on which they're all built. It sounds like most software projects too.

This structure engages audiences. The purpose of this pattern is to illuminate this structure so that you can adapt and apply it in your decks. If you do, your deck will be empathetically taking care of your audience, helping them hear your story, and see what matters, and make it more understandable, impactful, and memorable. And you'll get a green light.

So let's translate this for when we have to make a presentation proposing a new direction. Say you're making a Strategy Deck (see "Strategy Deck" on page 259) or an Ask Deck (see "Ask Deck" on page 256), or want to propose that we embrace a new software development method. Here's how to do it.

Establish the Status Quo

The status quo grounds the audience: we know where we are on this common ground. We restate our shared goals, acknowledge the current process, state a clear picture of our teams, and show the architecture diagram of the current state. We're getting buy-in here that this is Where We Stand Today. This is a level set of What We Know to Be True, and Our Shared Understanding.

Create an Inciting Incident

But something's rotten in the state of Denmark. There's a scratching at the door. We show the current state architecture with all its spaghetti mess of connections, leaving our teams debilitated. We point out the areas of exposure, weakness, and vulnerability in security. We show charts depicting the number of Priority One incidents: the trend is bad. In fact, if we stay on this course and do nothing, we are *doomed*. We show the effect of exactly what the state will be if we do not act. We have two years to migrate the servers, and then we're out of IP addresses and we can't add more customers. State clearly, with real data and projections, exactly what you expect to happen. The alien ships will land and enslave everyone they don't kill, we'll lose the family farm to the bank and end up on the street, the spaceship will go careening into the sun/black hole or run out of fuel, and everyone dies without a parent to raise their dear children. You show what bad effects are in store for the business if you don't act.

As in the movies, the stories in business are few. The effects are going to reduce to one of these:

- Our costs will go up, while our quality and availability go down.
- We will be slower to market, and the competition will win.
- We will lose this revenue opportunity.
- We will lose these key customers.
- We will lose these key employees.

You should illustrate these with data you cultivate, like the movie scientist with the white coat and pointy stick who warns everyone what will happen, but they're too dumb/lazy/entrenched in making money to heed his emphatic warnings.

You are showing, as vividly and truthfully as you can, what The Problem is and what the impact will be if we continue the status quo. If the problem you're solving doesn't reduce to one of these, you might be framing it wrong.

In Case It's Not Clear

I want to be crystal clear on this in case someone goes bananas with this and takes it the wrong way: with this pattern, I am in *no way* recommending or suggesting that you overstate anything, fictionalize anything, make a silly show of anything, or make your presentation somehow a drama. Quite the opposite. It is an organizing principle only, and should go completely unstated by you and entirely unnoticed by your audience. State only true facts and make the claims you actually believe. I reference this structure only as an unspoken frame on which to hang real data, actual claims, and logical and substantive arguments, as merely a hopefully memorable way for you to organize your concrete thoughts. There's no hyperbole and no manipulation of anything or anyone. You've got to organize your slides some way. I'm just saying that when you organize them *this* way, your audience will subconsciously interpret it as a story, it will make intuitive sense to them, and they will hear you better than they hear other people, and be more accepting and appreciative of your work. And secondly, if you struggle to fit your work into this frame, that means you haven't done enough homework, so doing it with this principle helps you to see the consequences and make better strategic choices

---

The Plan

The plan is how we state the way out. This is the "therefore" moment. The Rock has got to steal the helicopter, fly it into the dam, and defuse the bomb—we've got two hours until it goes off.

We were living on credit cards and never updated our legacy software, and now it's time to pay the piper. Here's how we decompose the monothlic system and turn it into a modern platform. Here's how our new tech will capture this market. Here's how we fix the quality and scalability issues that have plagued our mission-critical system.

Because the world changed in ways we didn't ask for, didn't anticipate, or weren't ready to confront, we must act. And here is the simple single statement of the path forward, the clear recommendation you're making, your plan: to fix the problem, we must do *this*. Make it a single sentence of your new goal. We were just going to live on this planet and be farmers, but now we have to go be Jedi Knights and blow up the Death Star to restore peace and justice to the galaxy.

Show what changes you expect across people, process, and technology. Who will be involved, what work will they do, what processes need changing, what tech will you buy or learn or add to, and what is the future state architecture?

Using Directional Costing (see "Directional Costing" on page 218), show how much the plan will cost, so they know what you're asking. Show how long it will take and who will do the work.

But much of this we'll look at in more detail in "Ask Deck" on page 256.

Shock and Awe

Shock and Awe was a military tactic developed in the late 1990s. Its goal is to paralyze the will of the adversary to fight. Using this as a metaphor, you overload your audience with such an onslaught of brutal facts about the status quo that they become incapable of resistance. Make a show of such *decisive force* in your deck—the painful succession of problems and bad outcomes for not agreeing to your plan, such that it's urgent that the executive make a decision now—they obviously will choose your path since you've so clearly gathered the facts and thought it through and they just can't wait for your plan.

Here, you all but crush the hero. You never use hyperbole or over-state the case or say anything false. Just be brutal in making the audience uncomfortable, confronting them with the real problems, as a Rented Brain would (see "Rented Brain" on page 163). Be specific about the bad things that will happen, using charts and graphs and projections in order to be clear on the time frame you have. How long until the bomb goes off? You pile on more and more in succession until they all but beg you to stop.

Finally, you state the following:

1. Your definition of done: this is the concrete statement and clear view of what the world looks like at the end of all this, the future state architecture once you're done.

2. How you will measure that success, how you'll show progress, and the metrics you'll use.

3. The structure you'll put in place to report back on those metrics and progress to a steering committee made up of these stakeholders. The executive is still in control: all she has to do is agree, and everything will be fine.

You have rocked their world with a cataclysmic event, piled on more and more pain like the Book of Job, shown them a path forward, and given them the assurance and mechanism of transparency that leaves them confident and relieved that this plan is in place and they are still in control and can't wait for the New Normal.

Here's a second great benefit to employing Dramatic Structure: if you can't honestly weave your request into this structure, if you don't know clearly what the real reasons are that you want to move to the cloud or make all the programmers learn AI, or you can't explain why everyone should stop doing Agile and start doing Fred's Cool New Software Development Method, then you might not have good enough reasons.

If you can't create the inciting incident this way, and don't know what will happen if the team doesn't follow your recommendation—or if what will happen is that Everything's Still Just Fine—then you might have a solution looking for a problem or you might have merely made a Shopping List of Shiny Objects that would be fun to put on your résumé. If you're not solving a real business problem for anyone, then it shouldn't be done.

I've employed this structure in every Ask Deck I've made for the last decade, and there have been many of them, requesting many tens of millions of dollars to go do important stuff that needs doing. With this structure, I've never been told no. It can work for you too.

Deconstruction

It ain't what you don't know that gets you into trouble. It's what you know for sure that just ain't so.
— after Josh Billings

When the blackbird flew out of sight,
It marked the edge
Of one of many circles.
— Wallace Stevens, "Thirteen Ways of Looking at a Blackbird"

Il n'y a pas de hors-texte.
— Jacques Derrida

As technology leaders, architects, and strategists given a problem, we are all too often devoted to directing solutions toward local optima. In computer science and applied mathematics, the *local optimum* is the best solution within a cluster of neighboring candidate solutions. Local optima are easier and quicker to find than potentially more impactful, global solutions. "Quick wins," as they are sometimes called, appeal to leaders of the short-term mindset, who are focused on quarterly earnings per share, willing to live on credit cards to enjoy the high life now, and content to defer larger problems to their successors.

Solving local problems is an important part of our jobs, and needs to be done. But architects and leaders who too frequently focus on too fine-grained matters, on small issues with few branches, can actually perpetuate and worsen the organizational dysfunction that they purport to address. This is one inherent contradiction in problem solving. Another, as Paul Virilio showed us, is that solving one problem concomitantly creates another.

In short, contradictions abound, and they do so in ways that subvert the scientific mindset of the typical engineer or data-driven analyst.

Three Levels of Problems

When you are faced with solving a scalability problem within an application, consider the very meaning of "scalability." Consider it across contexts. What other functions constitute the set of conjuncts of propositions that make up the domain of discourse? Said more directly, when you're solving a problem, look at three things:

- The local problem
- The category that this problem is in, the set this is a member of
- The associations in which this problem arises in other contexts

This is not a deceptive way of suggesting that you turn every mole-hill into a mountain. It is saying that if you have a scalability problem on this system, you have a scalability problem in general, and that solving the problem won't solve the problem, and you'll have it again. See further.

When given a problem, we seek solutions and seek to find problems in our own history that match this one. We are implicated in our own histories, which can harm as much as benefit us. We solved X this way in the past, so we might be able to apply that to new problem Y. We assume constraints, taking as necessary what may be contingent. Because of the way we bound the problem within a domain of discourse, we miss rich signals from other nearby clusters. We can upgrade to the latest version of some software and increase capacity on some server to solve a local problem of this bug or that throughput. Local optima might solve the problem at hand, creating the best situation for the here and now, but fail to find the global optima revealed by a cross-disciplinary approach to our mental model of the domain.

Moreover, this creates in us an overconfidence in the stability and veracity of our viewpoints. It is hard work to create a viewpoint, to come to understand complex systems, methods, and organizations. It seems therefore difficult, if not exhausting and cruel, to suggest that our path forward is to destruct, reconfigure, and reconstruct them at once, even in the act of building, improving, and honoring them.

Because we do not raise our visor to the horizon of context, we do not scale as well as we might, either in our own roles or in helping the organization do so. When we fail in this as leaders, we leave our organizations inefficient, because we need to solve problems repeatedly instead of addressing the context in which they arise to improve the overall state. We leave our teams anemic, with a few key subject matter experts as single points of knowledge and single points of failure. We cannot scale our business, growing from a $2M funded startup to a $100M attractive business, to a $300M market leader, to a $500M public growth company or $1B diverse holding. Scaling means seeing context and acting to create new contexts.

The problem of having the same repeated problem, which creates organizational inefficiency, is one thing the Deconstruction pattern addresses. It is the pattern for a different way to define our mental models.

Three Causes of Problems

As you approach your work, look not only to solve the local problem, but to see the broader frame in which it can obtain ("obtain" here is used to mean "obtain ontological status," or "come into existence"). To do that is to see those contradictions that adhere as you interpret data to create insights. The contradictions abound, and they abound in signs. If we are not aware that we are dealing with signs, that signs are the "water"—the ocean in which we swim—and that they are always already rife with contradiction, our vision and our methods, our ways and means, our strategy, and therefore our organization, will suffer.

I submit that there are three primary factors in technology organizations that account for most, if not all, of their problems:

- Lazy people
- People who are not lazy, but don't think about how they think about their work
- A misunderstanding of semiotics

Too frequently we may solve a problem directly, only to have it appear again later, in the same or similar form. We thereby make a fundamental mistake: we come to believe that this is our job, the repeated solving of this same problem, because we get better at solving it and better at seeing it in the first place. So we create an unhealthy attachment to it, in a sort of Freudian *repetition compulsion*. Freud first discussed this psychological phenomenon in 1914, stating, "The patient does not *remember* anything of what he has forgotten and repressed, he *acts* it out, without, of course, knowing that he is repeating it." Freud elaborates this idea in the later work *Beyond the Pleasure Principle*, which serves as an unfortunately relevant, if unwitting, discourse on the state of many work processes in modern organizations.

Left unwatched, our work is a mere variation on this theme, the diminishing drudgery of the same little riff, echoing into the eternal void. This is, in part, a mistake in our mental models, the assumption that the world is divided between two things: the signified and the signifier. We see this thing, and we name it. Signified, signifier. In the act of naming it we create a direct relation to it, and reinforce the tendency to solve the local problem. The label fixes the concept. We have then put in an honest day's work. A continuing collection of honest days' work is called our "job."

Organizations whose constituents mostly act in this perfectly reasonable-seeming fashion cannot scale. Your "job" gets in the way of your *work*.

This is a call to inspect our categories, in order to make a new order not for solving the same problems, but instead for seeing how to not have those problems, perhaps without ever "solving" them. Or to be able to solve the problem while concomitantly extending the context, such that you invite a bigger, more interesting, better problem to contend with. In doing this yourself with your team, you will build a better business, and have a better chance of growing and scaling the business. Another way of putting this to yourself is, "rather than solving it, how do we just not *have* this problem?"

If you are a knowledge worker, your job is not your job. Your job is to destroy your job. Employ metacognitive thinking: stand outside and consider how you do what you do, watch yourself and your organization, externalize what you know, share your knowledge as fast as you can, create a new context, templatize and automate yourself out of a job. If this is your personal aim, your business will start to scale better and your career will too. Another way of putting this to yourself is, "How can I work myself out of a job?"

Semiotics: Signs and Symbols

Semiotics is the study of signs and symbols, how they are interpreted to make meaning, and how they are used to communicate.

In semiotics, a *sign* is a pointer. It is not the thing itself, but refers to the thing itself, like a word, or a symptom of illness, or a stop sign. A signifier is the form a sign takes. The signified is the concept, the referent, the material aspect of the sign, the thing the word describes, the illness and not the symptom or its name. We point at a ball and say "ball," which refers not to that object so much as our mental concept of a ball. These differ from ball to ball, and from signifying agent to signfiying agent.

But signs take on meaning only in relation to *other signs*. We know something is "present" only because something else is "absent." That implies that there are traces, or residue, or material connection between these terms. It foregrounds the importance of context, and domains of discourse, and extra text—the relatedness and implication in each other of apparently contradictory elements. Recognizing this is a key to categorizing properly, to knowing what to include, where you'll be tripped up, how to create the most compelling products, how to make processes and organizations with proper degrees of conflict and harmony, and how to grow a business.

As noted designer, author, and artist Edwin Schlossberg said so wonderfully, "The skill of writing is to create a context in which other people can think." Likewise, the skill of leading an organization, or creating an architecture, or creating a strategy, is structurally analogous: you are creating a context in which other people can succeed.

The Netflix Culture Deck

The best treatise on setting context as a leader is Reed Hasting's wonderful Netflix Culture deck (*http://bit.ly/2LhKD1H*). I highly recommend reading this if you haven't already, since it was published in 2009. It is also an excellent reference as we consider the intersection of strategy, execution, and culture throughout this book.

If you see yourself as a context creator, which I hope you are coming to do, you must also consider yourself as this observer of systems and maker of models, keenly aware of the inherent impossibility of language and the infinite conjunct of interrelated signs. You are assigning labels to concepts in making a system architecture. This is that. Epistemology, as a branch of philosophy, is concerned with discovering what is knowable and our methods of knowing. *Metacognition* refers to the local act of thinking about your own thinking. This is the job of the architect-strategist. We ask ourselves: What is the context in which such a circumstance as this, which surely is only one instance of this phenomena, could come to be true? What category is this in? Can I just as easily solve for the category so our organization can get off the hamster wheel and scale? We consider the assumptions we make, the biases we have, and the constraints we see that are perhaps not necessary, but only habit.

This is not a beckoning toward the siren song of scope creep. Architects are not interested in what every programmer names every class. Strategists are not interested in this local optima. If you are not able to look at the big business problems alongside your leaders and bring your vantage as a technologist, and are overindexed on picking this JavaScript framework over that one, you'll win the battle and lose the war.

Scopes Without Center

Most of the people who will execute your plans do not report to you. As a strategist or architect, you must reach them by influence. Architects often used to be developers, so they see themselves as the most clever developers who then must rein in the wayward activities of the less clever developers. This is architect as traffic cop. It's not interesting and it's not necessary and it doesn't scale. You are *adjacent* to the big forces of development, product, strategy—but master of none. Your power comes from making the most important business decisions as if you were a technologist, and the most important technology decisions as if you were a businessperson. You deconstruct the false binary opposition between business and technology.

You influence your adjacent colleagues by the broadness of your vision, by the soundness of your arguments as to why that's the right vision and how your way is the best way to get there, and by stirring them to care for that vision for themselves.

This pattern is in the communication set because it serves as an offering, a possible plausible underpinning for how to approach thinking about thinking, conduct conversations, conclude investigations, make presentations, form teams, participate in organizations, and advise senior leaders. It takes inspiration from the work of Jacques Derrida, the post-structuralist French philosopher and focus of my graduate studies. Derrida is the originator of the philosophical approach to textual analysis called *deconstruction*, a term that is sometimes seen in popular culture, and invariably abused in dilution when it is.

In 1966, Derrida delivered a paper entitled "Structure Sign and Play in the Discourse of the Human Sciences" (*http://bit.ly/2nXYn8t*) (which is a wonderful paper, right up there with the original DynamoDB paper (*http://bit.ly/2LdfbBD*) and the Page Rank (*https://stanford.io/2o1Pk6C*) algorithm paper). The term *deconstruction* is not directly introduced in this paper, but the method of analysis he suggests is rather enacted.

Derrida's phrase "il n'y a pas de hors-texte," quoted in the epigraph at the top of this pattern, is French for "there is no outside-text." We consider our work not having been given this object, this center, but rather that we mediate signs around what colloquially is called a center, in "a series of substitutions of center for center, as a linked chain of determinations of the center." The center is not the center. It is at once within the structure, and outside it. It is the irreconcilable difference that we reject and live.

The World as System: Synthetic Decomposition

Ultimately, your endeavors in this work will be a matter of *synthetic decomposition*. This is a phrase I just made up. It means that you do two "opposite" things at once (let us suspend, or bracket,[1] for a moment that I don't believe in "opposites," but cede that I occasionally must make a grudging nod to convention). Synthetic decomposition means you consider a proposition, consider its opposite, and act from the opposing view simultaneously as from your original view. In so doing, you will realize the impossibility of signs. You will

---

1 *Suspension*, or *bracketing*, is a tool that Derrida frequently employed. See "Structure, Sign, and Play in the Discourse of the Human Sciences" (*http://bit.ly/2nXYn8t*), Derrida, 1966.

have seen into the universe, seen into its contradictions, the inadequacy of explanations, the tyranny of its confusion, and the fickleness of its attitudes, and the emptiness of its presumed virtues. You must go through this to see the relations, the harmonies, the firmness, the beauties, the soundness, and vitality. You have destroyed the signs you thought you knew, redefined the images on a broader canvas. In creating new signfiers, you create new signifieds. From such a vantage, your systems, your architectures, your designs, and your strategies will gather unstoppable force.

In synthetic decomposition, you build by destroying received categories. Like Vitruvius, you are concerned with all of the arts and all of the sciences, and see them together and seed your work with them. You are combining and composing across disparate patterns that seem at odds. This plies thinking across your team and is the germ of innovation.

The Maserati Gran Tourismo is one of the most perfectly engineered high-performance machines on the planet. It drives nearly 200 miles per hour, executing with unmatched reliability. Its engine block is made by Ferrari, a direct competitor. Its unifying inspiration is a Stradivarius violin. Its design was created by exalted Italian design group Pinninfarina, which for nearly 100 years has designed cars, but also wristwatches, bicycles, major appliances, and the Olympic torch. To believe you are a designer of *concepts* first allows you to bring multivariate sources and forces to bear, to engineer like a designer, to design by emptying yourself of care for design but total care and empathy for the user, to lead like a philosopher. This interdisciplinary mode of synthetic decomposition will help build your most powerful and innovative way forward.

You are always building a system: your architecture is a system, your strategy is a system, your organization is a system, your mental model as an observer is a system.

So the metamodel, the frame of mind that I encourage you to adopt in your work, goes like this:

1. Discover and analyze the problems and opportunities about you. Decompose them into their more atomic constituent parts, determining correlations and causations.

2. Hypothesize as we saw in Chapter 2. Catalog your hypotheses. Ask what broader context must exist in order for this circumstance to arise? What is the global maximum across clusters?

3. Observe yourself as an observer in an act of metacognition and decompose your concepts. See them as signs with false signifiers. Do your best to undermine your own hypotheses. Argue against them. Destroy them to find their weaknesses in a mock trial. Build them as a Logic Tree. Then build them as a poem. Beware of your biases and ask what assumptions you are making, what you know for sure that just ain't so.

4. Synthesize to recombine the problems and opportunities from across different frames: people, process, and technology as well as the different trajectories of temporality, velocity, and force. How can you look at the blackbird 13 ways? What threads, or traces, or residue can you observe in each that can be brought to bear in new, innovative, overarching, more impactful, global ways? How can you reconstitute, reformulate, reconstruct to create a new semiotic of your design?

5. Develop a model taking all of that up, one that represents a new frame, a new context, in which the constituent parts are optimized for their metrics, simplified, reduced. You're making a framework at the level of context. In this way, you're externalizing what you know, making a template every time you solve a problem, so that the problem can be solved again without you when next it arises.

The job of the architect, CTO, technology manager, or strategist is to determine how to create a context—design a system—in which new concepts can erupt and evolve (they're extensible) and people can do the best at what they do (they're fit for purpose). Such contexts involve the interplay between you, your department, your company, your industry, and the world, and how signs are mediated and how you participate in creating and destroying their structure at once, performing the synthetic decomposition, the dearchitecting, the destrategizing, the deconstruction of all these as an infinite conjunct of propositions with undermining contradictions, replacements, and evolutions at their core.

Scalable Business Machines

Organizations which design systems are constrained to produce designs which are copies of the communication structures of these organizations.
　—Melvin Conway

The spirit is a bone.
　—Hegel, *The Phenomenology of Spirit*

Does your organization have any of the following problems?

- You have a hero culture.
- You have many single points of knowledge.
- You have many single points of failure in processes.
- Your smart people who once really cared don't care now, are disengaged, are looking for jobs, or are on perpetual vacation.
- You bought a business that now is integral to your larger company's mission, but it still behaves like a startup.
- Your mature company is struggling to bring the old guard on board with a new vision.
- You need to be ready to grow your regional business into a national one, or national to international.
- You are considering adjacent markets to enter and need to have the real picture of your business to see how you can apply, reuse, repurpose, refocus, or modify existing elements to make it work.

If you have any of these problems, your business will struggle to scale. You need a *scalable business machine*. Before we say what that is and how to implement it, let's look a bit more at a few of these problems.

First, many of these problems are cultural. But the symptom is not the illness. Culture and strategy and execution revolve around each other in spheres of strong influence. And there are many ways to answer these cultural problems, which are typically the longest and hardest kind to turn around. This is not an HR book, or a ra-ra leadership book, and there are many maybe-helpful books to guide you in that method of addressing cultural problems. So we'll look at this from our architecture and strategy perspective: how we can design our business in order to maximize its efficiency and scalability, as well as to maximize our chances of any cultural work taking hold quickly and succeeding.

Hero culture is evident when your company lauds, promotes, and otherwise exalts the people that repeatedly save the day when some disaster strikes. Heroes get so many strokes for being heroes that they do not step back and think how to solve the context in which problems are created. They are rewarded, bonused, and publicly celebrated for pulling all-nighters, toiling alone into the wee hours, doing it all themselves. Again. Loads of otherwise competent people stand around doing nothing. They're essentially worthless to the organization at worst, and underused and alienated at best.

Hero culture is a disaster for a business that's trying to scale and grow. Without dismantling that, you can't scale your business, and it will be hard to see why it continues to be unable to break through.

Hero culture is vicious, because you don't want amazing feats of technical dexterity or brute force that save the day to go unnoticed. You don't want to alienate the people on whom Everything Depends. But if you can't break this cycle, which is a cross-organizational culture problem that starts with the leader and bad processes, then you cannot scale.

Without a scalable business operational model across your functions, you cannot be more efficient and maximize revenues and profits while minimizing costs. You cannot have happy workers who know they're doing stuff that matters, who don't get distracted and interrupted constantly, so they can focus and think a smart thought and do something great. Smart people are not interested in working in mind-numbing bureaucracies where they have to constantly scream to get anything done. If your processes are not right-sized, nimble, and efficient, you will be too slow to grow.

This pattern shows you how to create something that I just made up, called a scalable business machine. You want to use it when you need to create or revise a set of processes across business functions in order to grow and scale your business.

Business as System

Architecture is the broader purview over a system. Strategy is the broader purview over a line of business. Thinking like an architect, technology executive, or strategist is to look at the nexus of external forces and internal forces operating on our work as considered holistically, whether those be a software application, a process, or an organization. These take effect across various temporal trajectories, operating at various velocities, with various degrees of dynamism within the system.

To improve the organization, observe these forces and see them as a context to create a model of the world *as a system*. You are a maker of systems, which are built with an architecture, which desires certain properties: usefulness, firmess, and beauty. Attributes we tend to design explicitly for as architects include:

- Fitness to purpose
- Portability
- Scalability
- Extensibility
- Availability
- Monitorability
- Manageability
- Maintainability
- Resilience
- Security
- Auditability
- Performance
- Testability
- Elegance

We commonly employ certain principles in architecting and designing:

- Hide details behind an interface.
- Apply the principle of least knowledge.
- Create a strong separation of concerns.
- Ensure loose coupling.
- Isolate what changes independently.
- Look for opportunities for reuse.

- Explicitly manage risk.

Finally, let's recall the SOLID principles of object-oriented system design:

Single responsibility
Things should have one and only one reason to change, meaning that a class should have only one job.

Open-closed
Things should be open for extension, but closed for modification.

Liskov substitution principle
Objects of a derived class should always be substitutable for a parent class.

Interface segregation
A client should never be forced to implement an interface that it doesn't use, or clients shouldn't be forced to depend on methods they do not use.

Dependency inversion principle
Things must depend on abstractions, not on concretions. The high-level module must not depend on the low-level module.

You can architect an application, a data center, a project, or an organization. You design the interactions between software services with a protocol and a message payload; you design the interfaces between two departments to maximize efficiency, clarity, security, availability, monitorability, and speed. You design these systems according to SOLID and the desirable architecture attributes just stated.

The organization is a system.

The project is a system.

You can apply what you know from designing technology systems to business systems, like structuring the processes or the projects. The valued properties are similar across all of these system types. When you're designing a process, keep the architecture qualities in mind: I know of at least one Infrastructure department I'd love to have learn the principle of interface segregation.

Reread the SOLID principles and the architecture attributes just given, but this time seeing them through the lens of process designer.

This One's Fractal Too

As you read through this pattern, note that you can do this for one department only, or for all of them together and tie them together to view your business as a single scalable metamachine consisting of interrelated machines. It works locally, and works the same globally, like a fractal.

The Origin Theory

I have a theory I'll call the Origin Theory that might help you assess why your company behaves the way it does or has the problems it has when it's trying to grow. Sometimes a company starts its life as a support function. For example, maybe a big company had a little IT shop to support its real value creation work, and someone along the way made a software application for internal use that worked well enough that somebody else thought they could make more money if they were to spin off a company to sell it as a software product. That new company has its origins as a support function. The Origin Theory states that *it will therefore continue to act as a support function, even to its detriment. In essence, you end where you began.*

This happens because in the Olden Days, the little company hired leaders who matched its size and culture, which is typically one in which people must perform heroics, and must wear several hats. That's not a problem in a startup—it's a necessity of survival. So the people were nurtured through the ranks with everyone acting as participants in a support function. They do not think like product people. They don't think in terms of a P&L (profit and loss), or having clear guardrails and documentation and external supporting functions, and strongly separating responsibilities, and interdepartmental interfaces, because there's only one department and it's called Get Stuff Done. They think in terms of projects: those long, drawn-out loci for people doing activities instead of thinking in terms of outcomes. I have seen this in multiple companies, even multibillion-dollar public companies that act like private companies because even after decades in business and having gone public, there's really one or two majority shareholders: "Junior."

It is very difficult to turn around a company in this state. First you have to recognize it, then you have to get others to see it, then you have to rethink all your processes to define clear outputs and interfaces, and then you must make a cultural shift that will involve dramatically changing who is on your staff, changing how you manage and communicate with customers, and thinking of your products and services as independent of your heroes' hand-holding. Helping make such a transformation when you need to grow and scale your business is the aim of this pattern.

Aspects of the Scalable Business Machine

Implementing this pattern to create your scalable business machine (SBM) will mean making a project that you need to lead and track. Even if you are just implementing it within your own department at first, expect that this is a nontrivial amount of work. You should make a RACI and Stakeholder Alignment too. Before doing any work, make sure you've got your leader's buy-in and know who will make decisions. It's the kind of thing that you could pay consultants to do for you, but they wouldn't do it as well as you would, and the people wouldn't receive the change as well if you have this framework in mind.

Let's define some terms first. The following are the component parts of the SBM.

Action

An *action* is one atomic activity or local work process performed within a single department in aid of producing a deliverable. Each action produces something of clear and present value to be used by other members of the same department. Eventually, together these culminate in the creation of a deliverable for a customer outside this process.

For example, one action within the software development department might be to make a user story, another action might be to write code, a third might be to test it. These are three different roles within the same real or logical department. Testing on its own is not of value to anyone else. But all three work in concert to create the important deliverable that is demonstrable, working software that is high quality and fit to purpose. Each action (activity) has a deadline, typically one person responsible, and is a clear and discrete task. These are orchestrated together to form a process that makes deliverables.

Only one role is assigned as responsible to complete that action. Actions are typically not tracked by many other people, or maybe are analogous to a task or story in your Scrum tool. They don't require significant coordination with others. This is where much of the workday is consumed, transforming raw materials into an output of some value: you get a bunch of epics and make an architecture; you get a bunch of user stories and make working software.

Actions can be one of three types:

Create
> Make an initial result in partial fulfillment of a concrete deliverable output document or result.

Approve
> An approve action might be performed by a single person in a role such as the department head, or might be a virtual role comprising a governance body or other formal committee such as the "Project X Steering Committee." For virtual roles, it must be clearly defined what that virtual role is and the names of individual, concrete job titles that the virtual role or committee comprises. You have to know when you are done, which requires knowing who can approve or reject the work deliverable.

Review
> Check over the initial document to determine its validity, fitness to purpose, and relevance. This could be a single person in a named role, or a virtual role consisting of other concrete, existing named roles.

Tool

A *tool* is application or Software as a Service tool used to create a concrete deliverable that can be reviewed and used by someone else as valuable output, and sufficiently formally expresses that they don't need to participate in the process to make use of it. It's the means of making the output.

Examples: a spreadsheet, word processor, IDE, or project management tool, or Salesforce.

Deliverable

A *deliverable* is a concrete document, created with a tool that has value to someone else outside the department or process in which it was created. One or more related actions work together to create a deliverable.

A deliverable is something that stands on its own, and has value only within your process. It has no customer value. It's a work product you must track, assign to someone, and put a deadline on creating. But on its own, no one cares. Deliverables are necessary, and their quality can have tremendous impact on the overall eventual quality of the output. But they are a means, not an end.

Examples: vision statement, architecture definition document, release plan, working code, deployment plan, and project plan.

Don't involve customers in deliverables. They care only about outputs.

Output

An *output* is a collection of one or more deliverables. Outputs are the stuff we produce, whether physical or virtual, whether a product or coherent service. They are the What. These things matter to customers and are visible to them and tangible to them, and customers pay for them. This is your work product that *matters*. It's what customers need to get from you so they can go do their thing. It's why you exist: to make this output. You might have to make a project plan: that is your job. You might have to make an architecture document or type working code: those things are activities in doing your job. But they are not a total work product usable by a customer on their own. In themselves, they don't matter.

Outcome

The *outcome* is the difference your output makes to a customer. Outcomes are the Why. They represent the benefits your customer gets.

Outcomes will ultimately be some variation on a more refined version of one or more of these: increased revenue, reduced costs, quicker time to market, better positioning in a market, increased share of wallet, increased yield, higher margins, better reliability, and so forth.

One or more actions create a deliverable internal within a department. One or more deliverables together create outputs usable by a different department in the same business unit or company, or they are of value to external customers. Creating outputs of value for customers are why businesses exist.

Department

A *department* is a logical grouping of people who perform actions to create outputs of the same kind. As we learned in "Value Chain" on page 116, a department is one of two types:

Value creator
> They make the products and deliver the services the company sells.

Support
> These people do not create direct value for customers, but provide necessary functions to conduct business. These include HR, Legal, Finance, Infrastructure, and Procurement. They exist to serve the value creator departments and make their work quicker, easier, and compliant with law.

Companies that do not recognize the difference between these two kinds of departments will see a terrible imbalance of power play out, resulting in the support functions acting like bureaucrats who are so far removed from the customers that they think the value creators exist only to participate in their processes. This isn't hard for people in the trenches to see, but correcting it means the most powerful leader needs to see it and replace the relevant management team with people more clueful about where their bread is buttered.

Business unit

The *business unit* owns a slate of product SKUs it sells to customers and owns a P&L. The business unit can succeed or fail mostly on its own merits, with help (or interference) from the supporting departments that do not create value.

Company

A *company* is a legal fiction that has the status of a special person. The company itself doesn't make anything. It is an abstract class for holding business units or departments. There are no company outputs that are of value to customers that are not already defined by some specific business unit.

The company itself is not a value creator other than as a sum of the department parts. For a smaller company, say, those under $100M, you may not be subdivided into business units with their own P&L. In these cases, the business unit and company share an "identity" relation (they're the same thing). In such cases, treat their use here interchangeably.

Figure 7-1 shows a logical architecture of how these components all relate. In general, here's the idea behind the SBM: companies do a bunch of stuff that doesn't matter and on occasion need to identify those things and refine their processes to remember how to efficiently create value and make a difference in the market. They need to get out from under the inertia that sets in and focus on outcomes.

The SBM is engineered to help you identify where you are, separate the wheat from the chaff, focus on optimizing outcomes for delighting customers, and allow you to scale and grow.

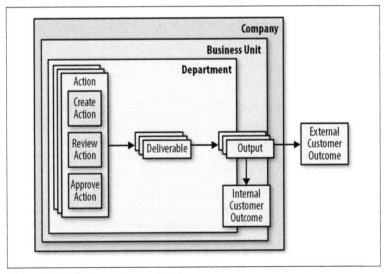

Figure 7-1. The terms in an SBM

Executing

Now that we have the relevant terms defined as we'll use them, here are the steps for creating an SBM.

Define vision and scope

First, state the vision and the scope.

The *vision* is a single sentence characterizing the end state. If you don't understand the problem you're solving, or the desired outcome you would get at the end, you will just rearrange the deck chairs.

This step sounds lame, but it makes a difference if you actually use it. You'll actually use it if it's not a platitude, but a proposition and something some reasonable person could conceivably argue against.

Define the departments and customer outcomes

Next you need to create the list of departments that are in scope. This sounds too obvious to do, but it is in no way obvious to the people in your organization what the different departments are, why they exist, what they do, and how they interrelate. Just name them for now and agree on scope. If you want to give each one a charter or mission statement, that gets you bonus points, but again, only if you really use it to organize your thoughts as a Logic Tree.

Start with your external customers first. What is the *output* of your business unit for customers?

Then identify the desired outcome for them. What would give them a benefit or delight them?

Then determine the outputs at a department level. What outputs does a department make to feed the next department as their necessary input? These are the internal customers you identify.

List these for each department.

Now you have an overarching vision, a validated list of departments, their mission for each, the outputs they create in support of it, and the benefits that will add up to great outcomes—the benefits for which you exist to give your identified customers.

We are ignoring for now deliverables and actions. That's on purpose, and it's important. We want to go from the outside in, focusing on what we create that's of value for someone else, and being clear on what that value is. We do not care at this point how we create that value. Companies all too often get focused on their own internal processes and forget about customers.

At this point, you have a burgeoning spreadsheet (a list of lists) with roughly the structure shown in Figure 7-2.

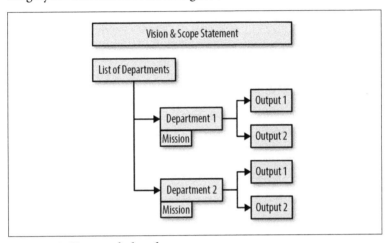

Figure 7-2. Your work thus far

It doesn't look like much, but getting this far is actually pretty great work. Remember, the key is to be outcome-oriented. Without measurable outcomes, there is no need for outputs.

At this point, we are hovering above the surface, going one inch deep across the entire field. Then we can dive deeper later, once this much is validated.

Define the activities and deliverables

Now, within each department there is the stuff you do to create the deliverables that add up to the meaningful outputs. In each department you must create a set of documents to proceed to the next step or hand off to the next role in the internal Value Chain within the department.

I use the term "document" loosely here to mean any tangible output. It could be an architecture definition document, a strategy document, a persona-based representation of customers, or a set of UI/UX wireframes. It is anything you give someone else internally so they can do their thing.

Customers of the department don't typically see these documents. These are what you hide behind your department's interface, adhering to the principle of least knowledge. This is "how the sausage is made" back in the kitchen. The waiters see some things coming together, but the customer doesn't.

Define the customers

This step is adapted from similar ideas in design thinking. You identify the customer of each department. Internally, the term "customer" is used loosely to mean someone who needs you to do your thing and be done so they can go do their thing.

Empathize with your internal customers. Think from outside in. This will help you be more outcome-based instead of activity-based.

To enact this, you can create a persona for each customer role. Give them a name and a picture, and state their attitudes and goals.

Give no thought to your internal process as it stands today or how easy it is. Consider your customers' pains: What is inconvenient for them? Difficult? What can't be done today? What do they complain about? What could be faster for them? More repeatable or reliable?

What *gains* could be realized for them? That is, what are new opportunities they may not yet understand or are not directly asking for but would delight them, go "above and beyond" for them?

Define the principles

We have discussed principles before in "The Principles, Practices, Tools Sankey Diagram" on page 142. These are not stated as passive values like "honesty" or "integrity" or articles of faith. They are not attributes of an ideal department.

These are claims about how we execute our processes.

Consider the following principles: Data as an asset. Automation. Scalability. These may sound obvious, but it costs time and money and adds complexity to be able to scale. You're making a trade-off. You act differently if you think these ideas are necessary and important. They are not principles or meaningful claims if some rational, knowledgeable person could not reasonably argue the opposite. The opposite of automation is manual. The opposite of "data as an asset" is data as merely something processed by applications, necessary to achieve user goals and otherwise uninteresting. Those are possible too. But good principles beget clear good practices that you can execute using appropriate tools. This is a good place to insert your Sankey diagram to map the three together.

Define the outputs

Make sure you know for each department what its products and deliverables truly are. It sounds too obvious to state, but it's amazing how infrequently these are actually agreed upon, even with salespeople of the same level but in different regions. These may be the outputs (if you're in product development). They may be some valuable component of the eventual output, but it must be concrete. For example, "goodwill" or other abstract ideas aren't outputs.

Start at the end, assuming all the other necessary components of the SBM have executed perfectly, and work backward, focusing only on outputs. Ask what the SKUs and applications are. Then list them and be sure everyone agrees.

Assess the Value Chain

At this point, you review to make sure everything lines up and is MECE before going further.

Now assess each input: What activities are required to come into each department so it has the raw materials to fulfill its role and create the deliverables?

List the required inputs.

Define the processes

Now ask yourself and your team: What are the processes within each department to make the transformation to that output?

List them at a label level without getting stuck in analysis paralysis.

Define the tools

Ask yourself: What are the tools that realize and support each practice?

Then make your Sankey diagram, or finish it now and refine it if you already started it.

Define the roles

Now ask the team: What are the roles needed to execute those processes? Who can do something individually, with minimum input from others?

Looking at all the roles laid out, ask yourself if the list is MECE.

What are the decision rights for each role? Who are the ancillary stakeholders supporting each, but not directly involved?

Make the RACI chart for the overall output from this.

Now you have your list of roles. That on its own is useful. But we need to go one step further.

Create a template that is identical, no matter the role, that your team can use to sketch out further what their own best practices are; capture their inputs, process, and outputs; and specify how they participate in the overall vision. This gives them clarity and helps them focus and feel tied to the big picture.

Define the metrics

Now you must determine: What are the metrics to show that each role is working?

Separately figure out: What are the data you need to create those metrics?

Make a set of metrics with dummy values in them. Ask other stakeholders if you were to actually produce those metrics with real values in them, would that give them a clear picture of how well you are delivering? Are those the most important metrics? Is the list of metrics together MECE? Do you cover all the ground for the different stakeholders? What behavior are you driving by stating those as the metrics? How will people game the system when the metrics are in place? Is there any way to deter that and ensure you're driving the right behavior overall?

List the metrics for each role, each product, and each outcome.

Create the templates

Now our machine is complete. But we need to see it altogether in its breadth and depth and full glory.

So for each department, use the same template (probably in a spreadsheet) to show the roles, the inputs, the internal processes, the outputs, the outcomes, and the metrics. For example, if part of the architecture team's work is to execute a Due Dilligence (see "Due Diligence" on page 232) for business development, make a template the first time you do it, assuming that's part of your job and you'll need to reuse it. That helps externalize what you know, automate your role a bit more, and make things overall slightly more efficient in support of the product rule we examined earlier.

Create templates to capture the metrics so the reporting is easier. Using this, you can visualize the metrics in monthly meetings and be sure you're getting the right data in front of executives who can help make the overall machine go smoother, as well as all the fractal machines within it.

Create templates for each activity with a deliverable. Once you're done, make them accessible on the wiki or the SBM internal website.

Determine the hotspots

For each role and process, determine the Process Posture Map as we saw in "Process Posture Map" on page 138. This will help you see what you need to address in your current state to improve and scale. You may have some areas you need to revise, or start, or assess. Do this assessment to tag each process with its posture so you know where you may need to refine, hire differently, or train or communicate differently.

Communicate the machines

Now you have a ton of material. You have the complete end-to-end process mapped out, all the subprocesses, role clarity, and a 360-degree view. You have a map of how and where you create value for customers both internal and external, and now you have the best chance to really optimize that.

You need to tell people about all of that. Put the work into decks to have local conversations. Present the big picture, without details. Then review a subset of the material in small groups with the stakeholder matrix. Take their input and refine if necessary. Check their level of engagement.

Now you're ready to discuss how to begin executing in this new model. It won't be easy. This will be a change management effort.

See "Fait Accompli" on page 174. You will need to roll it out in department meetings, review it regularly with staff, and talk to them individually.

Manage the change

This part is hard, and the length and complexity depends on the scope of your overall effort. If it's just within your department, that's easier than if it's your whole business unit. You'll talk in groups, listen carefully, listen actively, and consider your audience's suggested revisions thoughtfully.

But not everyone has an equal voice. Some people are smarter than others, have better insights, see further, have more diverse or relevant experience, have less of a chip on their shoulder, have less of a grudge, have more skin in the game, can think more objectively, can see the future, are less self-interested, and are motivated differently. You must listen to the people, but if you, the strategy program team, and, most importantly, your top leader are convinced that your machines are the right ones you need to realize the outcomes, transform your business, and build the future, you must accept that not everyone will be on board. Not everyone will make it through the journey. The old guard may have the hardest time seeing the future, believing in it. There will be passive-aggressive people or people who just don't want to participate in that future.

You will need to sort out the audience into roughly thirds: who is on board, gets it from the beginning, and is a believer and an ally; who will need to change their ways but can be retrained or nurtured if you spend the time to help the audience, and who is not on board and can't or won't make the journey. This is cultivating your garden, and you need to give those people a nice severance package and help them find the door.

The many other folks who want to be on board will still need help to manage through the change.

Congratulations: now you have a complete, end-to-end, templated, clear, visible, and measured scalable business machine that will work as a fractal for any department or company of any size that's focused on making great customer outcomes. That's pretty awesome.

Summary

In this chapter, we looked at several innovative ways to make a logical, persuasive argument and weave it into how you show the value and impact of your strategy. We examined the following patterns:

- 30-Second Answer (see "30-Second Answer" on page 161)
- Rented Brain (see "Rented Brain" on page 163)
- Ars Rhetorica (see "Ars Rhetorica" on page 167)
- Fait Accompli (see "Fait Accompli" on page 174)
- Dramatic Structure (see "Dramatic Structure" on page 179)
- Deconstruction (see "Deconstruction" on page 185)
- Scalable Business Machine (see "Scalable Business Machines" on page 194)

Taking the rhetorical approach presented here will help catapult your architecture and strategy work into messages that are understandable and meaningful to decision makers and a wider audience.

CHAPTER 8

Templates

This chapter and the next contain very specific templates that you can use directly in your work to help you advance your technology projects. The two primary vehicles for this are spreadsheets and slide decks.

Here you'll get the following collection of eight practical tools that you can modify or use out of the box. They're reusable rubrics to help you be sure you've covered the key aspects of strategy proposals and help you bring all of your technology project ideas into sharp focus. With these, you can usher the considerable raw material you've generated so far from the developmental concept realm into the material realm:

- One-Slider
- Use Case Map
- Priority Map
- Directional Costing
- Technology Radar
- Build/Buy/Partner
- Due Diligence
- Architecture Definition

These represent tools of my own device that I've used effectively. It's not a project management collection; there are plenty of tools for that elsewhere. They're most useful in the early stages of your project when you are trying to figure out what you're doing, and what you want to propose to executives or share with the broader team.

One-Slider

Challenge: You need to pull together the huge and diverse volumes of analysis work into a simple summary that you can use to inform teams and executives of the strategy.

Solution: You need to create a single slide that forces you to crystallize and succinctly state your strategic goals, the initiatives or practices as propositions that follow from them, and the supporting culture you will develop and encourage.

Recall that early in the book, I stated that a strategy must work together hand in hand with execution and culture in order to succeed. This slide is a distillation of how you can keep those three ideas front of mind and communicate them to your teams.

The One-Slider, as I use it, pulls together in one place each of our three aspects of strategy, execution, and culture. It might look like Figure 8-1.

At the top you state your vision. This is an aspirational statement describing what you want your organization to look like in the midterm or long-term future. This should be a one- to three-year time frame. Less than that won't give you time to do anything advancing enough. More than that, and you'll be befuddled by changing forces.

Next, all of your three or five strategic goals should follow as propositions that support and help realize that vision. This is where you will allocate resources, and your estimation of the best way to get to that desired vision.

Next you state the initiatives or practices. This is the execution part. These should be specific, and each will likely be defined as its own project or program and involve cross-discipline teams.

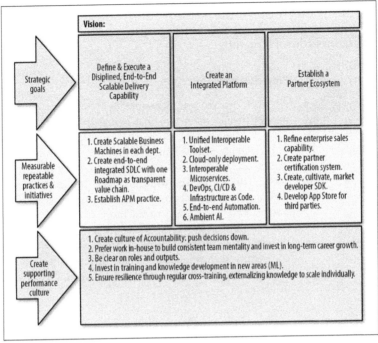

Figure 8-1. The One-Slider summary

The One-Slider does not include all the rich detail you have worked on throughout this book. That material should go in additional slides after this summary slide. Make one slide for each initiative you'll execute, and show how that decomposes into more localized specific actions and deliverables. They should include specifics about the toolset, and meaningful metrics, as we saw in "Scalable Business Machines" on page 194.

Figure 8-2 shows what your initiatives spreadsheet should look like.

Initiative	Actions	Deliverables	Accountable
Implement standard SDLC & software development practices	Define standard end-to-end SDLC process	Documented SDLC process	EA
	Define standard roles	RACI chart, Stakeholder Matrix, Role Template	PO
Drive consistency of development practices to support	Outline branching and merging requirements, pull request process	Documented pull requests and code operation procedures	VP Dev
flexible	Establish architecture review process	Architecture governance charter with reporting	EA
Improve efficiency	Establish design review process	Documented design review process with reporting	EA
Improve estimations' predictability	Establish code review	Documented code review process and reporting	VP Dev
	Establish metrics showing productivity, quality and predictability of Scrum	Published metrics	VP Dev
	Team work and individual team mates		
	Develop maturity improvement roadmaps for each discipline based on Process Posture outcomes	Published roadmaps	EA

Figure 8-2. The initiatives

You have headers for initiative, actions, and deliverables along with the named accountable role that owns that deliverable. The initiatives come directly from your One-Slider, and this represents something at a high-enough level that you can crank it out quickly as a communication tool, but it doesn't represent all the detail of, say, a Work Breakdown Structure.

Work Breakdown Structure

A Work Breakdown Structure is a standard project management tool that is defined in the Project Management Body of Knowledge, as a "deliverable-oriented hierarchical decomposition of the work to be executed by the project team." This works well with the Logic Tree and logical proposition approach we've taken in this book. I encourage you to read more at https://www.workbreakdownstructure.com/ and apply this tool if your project is of sufficient size and complexity that you would realize the benefit. Doing it on smaller projects doesn't make a lot of sense.

This isn't yet a project plan, but is a transition toward it to ensure that you are not just talking about these things in your teams, but that you can do just enough to have a token document for executive buy-in. Then you can manage the creation of the work as a project. Of course, you can add a column for due dates and so forth. If you have had a kick-off meeting and everyone is ready to start working, and you find yourself wanting to add much more detail, it's probably time to turn it over to the PMO, transfer it into whatever project management tool you use, and schedule regular meetings to get updates from those with deliverables.

Finally, along the bottom of the summary One-Slider, you have the culture piece. This is not separate for each initiative, because it's all-encompassing and you can't go creating distinct cultures for different cross-functional teams in the same world. There is the one culture, and you want to be explicit about what culture you want to form. I hope by now it's obvious that if you find yourself stating empty platitudes here, such as "winning teams," you are not digging deep enough. Make only statements as claims that someone else could reasonably argue against, put a stake in the ground, and be proud and go after it.

I hope it goes without saying by now too, but make sure that each section of the slide, and the comprehensive slide altogether, is MECE (see "MECE" on page 29).

Use Case Map

Challenge: You have a burgeoning, large system design that represents one of your strategic initiatives. You need to decompose the idea further into practical use cases of value to an end user. You need something to share with an extended team to ensure their alignment and buy-in with the initiative.

Solution: Make a set of Use Case Map slides, one for each major use case. You want to think through the use cases from a customer perspective to ensure it is outcome focused and not merely activity based.

Figure 8-3 shows an example.

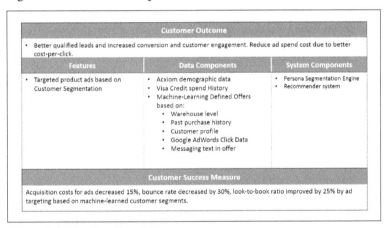

Figure 8-3. The Use Case Map

This map has five components:

Customer outcome
    Here you state the business benefit that this use case aims to achieve for customers. This is stated in clear, measurable terms, reusing the *outcome* aspect of the SBM (see "Scalable Business Machines" on page 194).

Features

Here you list one or more bullet points of the major features of the system. You will later use these to map to epics. It is something at the level an architect or tech lead can design further. Together, these describe a complete, usable, independent system as an *output*, as we saw in "Scalable Business Machines" on page 194.

Data components

These are the sets of data that are required to realize the output of this use case or to measure the metrics. This is high level in terms of data types, third-party data, or major kinds of data you'll need to purchase or siphon off the shopping system, gain access to from the data warehouse, or retrieve from third-party APIs.

System components

These are critical, big components of the software or process system you'll need to create. They may exist already as services, or you may need to refine or reuse some component. They're the building blocks of the system that are differentiating, complex, necessary, and important.

Customer success measure

These are the metrics, stated like SMART goals (*http://bit.ly/2M81N23*), with measurements you can aim for and later verify.

Note that this is particularly helpful in making sure you are thinking in a way that makes your use cases clear, measurable, and valuable as an outcome for customers.

From this stage, you or someone in Product can decompose your Use Case Map into a set of Agile epics or team features to begin transforming the strategy into architecture plans and executable project.

Directional Costing

In technology we get asked for estimates all the time. Everyone jokes about how bad we are at estimating when we will deliver some software module. That's for a variety of reasons, but an important one is that estimating is hard because we typically think only of the main parts of delivering something, and not the many auxiliary aspects that can take as much time or more. We think of how long it might take us to write the code, and don't think of how we'll write it again a different way when we're unhappy with the first time, handling errors gracefully, instrumenting, writing tests, writing documentation, doing deployments, clarifying requirements, executing builds, refactoring, profiling, browser checking, fixing some broken windows we discover along the way, coding for the six important alternate paths that weren't accounted for in the stories, learning a new framework, performance improving, and then hooking it up to the bigger deliverable. Writing the code itself is probably 33% of the work, even for a developer. Never mind the time we spend doing a load of unrelated things.

Projects often take two or three times longer than what we say they will. When 80% of the cost of a software project is intellectual labor, that's a serious financial problem for our leaders.

But the bad news is that as woefully poor as we are at estimating time, we're worse at estimating costs. That's because we're further away from the money, we're less used to talking about it, and we don't understand the nuances or even many of the terms nearly as well as we do our software discipline.

The good news is that the best executives tend to understand that the world isn't black-and-white, that estimates can be defined in stages and in ranges. An executive or salesperson asking for a single, definitive estimate early in the project is actually the sign of a clueless leader, and less the sign of a truly deficient architect who estimates badly. Put another way, a leader asking you for an estimate on the basis of a single-sentence description of a complex problem might deserve open contempt. A leader asking you how much this software project will cost to build can be met with, "I don't know. How much does science cost?" Refuse such idiotic questions. Much of our problem is that we don't refuse them—we throw out a number and shake the date tree until a fake deadline falls out—and the executive believes us (or pretends to for other motives), so all of a sudden we've chained a team of otherwise good people to a death march (*http://bit.ly/2Px6p4O*).

It's easy for me to say that you should refuse such questions, but the fact is that this has happened to me countless times in my career. We get backed into a corner. Some executive has a board meeting or the salesperson has a customer meeting or there's a quarterly review—there are always wonderful excuses—and like an addict, they just need one quick number, one little estimate; they *promise* this is the last time they ask for an estimate like this, and this time it will be different and they won't hold us to it, but they just need an idea. This is a dysfunctional relationship that sets a lot of people up for failure. But you can improve it.

The One-Night Estimate

I was once asked by a C-level executive to give him the cost estimate for a new software project we were considering doing. This was a multiyear project to replace the mission-critical 30-year-old system that ran the heart of the business. We didn't know a whole lot more than that at this point. Fine. Except he needed the estimate by tomorrow at 9 a.m. I was irritated at the time, because I felt set up to fail. In hindsight, this request is just astonishing. But in my ignorance and vanity, I thought I could do it. And anyway, he was the boss. What choice did I have? So I worked long into the night making an estimate like he asked. The estimate seemed like a reasonable amount, and the project eventually got funded, and we did it. By the time the project was concluded, that original estimate was —surprise—off. Way off. About three times off. The project took twice as long and cost three times as much as my initial estimate stated. We've all been there. This is the cycle we aim to break.

There are two things to do to improve this situation we somehow constantly find ourselves in: give a really good estimate or give a much worse estimate. Either of these is desirable, as long as you've set expectations properly.

Rough, Refined, Realistic Estimates

First let's talk about how you can do a really good estimate, whether it's wrong or not.

The first way you can give a better estimate is by realizing, and communicating, that *the act of estimating itself is a project*. Back in the day, I used to make money just to do the project of giving someone an estimate of how much their real software project would likely cost. Similarly, I've paid architects and builders to deliver nothing but a spreadsheet that is a really detailed, thoughtful, thorough, researched estimate that everyone could have a lot of confidence in.

Consider why estimating should be a little project. For the builder to make that spreadsheet took weeks. They made dozens of phone calls, got actual quotes from suppliers with current rates, had many conversations with crews and the architect, and spent hours with the blueprints figuring out the proper materials and how many square feet of everything they'd need, including overruns and thoughtful waste accounting. They included all the templated items that are the auxiliary parts we in software often miss, such as hauling costs, gas costs, site rentals, temporaries, and so forth. That all takes time, it requires thought and negotiation and research, and that's worth money. It's especially worth the cost because that really good estimate makes it clear that if the project is just too expensive to go forward with, you'll have to go ask the boss for a special dispensation to get more money, and now everyone can plan more reliably how to allocate resources. Good estimates matter, and bad estimates can really screw up a business.

The point is this: the weeks of work the builder in this example did resulted in a quote you can really hang your hat on, but that requires many hours of work to put together by a variety of people. If you don't charge for it, or don't treat it like a project, you can't set proper expectations.

So the first idea is that you need the *time* to treat the act of estimating itself as a project, if you're paying millions of dollars over years to make a building or a software product, and you really want to have your best chance of being close to the true number.

Second, you need a *form* to act as the deliverable of this estimate: you need a template so that you don't forget all those auxiliary things that constitute the majority of the product timeline. You can see the long math that went into the estimate and pick over the details and refine it.

The third thing you need is a *funnel* of time with stage gates. Instead of doing either a terrible, useless estimate off the top of your head or doing a perfectly refined and thorough estimate after six weeks of work, find a couple of stages in between. Here's what I mean. You might define three stages of estimating:

Rough
> This takes only a few days to produce, and everyone knows it's only within maybe 50%. If, say, your estimate is $10M, and it's labeled "rough," then you're not committing to anything other

than a range of $5M–$15M. Do this first, and see if that ballpark still allows enough interest from executives to move to the next stage in the funnel.

Refined

This takes a couple of weeks to produce, and includes more discovery conversations, and a clear understanding of requirements. Maybe this range has more documentation behind it, and is within 25%. It has no bearing on the original "rough" estimate. That is, your new flip of the coin—your new refined estimate—might reveal that you think the price is now $17M. That's fine that it's outside the rough range. But your range is now smaller. If you started executing now, you'd need to be between $12.75M and $21.25M.

Realistic

This has a lot of homework behind it, many customer conversations, and a clear understanding and a commitment on the functional and nonfunctional requirements: the epics and stories are written, and the Architecture Definition (see "Architecture Definition" on page 235) is done. This estimate might be within 5% or 10% range. Never go without a contingency.

These three labels (which I just made up, so use whatever suits you, of course) give an executive a good expectation, allow everyone to mete out the work with shoulder checks along the way to do only as much as is warranted, and mean that the executive has some more levers to control: if he's comfortable with a wide range because it's a smaller-risk project or he has more money than time, then he can start the project wherever he's comfortable. And you've kept your credibility.

The fourth thing you need in providing good estimates is to use *ranges* instead of precise numbers. Remember the logical fallacy of false precision (see "Logical Fallacies" on page 169). If we tell some executive the project will cost $18,535,716.34, that's wrong. We're already wrong. We can't possibly know the cost of a two-year project with 100 people working on it down to the penny. Of course people know this, but it sets up a bad expectation. What we can do is use ranges to instead say something like $18M–$20M. Then we're acting in better faith.

The fifth thing that you want in your estimate is a statement of your *assumptions*. All too often we skip this step, and a year later we get burned for circumstances beyond our control. Say the CTO declares that we're deploying everything in the cloud. Then that guy gets fired six months later, and along comes a new CTO declaring that we'll be deploying everything in new on-premises data centers we're building because as a paperclip company, running our own data centers is a competitive advantage. Such business regularly goes on, in which case you should state the sorts of things that could change but that a big part of your estimate depends on. Write them out as assumptions as you add up server costs and provisioning efforts.

Estimate Template

You'll be estimating things a lot. Remember that you don't want to solve only the local problem, but to do just a little bit extra to help scale yourself and the overall organization as well. That means that when we get asked for an estimate, we do it, and then we also want to create a template we can reuse.

To create a good estimation template in software projects, consider these factors: the labor and the data centers.

There are two kinds of labor: the development teams and the supporting cast. Let's start with the development team. Make a list of who is on your typical development team. I like to use the Margarita Mix team as a standard atomic unit: it's 4 parts developer, 2 parts testers, and 1 part analysts. So you can say a development team is seven full-time employees (FTEs). Find out the blended rate you use from your PMO or business operations folks. Let's say it's $70 per hour. Here's some third-grade math that will get us a long way: 7 people × $70 per hour × 40 hours per work week × 2 work weeks in a sprint = $39,200 per sprint. Let's round that up to $40K. That's the cost of a sprint.

Figure 8-4 gets more refined about the internal rate for the different roles. Your company may use some value that's fully loaded or not or the same blended rate, or Finance may have a rate sheet they use for doing these kinds of calculations. Use whatever is easy and close at hand for directional costing—it's more important to be quick at this point than it is to be perfect.

	A	B	C	D
1	Role	Yearly Cost	Quantity	Total Cost
2				
3	DBA	$92,580.00	1	$92,580.00
4	Server/Cloud Admin	$77,000.00	2	$154,000.00
5	Developer	$96,560.00	2	$193,120.00
6	Network Admin	$77,000.00	1	$77,000.00
7	Security Admin	$77,000.00	0.5	$38,500.00
8			Total	$555,200.00

Figure 8-4. Labor costs

Now we can turn our attention to what we know about the work itself. We look at the entire body of work as we understand it at this stage. You're looking for two things: what must be done in serial, and what can possibly be done in parallel.

Front-load the big blocks that are likely to be "showstoppers"—things that could sink the project if they don't go well. You want to short-circuit the spending if you can, and don't put off finding out that something critical is impossible or delayed or different than anticipated. You're designing the project just enough to be able to determine how many teams you can run in parallel. That will give you the number of sprints you need, the number of teams, and the anticipated duration. Let's say you can keep 10 teams busy, working on different aspects of the project so as to not interfere with each other. And if you had those 10 teams, the project would take 30 sprints. So you do some more math like this: 30 sprints × 10 teams × $40K per sprint = $12M.

Next you'll need to account for those auxiliary players, which is a bit trickier to do, since we usually have them only part time, their work is not divided up so neatly into sprints, and it's hard to see their direction relative to the work and therefore how much of their time we'll need. We'll have to consider these roles: Architect, Database Administrator, Networker, Scrum Master, and Project Manager. Put these in your spreadsheet and provide a simple calculator. Let's say that we'll need 25% of each of their time for the duration of the project. That would be 5 people × .25 × $70 per hour × 60 weeks × 40 hours per week = $210,000.

So our labor cost is around $14.2M. Figure 8-5 an example of how you might view those in a spreadsheet template on a summary page that you can pop into a deck quickly. This gives you the best of both worlds by showing the details and sets of assumptions as to how you got here, as well as recalculating when those assumptions change and giving you the quick answers that executives will ask about. You can get more sophisticated later and divide the world into capex and opex, but for directional costing, this is good for now.

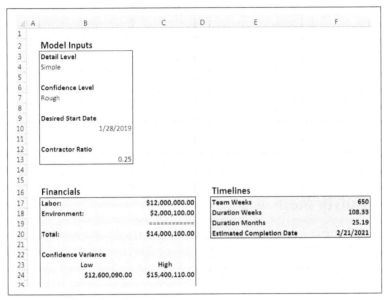

Figure 8-5. Directional costing summary

Now let's consider the data center business. If you're using a cloud provider, it will have costing spreadsheets that make this sort of thing easy. For example, the AWS Cost Calculator (*http://bit.ly/ 2Px40XO*) helps you plan out the fees you'll be facing monthly, which is great because it makes all the costs clear. You can fill it out quickly, get a number, and plug it into your directional costing spreadsheet.

The point of this pattern is not to mislead you with respect to the many sophisticated frameworks out there for estimating work. It's to say this: a lot of times what executives need is not a perfect number, but a *directional* cost. They really do want a rough ballpark and don't expect it to be perfect. They want to know if it's more like $1M or more like $10M.

So sometimes it's more helpful to produce an estimate quickly, even if it's not that great. Executives are used to big numbers and tons of ambiguity. So being able to tell them the project is likely around

$25M all-in is useful, even if it turns out to cost a bit less or a lot more than that. They are calculating things other than what they are asking you about. They are wondering if they should do the project at all. But they may be thinking of buying a company, and if they can buy a whole company with this capability for $50M and get it today instead of two years from now, and get all their talent and revenue now, then that might be a better option.

Which is to say that while the rough estimate may be maligned, it's often useful—as long as everyone has the same expectations around it. The Directional Costing pattern turns out to be more about setting proper expectations than about nerdy project management math. There's a time and place for that, and it's pretty well understood. So I lay out a different take on it here, in the hopes that this is useful too.

Priority Map

The Priority Map, shown in Figure 8-6 is a simple guide to help you prioritize your Use Cases (see "Use Case Map" on page 217) or your strategic initiatives as in your One-Slider (see "One-Slider" on page 214).

This pattern provides you with a mental map to quickly guide you through all the angles of both risk and opportunity as you prioritize strategy efforts and major projects during strategy season or big shifts. This won't be useful for prioritizing sprint backlogs or anything like that, but that's not what we're after here.

The map shown in the figure is not the only one you could draw of this kind, but it's a good start. You could use the Priority Map in conjunction with the Growth Matrix (see "Ansoff Growth Matrix" on page 95), Investment Map (see "Investment Map" on page 130), or a spreadsheet you devise to score each of your strategic initiatives across all of these items, weight them, and produce a number you can use at least as a starting point for the priorities.

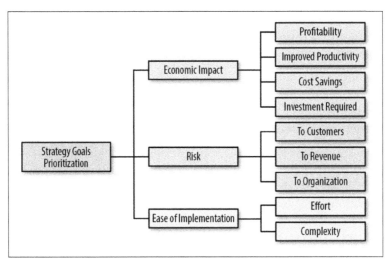

Figure 8-6. Strategic Priority Map

Technology Radar

How can we have a simple way to help us communicate our Roadmap for technology tools and practices to broad and diverse technical teams, collect feedback, and measure progress against advances on our strategy?

The Technology Radar (*https://thght.works/2NqU4AQ*) pattern was invented by ThoughtWorks. The company publishes on its website, every six months or so, the set of technology tools it is reviewing, and gives a summary of its view on that technology.

The radar is divided into four parts: Tools, Techniques, Languages & Frameworks, and Platforms. Then ThoughtWorks further divides the technologies within each of those areas into a category based on how the company advises you to consider them. These subcategories are Adopt, Trial, Assess, Hold.

I like to look at this radar on occasion to consider how Thought-Works is thinking about technology. But they company opened up its radar-making tool so that you can generate your own radar (*https://thght.works/2Corfko*) using your own categories and list of items. This is a terrific way for you to visualize and share with your teams how you're thinking about the set of tools out there. Depending on your culture, this can be more of a dictum or more of a guide.

The radar is not merely a frozen perfect tech future represented in boxes and arrows, but shows the tools and techniques together and presents them in a clear, easy-to-understand framework, and presupposes that you will evolve and update it.

The radar is a set of concentric circles representing criticality and standardization levels, showing what teams should start using now, what to learn about and test, and what to contain and avoid.

The Technology Radar will evolve over time, in a methodical, inclusive, transparent manner. This is a more evocative, realistic, and planful way to show your thoughts on technology features than a traditional single, pristine architecture target state as if it could be frozen in time. Figure 8-7 shows a sample from ThoughtWorks of what this pattern looks like.

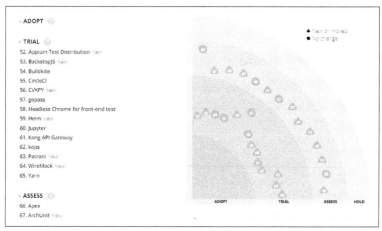

Figure 8-7. Technology radar

There's value in helping your teams see how you're thinking, topics they should be researching, or areas where they might suggest other items you weren't aware of. Instead of providing a merely beautiful, oversimplified, isolated, frozen snapshot of a future state (as architects all too often do), you can represent architecture as an evolving radar, improving the signal-to-noise ratio, and support a practice of directing capabilities toward a strategy. This can help us offer options through a variety of lenses.

Remember, too, that the radar-making tool can include any categories and items, so you could use it as a way of presenting strategy priorities in conjunction with the Priority Map (see "Priority Map" on page 226).

Build/Buy/Partner

Sometimes we're brought into conversations with the business development folks who do mergers and acquisitions. We can use the Build/Buy/Partner pattern as a way of framing our conversations with them. It's important to align these decisions with your technology strategy. Let's take an overview of each of the three options in turn.

Build

There are many reasons to build your own software application or product:

- You are, or want to be, a pioneer or leader in the market.
- You have some reason or desire to own the intellectual property.
- You have technologists in-house with the proper skills.
- You have time to build it.
- You want to own the technology for a long period because it's core to your business.
- You have expansion plans and you'd be in a more flexible strategic position if you owned the intellectual property.
- You think what you would do with the product is innovative enough that it could be patented and licensed and become a valuable asset long-term.

The advantages of building yourself are that it provides you with the most product control: you can have every feature customized just your way; it offers the best opportunity for profit if you can market it; it offers you the potential for lowest cost in the long term; and you get an asset with value.

There are a few disadvantages too: it's the longest time to market, and you'll need to keep a number of development folks around to maintain it. You could find yourself in a precarious situation if you later want to switch and have gotten quite used to having all your processes exactly customized to your company's nonstandard way of doing things.

If you're thinking of building a big software system yourself that someone else could sell you instead, consider these questions:

- Is this the way you want to use the time and resources of your organization? Are there other opportunities you won't get to pursue because of this allocation, and is that OK with you?

- Do you have the resources to not only pursue it, but to complete it, and do it in a significantly better way than what's otherwise available?

- Will you realize a meaningful cost savings?

Basically, it comes down to asking if this software represents a significant differentiating factor for your company that helps position you strategically and helps you compete in the market.

Buy

The Buy option represents the quickest time to market. You still have to face integration challenges, but not on top of making the system in the first place.

The biggest drawbacks are obvious: you don't own the software, you may find it very limiting in the options it offers in terms of customization, you may have to change your business processes around the software or have to do things differently than you really want to, and it's expensive. You also have the least control during the project, because there will be expenses of a different kind in terms of coordination and management, and there can be many lengthy contract negotiations and unmet expectations.

There really are two things meant by "buy": you can buy off-the-shelf software such as Workday or Salesforce to run noncore functions or functions that are important but don't differentiate you in the market. That is, no one is buying your software product because of the nuances of your HR system. But the other thing is that you outright buy the technology or the company that you want to get to market with. As an example, think of Google buying DeepMind. Google wanted to become an AI leader and start exploiting that capability, and would be years behind DeepMind, leaving it available for a competitor to pick up. Sometimes you want to buy a company or a key technology just to keep someone else from getting it.

The Buy decision comes down to determining what your core priorities really are. Ask if this is out of scope for the capabilities you are the best at, and if you bought another company's solution, whether you could improve your competitive advantage. If you look at buying anything, perform a thorough Due Dilligence (see "Due Diligence" on page 232) and hope the deal folks trust the assessment of the tech teams. If not, this can be a very painful, incredibly costly disaster.

Partner

This blended option means you work together with another company, and each brings something distinct that's of value, in an area that you're a leader in, thereby creating a new thing of value.

The advantage here is that you get to market quickest doing something complex. This lowers later switching costs, assuming you design the integrations properly and you get to save on resources.

The challenge with this option is that you get the least control over your fate, and will lose certain revenue opportunity, depending on the structure of the deal, of course. Partnering is nice because you have another company to share the risk with, to help popularize the product, and to extend the name recognition and reach of your own brand.

When evaluating a partnership, ask yourself:

- Is the potential partner financially healthy? Will they be able to hold up their end of the bargain and still be around in a few years?
- How important or strategic is this deal to them? What's in it for them to make sure this is successful?
- Relationship: How well do you know each other, have you done business before, will your styles of working and your systems be compatible?
- Execution: Will both of you be able to fulfill the obligations of the deal?
- Speed: Is speed to market the most important thing, and will this technology enhance your existing offering in a credible,

clear way? Does the partnership buy you time to get into a market and assess how much real potential there is?

With a partnership, the clear trade-off you're making is for control. It's also the middle road, the most compromising kind of decision.

I'm usually not a fan of partnerships. I've seen a number of them go poorly, and precious few go even well. Eventually, someone needs to decide if they want to be in this business or not, and if they do, they should own the solution and go be the best in the world at it. That said, partnerships can be a good way to test the waters if you really need to see more in order to make that determination. If there is no clear market leader, partnerships can allow you to work together as a longer-term way of deciding on an acquisition.

You can use the Build/Buy/Partner pattern in conjunction with Due Diligence.

Due Diligence

As part of the conversations we have during Build/Buy/Partner (see "Build/Buy/Partner" on page 229), if things advance to the Buy stage, we'll need to perform a Due Diligence. This is an assessment of the technology and operational aspects of the target company. It's very important, because it's used to determine if the company should be bought at all. Depending on the outcome of your assessment, it may suggest that you leave the company be, or pay a different price than what the company is asking, or go a more nuanced route and pick up only part of its software, or enter into a licensing agreement. There are too many variables to make those suggestions into a template here, so this pattern is confined to helping you consider all the technological aspects so that you can make an informed decision. I encourage you to make your own template as suits your purposes. This pattern offers you a strong starting place for performing this kind of analysis.

First make a spreadsheet that will represent your template. Create a summary page, as we did with the Directional Costing template (see "Directional Costing" on page 218). It looks like this:

Characteristic	Definition
Maintainability	Degree of effectiveness and efficiency with which the product or system can be modified to improve it, correct it, or adapt it to changes in environment and requirements.
Manageability	Degree of effectiveness and efficiency with which a product or system can be monitored, configured, and deployed.
Portability	Degree of effectiveness and efficiency with which a system, product, or component can be transferred from one hardware, software, or other operational or usage environment to another.
Security	Degree to which a product or system protects data so that persons or other products or systems have only the degree of data access appropriate to their types and levels of authorization, and demonstrates modern security.
Compliance	Degree to which a product or system complies with auditing and compliance requirements.
Privacy	Degree to which a product or system protects information deemed to be restricted due to privacy concerns.
Resiliency	Degree to which a system, product, or component performs specified functions under specified conditions for a specified period of time.
Compatibility	Degree to which a product, system, or component can exchange information with other products, systems, or components, and/or perform its required functions, while sharing the same hardware or software environment.
Performance	Degree to which a product, system, or component, relative to the amount of resources used under stated conditions, is performing.
Usability	Degree to which a product or system can be used by specified users to achieve specified goals with effectiveness, efficiency, and satisfaction in a specified context of use.
Functional suitability	Degree to which a product or system provides functions that meet stated and implied needs when used under specified conditions.

This is your master list of concerns in the assessment. You can add one for your own company's particular concerns, and how well the target aligns with your strategy and Roadmap, distinct from these generally reusable and standard categories.

You will create a set of questions in each of these categories and give the target product's answer a score. Make a legend like this:

0: Unsupported and not on the Roadmap

1: Unsupported but on the Roadmap

2: Implemented but weak

3: Implemented and suitable

4: Implemented and world-class

Add another column to reflect these scores, as summed on each section's individual worksheet.

These scores of 0–4 will cover most of the circumstances I tend to see when doing this kind of work. If the company states that a particular feature you're interested in is unsupported in the current system, and not on the Roadmap, that's a different signal to you than if the company knows it's important and has it prioritized but just hasn't done it yet.

Then create separate worksheets for each of those categories that have the drill-down questions. These will form the core of your assessment.

Each subsection spreadsheet (you'll have 12 of them) will look something like Figure 8-8.

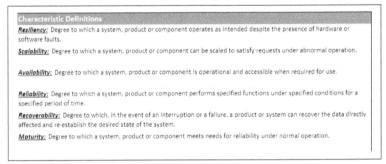

Figure 8-8. Due Diligence subsection spreadsheet

Make a similar worksheet for each of the remaining primary characteristics. You then score each one of these individual items with a value from your legend, 0–4. This should sum up to a score for that characteristic and then appear in the summary page. Together, these all add up to a score for the product.

There's a second use for this template: note that as a software vendor, you could also offer this to large enterprise customers as they assess whether they should license your software or not.

Internal Use

But wait, there's more—there's a third amazing use for the Due Diligence template.

Maybe you're thinking that you don't have the opportunity to go around buying companies every week like Oracle, and this pattern is maybe not that useful. I love to use this tool in a novel way. Recall from "Rented Brain" on page 163 that we sometimes (or often) want to act as if we are a consultant for our own company, so that we can be a bit more objective, stay out of politics, and speak truth to power. If you're a technology leader on a development or product management team, I encourage you to turn your sights inward, and execute the Due Diligence on your own products, as if you were from a different company and sent to assess the quality and state of the software product.

After making the assessment on your own products, you have an excellent Roadmap for fixing technical debt, improving features in lagging areas, and providing a communication mechanism for talking with other leaders about how well your software is positioned. In this sense, Due Dilligence acts like a Process Posture Map for a single product. While I frequently use this template for both purposes, I've found that we really get a lot of mileage toward improving quality by designating an architect to run this internally.

Architecture Definition

I'm going to have to contextualize this template a bit. Let's start with recent attitudes toward how we express architectures.

In my experience, the predominant form architectures take is in the clever people expressing their views over email and in meetings. This is too informal, too untraceable for architecture work. To be clear: I reject this mode of business unless the team is small, they all share extra-sensory perception, and what you're building doesn't require any physical load bearing. If you're building Yet Another Trivial Social App for neighbors to spy on and gossip about each other, that should work just fine.

But when this "method" finds its way into the enterprise, absent any formal means, teams in these environments will be confused or uncertain about how to do things. The role of the architect lacks clarity, and there is insufficient accountability for their decisions. The products will also suffer as a result, and thereby so will your customers. Moreover, the architect, and thus the organization, is unable to scale, since they're required to be present and speak to how they want things built. This is far too slippery and sloppy a mode for any really helpful architect.

Yet in recent years we hear formal architecture definitions—and perhaps even the practice of architecture itself—sometimes derided in the posh voice of maverick trendsetters, those impresarios of the modern software stage who denounce waterfall, reject RUP, and poison the well for any way of representing requirements that doesn't fit on a Post-it note. We mustn't plan because the world "changes" so fast, we are told. We have no problem spinning up 150 people to type their hearts out for two years, presuming to use $25M of someone else's money to build something without a plan or design. But we can't afford to have three smart people think about how to build this thing for three weeks. I find this irresponsible. We need to have a clear picture of what we're doing, why we're doing it, and how we're doing it, and we need to be able to refer to those things.

But the currently prevailing trendy attitude in some—not all—software circles can be very inefficient. It can create significant churn, waste, confusion, redundancy, alienation, and lack of alignment. Yet in the name of saving time, we sometimes dismiss formal architectures. "We don't have time to write this stuff down," I've had dev leaders tell me. There's never enough time to do it right, but there's somehow always enough time to do it over.

Other detractors would denude the art and science of software development methods or architecture documents down to a set of platitudes proclaiming "disruption" and "obsession with customer feedback" as if their "platforms" will spring to life without a clear picture of what they're doing, why they're doing it, and how they get there. "Move fast and break things" works if you don't think your customers are people, and what you're "breaking" is trivia within a predominantly closed system entirely of your own devising with no operational contractual responsibilities, and you hold people, relationships, and data as playthings. I wouldn't hope to get on an airplane built by software teams proclaiming this hollow creed.

For many practitioners, "Agile" seems to have devolved into "we don't have to write requirements," and "iterative" often translates to "we don't have to think about what we're doing." But since it's iterative, we can just revisit the same code and the same problems over and over, like a scene from *Groundhog Day (http://bit.ly/2MpYTdX)*, or enter a Sisyphean (*http://bit.ly/2wnIf46*) eternal return from which one day hopefully someone will rescue us.

Consider that Google was built on a tremendous architecture foundation. The many (publicly available) founding papers for web search and PageRank are 20 pages long each—including diagrams and math!—adding up to many pages of descriptive, specific, planful architecture that paid careful attention to business architecture (though they don't call it that, instead referring to the vulnerability of the algorithm as what eventually become known as "Google bombs"), and thoughtful and specific design around the scalability and the core components. Though the folklore likes to suggest that Silicon Valley is full of freewheeling geniuses who ride around on colorful bikes and don't need to think about how to build their systems because it will all "just work" as long as they're thinking about disruption, this is a false narrative.

This pattern represents a template to record architectural decisions and goals with the aim of guiding development teams working in an Agile environment. So it is up-front. In my experience, architecture is best expressed with a formality somewhere between a long hallway conversation and a full-blown Turing-complete intricate specification written in thousands of pages with Leslie Lamport's TLA+ (*http://bit.ly/2PxcrCs*). If you think even this middle-road way of recording architecture is too formal, this is how real companies are built: see the Google Search Architecture (*http://bit.ly/2nZEyh1*), the Google BigTable (*http://bit.ly/2wnKl3Y*) architecture, and the original Cassandra paper (*http://bit.ly/2OWYGvw*) describing its architecture from its creators at Facebook. Often these papers were written for the public after the fact to explain how the systems were built. When this level of forethought isn't applied initially, the software tends to quickly be rewritten and eventually scrapped. Consider the entire AWS website (*https://amzn.to/2MG6PHz*) Amazon has devoted to its whitepapers, or a talk (*http://bit.ly/2LnPUow*) by a hero of mine, Amazon CTO Werner Vogels, on scalable architecture and how architecture must work with the business. There are a lot of PhDs writing these architecture papers. And they didn't do it *after* the companies made their first billions. However people may talk, this level of detail, thought, and comprehensive planning is how the grown-ups do architecture.

In my view, to best help guide teams and direct systems toward demonstrating strong nonfunctional attributes, and to best scale the organization, the architect needs a template. This template might be called the Architecture Definition Document. It's the document analogous to the blueprints of a building architect.

The product management team owns the functional requirements: *what* the system does. These items are expressed in epics and user stories and stored in something like CA Agile Central. That's great. But the architecture team owns the nonfunctional requirements: *how* the system will be realized—and what's their form of expressing the architecture?

The purpose of the Architecture Definition pattern is to express in clear, executable, measurable, testable, directive text what the non-functional requirements (NFRs) of the system are. These are the -ilities," which we covered in "The Architect's Role" on page 7.

I've used the same basic template for well over a decade to express architecture requirements. It's based on TOGAF (*http://bit.ly/ 2MKkVHT*), but is much lighter and, I believe, more pragmatic. In this pattern, we'll walk through the major sections of this template. Then anytime you have an architecture question that needs answering, you can use this template. It scales from just several pages if you're making a change to a single component inside a system, to large documents that cover how to build entire new systems. I've used it to write architectures in just 6 or 10 pages, to 50 pages, to 150 pages. It scales in a different way too. The lead or enterprise architect might write one capturing the broad contours of a system, and then have local application architects on a team write "child" architectures that represent specific subsystems.

One question that comes up is: When should architects weigh in? I use the following informal little rule of thumb, and make sure the team knows it too:

- When something is going to cross a data center or other significant network boundary
- When something is going to cross system boundaries
- Anything architecturally significant

The question of what's "architecturally significant" (*http://bit.ly/ 2OXGty1*) seems slippery, but it's actually rather decidable. It breaks down to one or more of these, based on the Wikipedia list:

- There is high business value, it's highly visible across teams, or it has high technical risk.

- There is high risk of budget overruns or high business risk based on past experience with similar projects.

- There are outstanding questions or concerns from a key stakeholder or business leader.

- This component is new or first-of-a-kind to the organization— none of the responsibilities of existing components in the current architecture addresses it, or it must dramatically change.

- The requirement has Quality of Service or SLA (service-level architecture) characteristics that deviate from all the ones that are already satisfied by the evolving architecture.

If there's other stuff, architecture can be silent on it and let the team leads handle it. Now let's look at the template itself.

The Template

There are five primary sections to the Architecture Definition template I use:

1. Metadata or Front Matter
2. Business Architecture
3. Application Architecture
4. Data Architecture
5. Infrastructure Architecture

Metadata

First, you have the front matter, the document's metadata. Include the system name, author, and date. I don't care about version, because the date to me seems like the superclass of that data; the date a unique thing like the version number, and it tells you how long ago the document was written, which adds useful context. I also like to list the people who reviewed and contributed to the document to make sure that readers know who else was involved and how holistic the perspective is.

My favorite part of the metadata is the Internet Engineering Task Force (ETF) keywords. I always include "must," "may," and "should" as keywords and state that the document will use them with special status, like this:

Use of IETF Keywords

This document employs a subset of the Internet Engineering Task Force keywords found in RFC 2119 (*http://bit.ly/2MKSbi4*). These words are MUST, SHOULD, MAY, and their counterparts MUST NOT, SHOULD NOT, MAY NOT. They are capitalized throughout the document to draw attention to their special status as keywords used to indicate requirement levels.

I love the IETF keywords because they are MECE and clear. They nudge document authors toward decisiveness and specifics, and make the implementation path more sidirected for readers.

Business Architecture

This part is one of the least understood aspects of architecture for technical people. Its aim is to provide a map of the common understanding of the organization as a system, with its organizational models, processes, and capabilities in order to establish alignment with strategic goals and tactical plans. In that sense, business architecture has been an underlying focus of much of this book.

It answers, or at least collects and reflects answers to, the following core questions:

- What organizations do we have?
- What capabilities do we have?
- What are our Value Chain models (see "Value Chain" on page 116) and their attendant processes? What is the present posture (see "Process Posture Map" on page 138) of those processes in order to assess our preparedness to support strategic goals stated by the business or strategy teams?
- What information must flow through their processes as their fuel for them to run?

These are the basic building blocks. But any business architecture practice that stops there isn't creating anything of value. We have to take these raw ingredients and make something useful. This means drawing connections. We ask:

- What are the relevant regulations, applicable laws, rules, or corporate policies that might constrain our system?

- Who are the stakeholders (see "Stakeholder Alignment" on page 99)? Who owns what decisions? What events are generated when a decision is made?
- What initiatives are under way, and how well aligned are they with the strategy and each other?
- What are all our products and services, as listed in our APM (see "Application Portfolio Management" on page 146)? How well aligned are those with the strategy and with each other?
- What training might be required by the new organization or new system or component we're architecting?
- What metrics will we use to measure how well we are doing toward achieving our desired outcomes? What data do we need to support those metrics? How well aligned across organizations (or machines) are they? What behavior do they drive?

Now you can start to determine the gaps between your current state business architecture and where you need to be to support your initiative. Recall our model in Chapter 2. In this way, you can view the first set of previous questions as your data findings—the collection of research and raw materials—and the second set of questions as being occupied with the insights you can draw from it.

For me, any good business architecture will answer these two questions—different sides of the same coin:

- What business constraints exist that will inform or modify the proposed technology system? How will they do so?
- How will our business need to change in order to support the proposed technology system? What training will teams need to successfully realize the system? What governance will need to be in place through the large project or subsequent to its completion? What processes or teams will be impacted by the system?

When you make a scalable business machine (see "Scalable Business Machines" on page 194), you are making an executable model of your business architecture.

As with many things in this book, the business architecture as I describe it here is fractal: each part has the same statistical character of the whole. That is, you can ask these same questions about a single component that you're writing an Architecture Definition for, or for the architecture of a new greenfield application you're building.

Such a template could look like this:

Major Features
> Describe the purpose of the system and its high-level feature set. What will this system do? What current capabilities can we draw on? What must be repurposed or modified?

Strategic Fit
> What aspect of the business and/or technology strategy does this effort and design support? How does it help realize strategic goals? If counter to the goals, how is that justified?

Business Drivers
> Make a bullet list of the reasons for doing this project. What money would be saved, what efficiencies would be created, what process improved, what customer opportunities enabled?

Business Priorities
> Given a conflict of priorities, what is the stakeholder bias (time to market versus quality, performance versus security, SLA versus costs).

Assumptions
> Make a bullet list of your assumptions about the current state of the world, your organization, and your systems that, if later proved false or changed, could dramatically impact this system. Consider people (what existing roles or new roles do you assume will be in place that you might require), process (consider Procurement, HR, Finance, approval gates, ETO, GNOC, Security), and technology (consider stated drivers, standards, or architectural direction or patterns from the leadership team).

Constraints
> What are any applicable laws governing the data or processing of this system? Consider GDPR, or other European personal data laws, for example. List applicable regulations, such as ADA, PCI, and PII.

Risks
> List business risks in doing the project as envisioned, and risks to the customer or existing business prospects or processes. Can the project be maintained and operated properly, are staffing

resources easy to find, is funding secured, what countries or markets will be targeted, what risks are inherent in trade-offs made?

Impacts
What will this project or this architecture create in terms of the organization, training, and process?

Stakeholders
List internal and external business partners who are concerned with or impacted by this project.

Governance
How will the project be governed? Is there an executive steering committee, or a responsible stakeholder committee? What cadence and form will they take, with what explicit purpose?

The Business Architecture section should be the first primary section of your burgeoning Architecture Definition Document, after the headers or metadata.

Application Architecture

This is where you describe the software components and how they are built:

Applicable Standards and Policies
Make a list of links to published guidelines and conventions for dev teams to follow (e.g., any internal policies, OTA/HTNG specs, PCI guidelines, ADA guidelines).

Guidelines and Conventions
Make a list of links to published guidelines and conventions for dev teams to follow, most likely published internal standards documents, Google Java coding guidelines, JavaScript conventions, code quality guidelines, and the like.

User Interface
Specify the anticipated impact of UI/UX to the project, existing design work, wireframe method, and libraries to be used. You may have a Concept Model (*http://bit.ly/2NcuFHI*) to reference.

Services

List services to be created or existing services to be reused, and the owners of those services. This one requires some real analysis beforehand.

Security

Specify the security requirements and design: how data will be secured, encrypted, authorized, authenticated at rest, in transmission, or in processing. Outline the use of OWASP Top Ten and how those are addressed. Cover user roles and authentication methods and authorization. What security groups are required? How will credentials be stored, and how will keys be managed? Will you use two-factor authentication? Highlight security requirements for development such as bastion hosts. List transport or TLS/SSL requirements.

Availability

Target SLA in terms of 9's uptime and how specifically the architecture will support such numbers. Document how recoverability, disaster recovery, and the like is being supported. What compensating actions are taken? Will a circuit breaker be used? What redundancy is there? What caching? Health check page? Multideployments?

Scalability and Performance

List the number of transactions per second at this latency and CPU utilization. What is the unit of scale (container, VM, cluster)? What are the ways the application and services can scale through statelessness, autoscaling groups? State thresholds.

Extensibility

List APIs, ways that the application affords future change, how the application supports customizing per customer, and how configurations are afforded.

Testability

How will this be tested, what tools will be used, and what specific automation and targets will be in place? Include functional testing, regression testing, automation, tools used, chaos testing, and resilience testing. What is the load-testing plan?

Maintainability

What software guidance for developers will help make the code base easier, cleaner, and simple to maintain in the long term?

What are the code repository needs or project needs? What is the maintenance schedule anticipated or downtime for upgrades strategy?

Monitorability and Metrics
What tools and dashboards are required, and what are the logging requirements? State how the software itself must support event publishing to increase visibility. What are the specific metrics that will indicate system uptime, health, and proper performance? How will alerts be triggered, and at what threshold? Consider CPU, memory, drive/filesystem volumes, database process monitoring, logs, event logs, and required procedures. These will end up in an operational playbook or hopefully getting automated.

Data Architecture

The next aspects of the template are all about data: how to get it, what to do with it, how much there is, how long to keep it, how to move it, and how to get rid of it.

This section might include the following:

Data Sources
Where should the team get key data from (existing services or databases or new)? Where is data stored? What database software will be used to store what data? Which instances of those databases should be used?

Data Strategy
What are the hard limits on the number of key data rows? What are the key data transaction size limits? What is the tolerance for eventual consistency for key aspects of the solution? Include data warehousing, storage and management requirements. Transfer requirements. Long-term storage.

Transactional Requirements
What are transaction requirements such as two-phase commit, eventual consistency? What data volumes must be supported? Include data movement policies and requirements.

Volatility
How often will key pieces of the data change?

Data Maintenance

Describe how data will be maintained, data retention policies, scripting to offload, data restoration. How will data be populated for different environments for this application? Will data be truncated? At what interval? How will data be encrypted? Are there GDPR or PII/PCI requirements to be stated for dev teams or infrastructure admins?

Data Migration

How will data get into the system? Is connecting to a legacy system required? How will you replicate data? Is Golden Gate or Kafka or ETL or another tool in use? What time period is anticipated for this? Will data have to be synchronized over a certain period time?

Data Volume

How many rows are anticipated to be added daily for the key services? What size database is anticipated? Will there be multiple data stores?

Logging

Log rotation policies, Splunk requirements, and indexes.

Analytics

What data must be exposed by the application to support business analytics? How must that data be exposed to support analytics tools?

Caching Strategy

Requirements for caching and the locations and technology to support caching.

Infrastructure Architecture

These aspects of the template are about the data centers, the network, the hardware, and the operational aspects. We can't leave these out: the application and its environment are all of a piece, and the architecture must consider the full stack.

The key sections here might include:

Cloud and Data Center Requirements

Which data center will this be deployed to? How many? How will communication between data centers be supported? Will this be a cloud-based application? How will that be supported?

What about cost management strategy? Deployment pipeline requirements? How will the infrastructure be stood up—are there infrastructure-as-code or containers and orchestration opportunities? Do you need to be "cloud-agnostic" (good luck)?

Deployments
List how deployments will be executed, outlining any blue/green deployments, deployment pipeline, and CI/CD.

Disaster Recovery
Is DR required by this solution? Will it be built-in DR based on data replication and redundancy?

Network
Describe and diagram networking with firewalls, gateways, load balancers, VIPs, zones to be used (e.g., PCI, DMZs, routing), and DNS-specific needs.

That's the template. It's a lot, but not all sections are equally important, of course, depending on the size and nature of the product. I really hope that thinking about your architecture this way helps you make great systems.

Executable Architectures

I can see you rolling your eyes already: making a document like this would take too long! No one will read it! Documents like this just wither and die when we post them on the wiki. They'll languish at the edge of the known universe for years. I urge you to think otherwise. Here's why. I have used documents like this for a decade, at different-size companies, and they work. But not in a vacuum—they must be used as a first step to translate them into what will be executable within the project team.

But the NFRs need a system for their expression, and we just have to close the gap between that formal expression of your architecture and the teams typing the code. We can do that. Depending on the size of the system or component you're architecting, there are different ways to handle this.

First, I encourage you to work with the product team and the analysts to get your NFRs into the acceptance criteria of user stories about functional requirements. This is the best way to make sure your architecture work isn't ignored. That also ensures that you are writing the architecture requirements in such a way that they are easily transferable to story form, demonstrable, and testable.

The second way you can do this is to help guide the analysts or product teams to write stories specifically for the NFRs. If you've defined your NFRs properly, as measurable and specific and testable and demonstrable, this should be easy to do. I like this way much less, because it tends to make some of the teams think they aren't responsible for thinking about the NFRs, and it means that you can't have the proper sense of ownership and delineation.

The definition defense

You cannot simply write an Architecture Definition Document, hand it off to the development teams, and expect anything good to happen. Your architecture won't be realized. We all know that won't work. The teams won't implement it, and you will be viewed as (and unfortunately actually be) irrelevant.

A critical part of success here is to actually talk to the teams, but with the document as a center piece of these conversations. This lets you eat your cake and have it too: you get the formality of the document and the engagement and understanding of the two-way conversation.

Dissertation Defense

If you're not familiar with the term the "dissertation defense," it's the final committee meeting before a PhD candidate is granted her doctorate. The candidate has written a book-length document on her subject, called a dissertation, and must defend her claims in person before the committee in a process that takes hours, to ensure that she really knows the material and that it makes sense. She must defend her methods and research and choices to the committee.

To aid in this eating our cake and having it too with the formality and the conversation, some years ago I came up with borrowing the idea of a dissertation defense for us as architects. You need a forum for people to argue things over, ask questions, clarify misunderstandings, and agree to move forward. This will act too as a refining opportunity for you to gain insights into where the architecture isn't optimal or the constructs make sense but aren't expressed clearly.

Have meetings to walk through the document. Invite application architects, enterprise architects, devlopment leaders, analysts, product managers, and relevant technical stakeholders. These are long forums in which the teams can ask clarifying questions of the architect, similar to a dissertation defense in graduate school. It's similar to an architecture review board, but inverted, because the architect who authored the document presents the material instead of being merely a passive participant as some "star council" sits in judgment.

The dissertation defense meeting has a form similar to this:

- Write your definition document.
- Schedule a meeting that has a clear agenda—a definition defense meeting. People should know what that is. Your invite should include the definition document in the meeting agenda as an attachment.
- Give people a week or few days to read it and remind them to do so before the meeting.
- Many still won't read it. Chastise them roundly, and then spend the first bit of the meeting reviewing your document's major decisions and most different, key aspects.
- Open the room up for discussion and welcome questions from the group. Clarify for them, and take criticisms without defensiveness.
- Take notes and after the meeting revise the document as applicable and resend it to everyone, thank them for their time and great ideas, and then follow up in the ways we've discussed to be sure their feedback is incorporated into the work.

If all this sounds very too-too much, my view on that is, "If you think education's expensive, try ignorance." Having a coherent, unifying vision is the best way to help people understand what they are doing, why they are doing it, and how their work maps to the bigger picture and the work of their colleagues. Of course the length and depth and most relevant sections will be different depending on the size and nature of the system you're building. I've made versions of these documents that were five pages and took a day to write, and I've led large greenfield systems representing a major overhaul of a core business product for which our architecture team produced hundreds of pages of architecture definitions, suitable for different teams.

If you still don't like it, consider the alternatives: you could put it all in software. I've never been a fan of the software that purports to make your architecture executable. It seems forever grandiose, out of touch, and really disparate to the way teams actually work. It takes a long time, is forever out-of-date, generates suspect code, and rarely maps to the real requirements. These approaches are for people who think a commercial tool will solve their problems more than rigorous thinking, pencil, and paper. Those people struggle on my teams.

Treating your role, your department, as a scalable business machine (see "Scalable Business Machines" on page 194) with a clear output in the form of this document and attendant local requirements in stories is the best way to ensure that your architecture features are realized in the final product.

You have now made your templates because you know you will frequently repeat this kind of work and need to externalize what you know so you can move on to the next big, exciting work. Then you've filled them out in collaboration with knowledgeable colleagues so you have a mass of insights to use in myriad ways as you weave together your final strategy in a coherent, compelling set of decks.

Summary

In this chapter, we covered eight patterns to help you talk about your strategies and architecture decisions to a wide variety of audiences at different levels. The tech teams, management and decision-making executives, and customers will all benefit from the patterns presented here:

1. One-Slider (see "One-Slider" on page 214)
2. Use Case Map (see "Use Case Map" on page 217)
3. Priority Map (see "Priority Map" on page 226)
4. Directional Costing (see "Directional Costing" on page 218)
5. Technology Radar (see "Technology Radar" on page 227)

6. Build/Buy/Partner (see "Build/Buy/Partner" on page 229)

7. Due Dilligence (see "Due Diligence" on page 232)

8. Architecture Definition (see "Architecture Definition" on page 235)

The next chapter will show you different types of slide decks that you can use to tell others about your great ideas and how to structure them so those people understand them, like them, and fund them.

CHAPTER 9

Decks

It is like a finger pointing away to the moon. Don't concentrate on the finger or you will miss all that heavenly glory.
   —Bruce Lee, *Enter the Dragon*

In this brief chapter, we look at the different kinds of slide decks that come in handy for the strategist, as well as the structures and key elements you can use to make them.

Decks can be surprisingly useful as an architecture tool to draw pictures that communicate succinctly. They're even more helpful if you present to customers a lot and need to have something that you can read from a screen.

But this chapter is more concerned with how you can take up all of the work that you've done throughout this book, and then pull it into decks that will make your data, insights, hypotheses, and overall strategic messages really soar.

Here we won't talk about content—that was the first part of the book. We'll just look at structure, assuming along the way that you've done the work from earlier patterns to populate the content as you need to.

Ghost Deck

The *Ghost Deck* is also called a *Blank Deck*. It's a special way of making an initial deck that has a certain purpose. It's a wireframe. There's no audience but you and your management team, which you'll subsequently work with to fill in the details of the simple narrative. The Ghost Deck is a storyboard made for creating a movie: you're making sure you have figured out what all the important shots are before incurring the major expense of shooting them.

Say you need to make a big Ask Deck (see "Ask Deck" on page 256, or propose an initiative, fulfill the boss's request to make a "get well" plan, or illustrate the story of what should be done. You need to craft the story itself without knowing all the data. You need to make sure that you have written an outline before you do any of the work, as we did in elementary school composition class.

The Critical Difference Between a Ghost Deck and an Outline

Let's be clear on this important distinction. If, when you go to make an argument for something, you first write out the structure of what you want to say with no content in it, making sure that your argument has strong bones, as our teachers in grade school told us to do, then that is called an *outline*. If, on the other hand, you do the identical thing in PowerPoint and work for McKinsey and get paid $400 per hour to do it, then that is entirely different and is called making a *Ghost Deck*. The differences can be subtle, so please try hard to keep them straight.

Ghost Decks help you when you have three or four colleagues, maybe on your team or a cross-functional set of leaders, and you each have different perspectives on the situation. If you need to make a deck for the board, and you've got the tech person and the strategy person and the boss and the product person all there, it would be imposssible to open up PowerPoint and start typing a good deck from the first word.

Here's how you do it:

1. Make an outline on a whiteboard or some nondeck surface. You need to stay at surface level and go one inch deep across the whole football field first.

2. Write only the headline for all the slides in the deck. Look at them to make sure they still make sense. Back in composition

class, we all called this the "topic sentence"—it's the claim you're making. Make sure the headlines have rhetorical punch.

3. Once you've written all the headlines, review them, making sure they are impactful, make a bold claim, and build together, as we learned in "Dramatic Structure" on page 179 and "Ars Rhetorica" on page 167.

4. Now you can assign someone to go get the research and write up the actual content in stages, make the charts and graphs, and write up the bullet points that prove the headline.

5. Have that helper send you the work in stages for frequent shoulder checks and revisions (or maybe it's you playing both roles, and that's fine too).

The guide I use for structuring a Ghost Deck is this: if your audience could believe everything that you say only by reading your headlines, they would have the entire story and wouldn't need to read the body of the slides at all. Be disciplined enough that the body of the slides you are making is packed with facts backing up your headline claims. The bodies are all data, data, data. The headlines are all bold rhetorical claims.

Here's a key to this pattern, as I see it anyway: most people treat headlines as these passive summaries that are a weak restating of whatever content they dumped into the deck. We, however, treat headlines as audacious, eye-popping claims like "Our company should buy company Y" or "We should get out of the coffee business and into the paperclip business" or "We must move the data center to the cloud within two years" or whatever that part of the argument is about. The point is that you're putting a stake in the ground, advancing the argument, and not ever writing tepid generalizations like "The Plan."

The advantage is obvious: you get to adjust the thrust of your argument and make changes to the main hypotheses you're presenting before investing a lot of work in substantiating them, making beautiful charts, and so forth. I suppose you could think of this metaphorically as creating a backlog for yourself in the form of slide headlines.

If you're working with a cross-functional group to make the deck, this can be a good way to align quickly with them without too much fuss and agree on the message you're composing. This is valuable, because otherwise it could look like a Frankenstein's monster all patched together with different styles and depths. And it wouldn't be MECE, which would weaken it and take precious time to straighten out.

The big thing about Ghost Decks is that they are very helpful in maximizing your efficiency, organizational clarity, and impact of your eventual deck. You're making the wireframe, the storyboard, first. Then you're making sure that it makes sense at the wireframe level. Then you substantiate it in a separate step. I love Ghost Decks and use them every time I make a deck because the bang-for-the-buck ratio with them is terrific.

Ask Deck

The *Ask Deck* is the deck you use when you need to ask an executive to give you a big bucket of someone else's money to go do your project.

By now, it should be clear that you can use the patterns we've discussed throughout this book as the building blocks for your local arguments within the Ask Deck.

When making an Ask Deck, first make a Ghost Deck, as described earlier. The basic structure is as follows.

The ask

The first slide says it all. You write your first slide *last*. Don't write it first. Write it at the very end, only after you know everything. Structure it with a single sentence in the headline stating exactly what you want to do. Then, in the bullet points of the body, state a summary of all the things the executive would need to know to give an answer. Those are:

1. The current state is this: X, Y, Z dramatic data points.

2. Therefore, executive, you do this: X important project described in a single sentence with a name.

3. Here are the milestones so you know what you get along the way.

4. That will take X duration, require Y number of teams, and cost $X capex and $Y opex.

5. Here is the end state that you will have bought for that money: something awesome, and now the bad current state is over.

That is, if the executive believed everything you said, he wouldn't have to look at the rest of the deck. So the entire rest of the deck is just a double-click of the first slide.

This one is totally counterintuitive. Most people wait for the big reveal of the number at the end: they think they're being smart to write all the reasons why their project is so great and their thing is so important and they really want you to fund it, and then they reveal the number at the end. But you are not on the sales floor at a car dealership. This is a mistake. If you do this, I bet you dollars to donuts the CFO picks up his copy of your deck as you're trying to present it and just starts flipping back to the end to read the bottom-line number. They're grownups. They're used to seeing big numbers. They know you're not going to rebuild the legacy ecommerce system for $50,000. Give them the news up front so they can contextualize and adjust how hard they need to pay attention and to what. If they had the rough idea you were going to ask for something like $10M and you ask for $12M, then you'll be having a different conversation with different levels of scrutiny and focus than if they walked into the conference room expecting a $1M ask and it's a $5M ask. They will hear you better, and you'll have a more productive, relevant conversation if you get all the bad news out of the way up front.

In fact, here is how I like to think about making these decks: write it all but the first slide, then write the One-Slider that says everything the executive needs to know. The test in my mind is that if he says "OK" on the first slide, you never need to look at the whole rest of the deck. You are not at a meeting to force executives to slog through your PowerPoint. You're there to get a deal. They are punished enough by PowerPoint. If you can get a deal after one slide, fantastic. Let that be the goal, and drive what you pack into the first slide.

Imperil the hero

Employ the Shock and Awe and Book of Job techniques from "Dramatic Structure" on page 179 to show the dire situation your company will be in without doing this thing. Here you're making a statement to show how we are in bad shape or how there is a new super-exciting opportunity.

Let the data drive

Now let the data drive. Just be very methodical and objective, presenting the data that illustrates how any reasonable person would come to this same conclusion. This is the logical argument of Ars Rhetorica (see "Ars Rhetorica" on page 167). Examples:

- X number of P1, P2, P3 contributed to Y amount of downtime YTD
- Trends in P1, P2, P3 total up X% over past three years
- 60 items of technical debt (all detailed in the appendix)
- 12 most impactful things of kind X

Save the hero

Now that you've imperiled the hero, you have to offer the Path Forward. This is your vision of how you can claim the prize of the opportunity or how you can get out of this awful predicament.

To make sure that you have covered all the bases, your Path Forward should include details on all these elements:

- The roadmap (see "Roadmap" on page 260).
- How long will it take?
- How much will it cost?
- Who will do the work?

Make the plans for these elements first, and do it in detail. Then you refer back to them as you build out the project plan.

The ask

Now you ask for a decision. Ask them explicitly for a yes answer. Any salesperson will tell you that the reason you don't get the sale is that you never actually *ask* them to buy.

Appendix

Include an appendix, which might be longer than the deck itself. The appendix includes all charts, graphs, query results, and any substantiating data supporting the claims you made in your main deck.

You will want these yourself later too when you won't be able to remember the details.

Your main deck should be 12–15 slides. Executives will talk too much, and you will definitely never get further than 18 slides, and then you won't have presented the whole force of your complete argument. But the appendix can be any length. You can include the appendix after the main deck in case the executives find themselves on a cross-Atlantic flight and want to vet your numbers.

Just use the patterns we've worked on. Using this structure has helped me a dozen times. With this structure, I've asked executives for millions and tens of millions of dollars to make sweeping changes to entire organizations or do multiyear heart surgery projects on mission-critical systems. I've never been told no. Not once. You can do it too.

Strategy Deck

The *Strategy Deck* is the simplest pattern of all. And the most complex. This is, ostensibly, the center of the book, yet it's empty. That's because, counterintuitively, when you've done all your homework, making the Strategy Deck will be practically a non-event. Here is how you do it:

1. Execute all the applicable creation patterns of this book while keeping in mind the analysis patterns along the way. See "Patterns Map" on page 265.

2. Collect your output from doing that.

3. Do a MergeSort of the output (see "MergeSort Meeting" on page 262) and make it into a deck with a smooth, comprehensive story using the communication patterns in this book.

Now you have a terrific strategy. That's it. This is not intended to be flip. This is the case. The simplicity is lovely.

Roadmap

I have an existential map. It has "You Are Here" written all over it.
—Steven Wright

The Roadmap (see "Roadmap" on page 260) is generally for executive alignment and is of little use to dev teams. It shows in broad terms your milestone deliverables and is clear on indicating the end state. You're stating less of a timeline here and more of the big building blocks, the meaningful work that you can release incrementally that together make up what you hope to achieve.

The teams won't be interested in a view this broad, except maybe at the quarterly town hall meeting. It is of use to you, however, as the initiative planner: requiring yourself to state milestones like this makes you think in terms of deliverables (outcomes) that will be of benefit to your customer and can ship without dependencies on the rest of the program.

You should start at the end, and use a modified Backcasting (see "Backcasting" on page 83) technique to determine the right antecedent milestones.

You've seen these before. But Figure 9-1 shows an example. You want the roadmap to fit on a single slide.

If you're presenting your overall roadmap to customers, I suppose you're just putting quarterly releases on a timeline with the major releases, and that's simpler. But if you're embarking on a major initiative, stakeholders will need to see what they get when in more detail, how the planning and building blocks are expected to accompany this, and internal details such as when you plan to ramp up teams, when other teams are required to deliver their dependent part, and so forth, along with the milestones.

Once you have an approved roadmap, and you have done your costing and made a conceptual architecture, then make a Tactical Plan (see "Tactical Plan" on page 261). This is necessary to estimate durations, and to figure out how much can be done in parallel versus what aspects must be done in serial. That is necessary to determine your Directional Costing (see "Directional Costing" on page 218), which you need to make an Ask Deck (see "Ask Deck" on page 256). It's all of a piece.

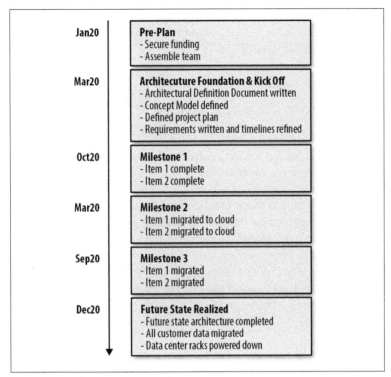

Jan20	**Pre-Plan** - Secure funding - Assemble team
Mar20	**Architecuture Foundation & Kick Off** - Architectural Definition Document written - Concept Model defined - Defined project plan - Requirements written and timelines refined
Oct20	**Milestone 1** - Item 1 complete - Item 2 complete
Mar20	**Milestone 2** - Item 1 migrated to cloud - Item 2 migrated to cloud
Sep20	**Milestone 3** - Item 1 migrated - Item 2 migrated
Dec20	**Future State Realized** - Future state architecture completed - All customer data migrated - Data center racks powered down

Figure 9-1. The initiative roadmap

Tactical Plan

The point of the *Tactical Plan* is to say, more as a reminder than any-thing, that the strategy work cannot stop here. This is only the beginning, the commencement of the strategy work. Stopping at this point will have achieved nothing.

You must turn your strategy, once approved, into a Tactical Plan. Remember the words of Sun Tzu: "Strategy without tactics is the slowest route to victory. Tactics without strategy is the noise before defeat."

This can happen in two steps (see Figure 9-2). The first is that you figure out only the durations. Resist the temptation to put hard dates on the plan at first, but then you'll need to do that as a second step. If you start with dates, you'll get a worse estimate of timelines.

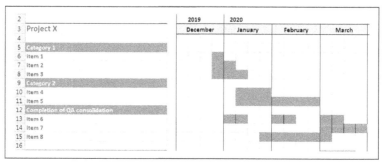

Figure 9-2. The basic Tactical Plan

Of course, there are many management books, courses, certificates, and software programs devoted to making great project plans, and you've surely participated in many of them. I include this pattern here mostly for completeness, and to suggest that making a preliminary Tactical Plan in this way forces you to think through everything: you can't get a good idea of the project to propose in your Strategy Deck (see "Strategy Deck" on page 259) if you don't do this step.

MergeSort Meeting

The *MergeSort* planning method is a novel way of working through plan-making meetings for managers that I made up and use on occasion. It works great if you, like I am, are a huge fan of making lists, as discussed in Chapter 2.

You use this method to solve problems when you are at the early stage of planning a large project. You have a mountain of brainstorming work you've done, or a Strategy Deck or set of ideas on lists you've been building, and you need to turn it into a plan. You want everyone's ideas in a quick, unbiased fashion.

When the time comes to make a plan, I like to get everyone's independent ideas. This could be a "get well" plan or the yearly strategy; anytime you want to brainstorm with your team, you can use this method to prevent groupthink from taking over.

You might be familiar with the MergeSort (*http://bit.ly/2MIcM6I*) algorithm, invented in the 1940s by John von Neumann. It's a way of sorting elements in an array as opposed to BubbleSort, QuickSort, and others. The basic implementation of MergeSort works kind of like this:

1. Take an unsorted list. Recursively divide it into sublists, which are trivially sorted.

2. Repeatedly merge these sublists back up the call chain to produce new, sorted, combined lists until only one list remains. This will be the sorted list.

There are different ways to implement it, and there's a terrific animation of the process on Wikipedia (*http://bit.ly/2MLJdRB*). But for our purposes, we're using it as a metaphor to help you create your tactical plan.

I use MergeSort as a keyword with my team, like a shorthand for this process. Here's how to do it:

1. Call a MergeSort meeting to make your plan, and make sure you clearly state the scope of what you need to build the plan for.

2. Have everyone make a separate list of lists, perhaps categories focusing on different aspects of the project such as "business," "data," "infrastructure," or whatever are the main categories of your project as outer headers. Use a common set of categories such as people/process/technology for the inner loop's set of headers.

3. Give everyone time to populate their lists of lists independently. You will generate a lot more ideas this way, and be more inclusive of shy people in the group and flatten out the louder voices.

4. Bring the raw material lists together in your MergeSort operation meeting.

5. Now you have a single merged list and you want to prioritize it. So use some other lenses you've learned in this book (like making a 2×2 matrix for likelihood/impact) to help prioritize things.

6. The project manager takes over the meeting to take the now single, merged, prioritized list of lists and assign who does what by when into a spreadsheet.

7. Now you've got a really comprehensive plan that the PM can track and someone can go execute.

Maybe this is too idiomatic, but I like it. It seems to work when called for, and I honestly hope you find it useful.

As you have seen in this chapter, your Tactical Plan generally will look like ones you've seen a lot before. But strategy without execution is just like the kids in the backyard making neat rules for the fort with no bearing on reality. A clear Tactical Plan is key to successfully carrying out any strategy.

CHAPTER 10

Bringing It All Together

Patterns Map

This completes the discussion of our 39 patterns. Now that you have a good understanding of each individual pattern, let's look at them all (well, all the creation and communication patterns, anyway) together in a map. When viewed all at once, the patterns in this book are devised to work on three levels:

Individually

For many of the patterns, you can just implement one pattern on its own and get real value from it. The Architecture Definition (see "Architecture Definition" on page 235) is a great example of this; you can write an architecture for a specific new project you're undertaking, and that would be very useful on its own. And in a different context, the SWOT (see "SWOT" on page 87), Technology Radar (see "Technology Radar" on page 227), and APM ("Application Portfolio Management" on page 146) are great to use alone too, depending on your need and your audience. So feel free to do that. On the other hand, some of them, such as the Investment Map, might not be as fully realized if approached in a vacuum. And then there is no value really in doing a Ghost Deck (see "Ghost Deck" on page 253) by itself—its value is in helping structure the other kinds of major decks, such as the Strategy Deck and Ask Deck (so that's why it's represented twice in Figure 10-1).

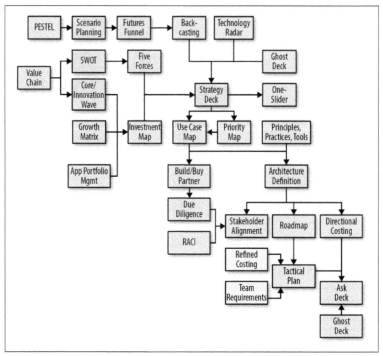

Figure 10-1. How all the patterns fit and flow together

In clusters

You can alternatively use several patterns together in clusters of three or five, if you have a medium-scope problem that is contained to the technology side or the business/operating model side. For example, if you're doing a broad industry analysis, you can pick patterns from Chapter 4 and use those to make a strategy recommendation. Or your marketing or product management department may have already created analyses for you to use as world and industry context and you're not interested in that; you might instead just need to do the technology work. In this case, you could use only the Build/Buy/Partner pattern (see "Build/Buy/Partner" on page 229), Use Case Map (see "Use Case Map" on page 217), Architecture Definition (see "Architecture Definition" on page 235), and Due Diligence (see "Due Diligence" on page 232). If you have a clear idea of what your technical pursuit is already, you might be more focused on this occasion on the project-oriented cluster: the Stakeholder Alignment pattern (see "Stakeholder Alignment" on page 99), Roadmap (see "Roadmap" on page 260), Directional Costing (see "Directional Costing" on page 218), and Tactical Plan (see "Tactical Plan" on page 261).

Comprehensively

Finally, you could use the patterns all together. If you do this, it's almost certainly for one of two main reasons: to create a broad organizational strategic plan leading up to a Strategy Deck (see "Strategy Deck" on page 259), or in order to create an Ask Deck (see "Ask Deck" on page 256). In one sense, these are the most important patterns here, inasmuch as they're the two that all the others exist to serve. It's the way you get funded, and to make a good Ask Deck, you really have to do many of the other patterns first.

The map of how they all work together is shown Figure 10-1. This can give you a sense of how they might flow or depend on each other. You can see how they cluster in a few smaller groups as well.

How many of them you implement depends, of course, on the size, expense, novelty, risk, and complexity of your project.

I submit that architects (and technology managers and practitioners) can move up the value chain, and help their companies to compete and differentiate, if they spend less time policing developers and more time visiting each of the boxes on this map and executing these patterns as discussed throughout this book. Use the results of these patterns to work more closely and meaningfully with your partners in product management, sales, business development, and strategy.

Conclusion

That's it! Thank you so much for reading this book. I really hope you enjoyed it and that you found it useful. We've come a long way together and covered amazing ground. There is so much more to say on these topics. But my hope is that, in having read this book, you now have greater awareness of—as David Foster Wallace might call it—the "water," the context in which we work as technology strategists. I hope too that you now feel greater mastery of the art of creating power for you and your organization, and you see how these tools can considerably improve your ability to differentiate and compete in a crowded market.

As you advance in your career, remember that these waters never stand still: different patterns will make sense for you and your teams at different times, and you'll need to frequently adjust. It may seem daunting, but I promise you: the tools and strategies presented in this text will help you navigate deftly through this exciting, challenging, fabulous ocean.

I'll leave you with these parting words:

> *The whole interest of reason, speculative as well as practical, is centered in the three following questions:*
>
> 1. *What can I know?*
> 2. *What ought I to do?*
> 3. *What may I hope?*
>
> —18th century German philosopher Immanuel Kant, *The Critique of Pure Reason* (http://bit.ly/2N7TV1T)

> *Thoughts are things.*
> —Bruce Lee

Best wishes, my friends.

Recommended Reading

These books were helpful in considering the ideas in this book, and I recommend checking them out to gain further ideas and different perspectives on these subjects.

Strategy Books

Lawrence Freedman, *Strategy: A History* (Oxford University Press)

Walter Kiechel III, *The Lords of Strategy* (Harvard Business Review Press)

Matthew E. Gladden, *From Strategic Analysis to Organizational Foresight* (Synthypnion Business)

Avinash K. Dixit and Barry J. Nalebuff, *The Art of Strategy* (W. W. Norton & Company)

Richard P. Rumelt, *Good Strategy, Bad Strategy: The Difference and Why It Matters* (Crown Business)

Aligning Technology with Strategy (Harvard Business Review Press)

On Strategy (Harvard Business Review Press)

Strategy: Create and Implement the Best Strategy for Your Business (Harvard Business Essentials)

Michael E. Porter, *Competitive Strategy Techniques for Analyzing Industries and Competitors* (Free Press)

Thomas Pyzdek and Paul Keller, *Six Sigma Handbook* (McGraw-Hill Education)

Babette E. Bensousson and Craig S. Fleisher, *Analysis Without Paralysis* (Pearson Education)

Consulting Books

Shu Hattori, *The McKinsey Edge* (McGraw-Hill Education)

Victor Cheng, *Case Interview Secrets* (Innovation Press)

Ethan M. Rasiel, *The McKinsey Way* (McGraw-Hill)

Marc P. Cosentino, *Case in Point* (CaseQuestions.com)

Duff McDonald, *The Firm: The Story of McKinsey and Its Secret Influence on American Business* (Simon & Schuster)

Mikael Krogerus and Roman Tschappeler, *The Decision Book* (W. W. Norton & Company)

Jeanne W. Ross, Peter Weill, and David C. Robertson, *Enterprise Architecture as Strategy* (Harvard Business Review Press)

Philosophy Books

Ian Hacking, *An Introduction to Probability and Inductive Logic* (Cambridge University Press)

Paul R. Halmos, *Naïve Set Theory* (D. Van Nostrand Company, Inc.)

Jacques Derrida, *Of Grammatology* (Johns Hopkins University Press)

Peter Bruce & Andrew Bruce, *Practical Statistics for Data Scientists* (O'Reilly)

Gary Klein, *Sources of Power: How People Make Decisions* (MIT Press)

Leslie Lamport, *Specifying Systems* (Addison-Wesley)

Alec Ross, *The Industries of the Future* (Simon & Schuster)

Index

L

labor costs, estimating, 223
language game, 46
language, scrutinizing for meaning, 63
legal analysis (PESTEL), 74
life cycle stage (companies), 111-116
    value stages, 111
Liskov Substitution Principle, 197
lists
    MECE, 29, 31
        applying, 34-37
        composing, 30
        knowing audience and why
           they care, 30
        rule of three, 33
    RACI, 30
    (see also RACI)
local optima, 185
Logic Tree, 27, 37-41, 79
    creating the tree, 38
    Diagnostic Logic Tree, 38
    problems vs. opportunities, 40
    Solution Logic Tree, 38
logical arguments (logos), 167
logical fallacies, 169-173
    ad hominem (against the man), 169
    affirming the consequent, 169
    blind authority, 170
    blinding with science, 171
    hasty generalization, 171
    petitio principii (begging the question), 172
    post hoc, ergo propter hoc (after this, therefore because of this), 173
logical operator AND, 43

M

machine learning, strategic analysis as, 66-67
maintaining confidence (of stakeholders), 107
market development strategy (AGM), 96
market penetraton strategy (AGM), 96

marketing and sales, 117
The Mathematical Analysis of Logic (Boole), 41
matrices (2×2), 106, 126
mature companies, 112
maturity stage (companies), 114
McDonald, Duff, 163
McKinsey, ix, 19, 28, 29, 41, 42, 45, 73, 75, 78, 163, 165
McKinsey Insights report, 45
MECE (Mutually Exclusive, Collectively Exhaustive), 27, 29-37
    applying MECE lists, 34-37
    in Process Posture Map, 141
    lists, 29
        determining audience and why they care, 30
        rule of three, 33
    PESTEL as, 71
meeting before the meeting, 176
mental models, locking into, 15
MergeSort planning method, 262
metacognition, 190
metacognitive thinking, 188
Metadata section, Architecture Definition template, 239
metapatterns, 27
metrics, 241
    customer success measure, 218
    defining, 208
Michelin, marketing at, 3
Microsoft, 115
milestones, 260
ML (see machine learning)
models (in ML), 67
monitoring stakeholders, 107
Mutually Exclusive, Collectively Exhaustive (see MECE)

N

NASA strategy, 137
    Application Portfolio Management (APM), 158
necessary but not sufficient condition, 59, 83
necessary relation, 59
negative revenue growth, 113
Netflix Culture deck, 189

About the Author

Eben Hewitt is CTO at Sabre Hospitality, a global technology company. He has led tech organizations as Chief Architect, CIO, and CTO. He is the author of *Cassandra: The Definitive Guide* (*http://http://bit.ly/cassandra2e*) (O'Reilly), and several other books on architecture, services, and software development.

Colophon

The animal on the cover of *Technology Strategy Patterns* is the sharpbill (*Oxyruncus cristatus*). This small, stocky songbird lives in the tall, dense rainforests of Panama, Costa Rica, and parts of Brasil, Columbia, and other regions of Tropical South America. The bird gets its name from its conical, pointed beak.

The sharpbill is colored olive-green on the back and tailfeathers with an orange-red crest. The underside is yellow with black polka-dots. It eats fruit, occasionally supplemented by insects. With toes well-suited to perching, it can hang upside down to catch insects and their larvae.

The male has a larger, erect crest and a loud, buzzing song that descends from high to low in pitch. Until 1980, when the first sharpbill nest was discovered, little was known about this bird's habits. The sharpbill is polygamous, with males traveling in groups (leks) to vie for the females' attention during mating season.

Many of the animals on O'Reilly covers are endangered; all of them are important to the world. To learn more about how you can help, go to *animals.oreilly.com*.

The cover illustration is by Karen Montgomery, based on a black-and-white engraving from *Shaw's General Zoology*. The cover fonts are URW Typewriter and Guardian Sans. The text font is Adobe Minion Pro; the heading font is Adobe Myriad Condensed; and the code font is Dalton Maag's Ubuntu Mono.